UPDATE ON
CHRISTIAN
COUNSELING

Titles in the Jay Adams Library

UPDATE ON CHRISTIAN COUNSELING

VOLUMES 1 AND 2

Includes *Matters of Concern to Christian Counselors*

Jay E. Adams

Ministry Resources Library

Zondervan Publishing House • Grand Rapids, MI

UPDATE ON CHRISTIAN COUNSELING
Copyright © 1977, 1979, 1981 by Jay E. Adams

MINISTRY RESOURCES LIBRARY is an imprint of Zondervan
Publishing House, 1415 Lake Drive, S.E.,
Grand Rapids, Michigan 49506.

"Does the Behaviorist Have a Mind?" by Wm. Hallock Johnson was first published
in the *Princeton Theological Review*, January 1927.

Library of Congress Cataloging in Publication Data

Adams, Jay Edward.
    Update on Christian counseling.

    (The Jay Adams library)
    Includes bibliographical references and indexes.
    1. Pastoral counseling. 2. Counseling. I. Title. II. Adams, Jay Edward.
Matters of concern to Christian counselors. III. Series: Adams, Jay Edward.
Jay Adams library.
BV4012.2.A35   1986   253.5   86-8585
ISBN 0-310-51051-1

Printed in the United States of America

86 87 88 89 90 91 / 10 9 8 7 6 5 4 3 2 1

Contents

Update on Christian Counseling
Volume 1

To My Mother
With Love

Introduction

Over the years I have discovered myself focusing on certain problems (or aspects of problems) in counseling that I have not treated before. I often speak about these matters at pastors' conferences, and I have written about them in magazines, or have taken notes on studies made for my own benefit, etc.

Now, I have begun to see the need for an open-ended series of volumes, published whenever sufficient material becomes available, that include such emphases. That is why I have published the first volume of *Update on Christian Counseling*. If this course of action commends itself to my Christian readership, I shall continue to do so.

Actually, what should have been the first volume in this series was published under the title, *Matters of Concern for Christian Counselors*, but at that time I had no notion of a series at all. There is another difference between the two books. Articles in this volume are, on the whole, longer than those in *Matters of Concern*.

With this explanation, let us plunge ahead; my goal (as always) is to try to keep the pastor (and other Christian counselors) updated on late developments, ideas, concerns, etc., in the field of Christian Counseling. I hope I shall (in part, at least) begin to achieve that goal through this book.

I
How Does Counseling Affect the Counselor?

Frequently, in pastors' conferences (I hold a number each year), I am asked the following questions:

You have done a lot of counseling. When you are talking to people about their problems day after day, how do you keep from becoming unbalanced or morose yourself? And, while you're thinking about that one, how about addressing yourself to this one too—How do you keep from carrying the weight of people's problems away from the counseling room with you?

These are both good questions, and deserve a thoughtful reply. Fortunately, they can be answered together as one combined question to which there is one combined response that covers both. What answers the first question is precisely what answers the second as well. Therefore, I shall treat these questions as one.

Statistical studies show that psychiatrists have the highest suicide rate of all medical professionals.[1] One can understand why. A major reason, I am convinced, is psychiatrists' failure to solve people's problems. When one's profession has as its *raison d'etre* solving other people's problems, and when he doesn't even know how to solve his own, that could be most devastating. Think of the discouragement, doubt and self-accusation that could result. Think of listening to tragic and unsolvable human predicaments, day after day; think of prescribing hopeless and ineffective remedies, few of which bring peace or satisfaction, and many of which seem only to aggravate the

---

1. Cf. *Bulletin of Suicidology* (Washington, D. C.: Government Printing Office, December, 1968), p. 5.

difficulty. No wonder many psychiatrists, daily immersed in human sin and its misery, themselves despair of life itself. Without Christ, what meaning or purpose is there?

So, in answering your questions, I have begun by emphasizing afresh the difficulty you raise. But I have done so in this form to set forth a contrast. The first difference between a truly Christian and a non-Christian counselor is that in Christian counseling the counselor does not offer human solutions (or, as they might more accurately be called, "non-solutions") to human problems. That means (1) they do not rely upon their own persuasions, wisdom and insight; (2) they do not counsel alone. Those who are really engaged in biblical counseling also are involved in the daily use of the Scriptures.[2] *That makes a great difference!* To be reminded of hopeful solutions that *do* work, to share *God's* solutions with others, to actually see the power of the Holy Spirit demonstrated in lives that are transformed in counseling, can be an exhilarating experience! Of course, if under the Christian label, non-Christian counseling is done, that change—because it is a change in name only, and not in fact—will not bring this result. Some Christians, therefore, who ask the question, ask because (like the pagan counselors around them) they know nothing of the joys and victories of the ministry of the Word in counseling.

Many times, after ten hours of counseling, I have returned to my home happier, more excited about the Bible, and actually feeling more rejuvenated than when I began in the morning. Biblical counseling doesn't leave one morose; indeed, it can be one of the greatest encouragements you will ever experience.

"But it can't all be sweetness and light. Aren't there sad times too? Surely, every session isn't exhilarating, is it?"

Of course there are rough sessions, disappointments, heart-breaking events. I had no intention of denying this. I was speaking of the overall impact, the general result—how one is affected by a *ministry* of counseling as a whole.

---

2. For more on this, see my *What About Nouthetic Counseling?*, pp. 41ff.

2

"Well, then, how do you handle the bad times?"

I'm not avoiding the question; I simply want to look at these matters step by step. Let me say at once that the solution is not the one offered by many who try to assume a "professional" manner, keeping themselves at a distance, never daring to become involved. The idea that I may not feel deeply the hurts and struggles of my counselees is (to me) a totally abhorrent one. Paul spoke of weeping with those who weep and rejoicing with those who rejoice; that is how Christians must minister to one another. So the answer is not in donning the white coat and assuming an air of clinical objectivity.

"But, how does the counselor avoid carrying more burdens than he can bear?"

Certainly not by becoming aloof. Many people think that the sort of involvement Paul described as "weeping" and "rejoicing *with*" surely would lead to utter despair. That's why they try to keep their distance. They are very wrong. It is the person whose emotions are not spent in the counseling session who finds them troubling him later on. While I am not advising counselors to lose control of their emotions (Paul didn't intend that either), it is necessary to enter into the counselee's problem as fully as one can; that means in thought and emotion—yet without losing perspective. The counselor's proper stance is empathetic disagreement (not empathetic agreement).[3] On this stance, he appreciates every feature of the counselee's problem as fully as he can; he tries to understand all dimensions, *in depth*. But—and this is *critical*—he refuses to see the problem only as the counselee does. If the counselee declares, "My situation is hopeless," he replies, "No, you are wrong; although the situation is *very* serious,[4] it *isn't* hopeless. God has an answer even to this. . . ." Because the counselee *knows* that there have been true understanding and empathy *in depth*, he cannot dismiss the coun-

---

3. For a fuller development of this concept, see my *Lectures on Counseling*, pp. 85ff.

4. He never minimizes the problem; in the spirit of Rom. 5:20b, he maximizes the Savior.

selor's disagreement. (If the counselor remained "professionally" aloof, the counselee might readily wonder whether he truly understands.)

The counselor, then, acknowledges the problem for all that it is. (At times, he will even point out other aspects of the problem that the counselee has missed and that make it even more serious than he supposed: "You see, this isn't only a matter of your relationship to your wife; it is also a question of your relationship to God.") But the counselor is never problem-oriented. Having adequately ascertained the true nature of the counselee's difficulty (and even when analyzing it), he offers hope from God. That is to say, his basic stance throughout is redemptive—he is solution-oriented. Always— from the outset—he holds forth the truth that God has answers, even to a problem like this. Non-Christian counselors cannot do this; they have no such stance.

Empathetic disagreement makes a great difference. He is empathetic (he doesn't downgrade the difficulty), but he always disagrees with the counselee who sees his situation as hopeless. Instead, his focus is upon biblical solutions. He believes that there is hope (forget everything, if you don't) and, in all he says and does, he conveys it. Counselors who have no such hope to offer doubtless become as discouraged as their clients. Often they advise divorces (for example) because they can see no other (better) way out. They know nothing of God's solutions to marital problems and can offer no hope. No wonder they carry a shoulder-full of burdens around.

So, summing up what we have discovered so far, we have seen:

1. The Christian counselor has the exciting and satisfying advantage of doing counseling in which he can see the results of the Holy Spirit transforming lives through the ministry of His Word.[5]

2. He has hope to offer.[6]

---

5. Incidentally, biblical counselors everywhere testify to the joy and satisfaction that they find in this ministry.
6. For an exhaustive study on hope (its importance, place and source), see pertinent passages in my *Christian Counselor's Manual.*

3. He is solution-oriented, not problem-oriented. (Some psychiatrists must content themselves with the dubious task of affixing a label to the person or his problem.)

"But what, now, of his failures, and the failures of his counselee? They don't all come through this with flying colors. What about those heartbreaking incidents you mentioned earlier? You haven't dealt fully with my questions yet."

O.K., we're now ready to move on. The Christian counselor knows from the outset that both he and his counselee are far from perfection. But he also knows that God is perfect. So, he counsels not from his own imperfection but from the stance of God's trustworthiness and power. That is, he points always to hope in God (never to himself). From start to finish the hope that he holds out is found in the Scriptures, where God has gone on record about life and the solutions to the problems posed by sin (cf. Rom. 15:4, 13— hope comes from God through His Word).

Because of this basic stance, the counselor himself can take seriously the advice that he gives his counselee about worry (cf. Matt. 6; Phil. 4).[7] Having worked hard at ministering God's Word to a counselee in any given session (and biblical counseling is *hard work*[8]), prayerfully, at the close of the session, he commits the counselee and the outcome of the session into God's hands and *leaves the matter there.* He has been doing the Lord's work; the Lord will watch over its results. Then and there he turns his mind to the next counselee (or whatever other responsibility that he has at hand). He *refuses* to carry problems home because to do so would be sin— he asked God to carry the burden; how, then, can he take it back from Him? Worry will do no good. He can do nothing more than what he has done; but God can. In the final analysis, you see, it boils down once again to *faith*—does he *believe* that God cares and will act? Worry is connected intimately to unbelief. But if he believes

---

7. See my pamphlet, *What to Do About Worry,* for a fuller explication of these verses.

8. I have discussed this matter in *What About Nouthetic Counseling?,* pp. 59ff.

5

that God will work through His Word *in* counseling sessions, why shouldn't he believe also that God will continue to work when the session is over? In a sense, what he believes about his counseling in general (God is/isn't at work in it) makes all the difference about his attitude between sessions. The answer, then, is not to stand aloof, or develop an insensitive and callous attitude or anything of the sort. The answer is trust—trust in God's promises both within and outside the counseling session.

Now, one other factor of importance should be mentioned to assure balance in what I have said. The counselor must make sure that he has given all that he can of himself in the counseling hour; this is vital. He must begin counseling prayerfully, asking God's help (after preparing for it thoroughly), and during the hour-long session must concentrate all his efforts on determining (in biblical terms and categories, according to scriptural values) what the problem is and what God says must be done about it. He must work hard at developing creative and concrete applications of biblical principles that are appropriate to the circumstances peculiar to each case. He doesn't confine his approach to rubber-stamp solutions, which are supposed to fit all cases (see the chapter in this volume on "Adaptability in Counseling"). Now, when he has done all this, he knows that he has done all God expects of him—so, why worry?

However, he will fail. When he does—and recognizes it—he confesses this to God and to the counselee. He knows, and has made it clear to the counselee in one way or another (usually by stressing hope in God, not in himself), that he isn't perfect. That is why it is essential to orient all hope toward God and the promises of His Word. There is little wonder that psychiatrists who must counsel exclusively by human power and wisdom often come to despair. The counselee's hope and faith is placed in *them*. Not so with the Christian counselor; while he is to prove himself eminently trustworthy, nevertheless, at times he will fail. Therefore, he directs the counselee to place all his trust in the unfailing Creator and Sustainer of the universe. God can succeed, even when the counselor fails.

There is one more matter worth raising. All biblical counselors

6

know that there is usually a point where things get worse before they get better. Counselors unfamiliar with this phenomenon often give up (or allow their counselees to give up) when this happens. Nathan had his rough session with David before the daylight of Psalm 51 flooded in! Do not despair, therefore, when difficult sessions occur. Indeed, wise counselors sometimes warn, ahead of time, of the likelihood of such an experience:

"There are going to be some difficult things God will require of you. You may feel worse before you feel better (like when you go to the dentist, or have an operation). Sinful patterns are stubborn and do not budge easily. At times, when they finally come loose, it is painful; there may be bloodshed. But don't despair—this is the darkness before dawn; this is the valley of the shadow of death that leads to the green pastures and still waters."

So, you see, biblical counselors expect difficult sessions and are not thrown for a loss when they have them. It is all part of a day's work in counseling!

"But what if a counselee messes everything up, or quits counseling—or, commits suicide?"

No one likes to think about these things, but we must, of course. I have had counselees go the wrong way in spite of the hope God offers; I have never (yet) had any commit suicide. But I have had to think about that possibility.

Jesus knew what it was like to have counselees quit. The rich young ruler walked away. And Judas committed suicide. So the problems are not unique; they have been faced before, and handled rightly by Jesus Himself. Obviously, Jesus didn't go all to pieces, or give up. He showed sorrow for the young man, but in both cases He clearly *placed the responsibility where it belonged*—on the young man and on Judas.

Jesus, Himself, did not fail. The failure belonged to the one who turned away. And *that is how Jesus viewed the situation*. The play was a success; the audience was a failure.

It is the counselor's obligation, as God's steward, to minister (or dispense) the Word accurately and faithfully (I Cor. 4:1, 2); it is

7

the counselee's responsibility to obey the Word. The counselor can explain the Word, encourage the counselee to obey it, warn him of the consequences of disobedience, but he *cannot make him obey*. If the counselor has discharged *his* responsibility, then he is clear. How the counselee responds is *his* responsibility, and his alone. If the counselor has failed in one way or another to assume his responsibility in the relationship, that makes him responsible (not for the counselee's failure but) to repent, to seek forgiveness and to rectify his failure as he is able to do so. The counselor *never* bears responsibility for the counselee's actions; the counselee *alone* bears such responsibility. The two responsibilities must be sorted out. Even if the counselor fails (he's responsible for that), the counselee is responsible for making a proper response to that failure. If he gives up on God, or even commits suicide, the counselor must not hold himself responsible for that. Poor counseling, though tragic, is not an adequate justification for the counselee to do either of these things in response. The counselee bears full responsibility for his sinful response, just as the counselor must for his sinful failures.

While the two responsibilities are separate, they are related. Any true counselor would deeply regret any failures on his part that the counselee used as an occasion to turn from God or to commit suicide. Yet it is wrong for the counselor to bear the guilt of the counselee's action. He has enough guilt of his own to deal with. Sin by one person neither causes, nor justifies, nor necessarily occasions sin by another. Because there is so much confusion abroad in society today, it is important to recognize this truth, and to understand Jesus' approach to the problem.

All in all, then, the Christian counselor takes a biblical stance, and has an approach to counseling that is coupled with hope and powerful resources that keep him from becoming unbalanced about life, or morose. He finds that if he is a hard-working person who assumes his obligations both in counseling and at home, he will not have time to sit and brood and become morose. He doesn't carry problems home. When he fails, and does carry problems around, he has no one to blame but himself. In that case, he must do some reorienting of his counseling schedules, procedures, attitudes, stance (or whatever else may be at fault) to become more biblical. He will find that he must apply to himself some of the principles that he uses in counseling (especially those relating to self-pity and worry). And, in the event that this doesn't help, he may find it helpful to chat with other Christian counselors who have overcome the problem.

2

Failure in Counseling

I have mentioned this phenomenon before,[1] but it seems necessary to say more about it in some depth.

"I agree with you entirely about avoiding a feeling-orientation in counseling, and I know that I must not allow counselees to say 'can't' if they are Christians, but listen Jay, aren't there still some persons who really *can't* do some of the things they say they ought to do?" Such were the words of a faithful pastor who has been trained in nouthetic counseling and who has been successfully using it in a fruitful ministry. Because his problem is not an isolated one, it ought to be addressed.

In the vast majority of the sort of cases that he had described, the answer (I told him) is not that the counselee *can't* do what he knows he should, but that he *won't*. In spite of clear-cut, concrete assignments, willingness to help on the part of the counselor and others, and a desire by the counselee to be helped and to follow scriptural counsel, in the end counseling fails because *the counselee persists in following counsel in his own way.*

When asked, "Did you do what I said?" he will invariably reply, "Yes, I did; but it didn't work." He isn't always sincere in this answer, but often he may be in spite of the fact that the reply is misleading and actually is a distortion of the truth. His own patterns of selectivity may be so dominant that, without explicitly focusing upon the fact of what he is doing, he may really hear only that part of a

1. *The Christian Counselor's Manual*, pp. 233ff., 245ff., 459-461.

counseling assignment that he wants to hear.[2] So, as a consequence, he winds up doing only a part of what he has been told, doing it in a different way from the way that he was advised, or substituting something apparently similar but essentially different from[3] what he was counseled to do.

There are people who (when advised to get a product), always end up purchasing a substitute; and usually they find it unsatisfactory.[4] For instance, a mechanic says that a Toyota oil filter will handle the oil better than any substitute can (and warns that the latter could lead to a $200-plus motor job if the owner persists in replacing the filter with a cheaper substitute). The owner hears (the problem is not selectivity), but he isn't sure, indeed, doesn't *want* to believe, or tells himself, "That's what they all say; he just wants to make a buck." He is a fool not to take such advice (or at least to carefully check it out before rejecting it) and run the risk of ruining his motor. Yet, there are any number of people who do just that because that is their pattern of thinking. In a sinful world where people do lie, and as sinners themselves, they have adopted this attitude. Then, when they come to God's Word, the same attitude is carried over. For one rationalized "reason" or another—there are any number of possibilities here—the basic perversity of sinners manifests itself by saying, "I know better; I don't really have to do *that* (or do it *that* way)." Then, when things fail (as inevitably they do), they blame the person whose counsel they did not follow. They complain that his advice was inadequate, conveniently omitting the fact that they failed to take it!

Physicians are acutely aware of the problem. A physician told a woman with high blood pressure, Hodgkin's disease, and a number of other related problems, "Don't drink coffee." She said in my

---

2. There is evidence that sense data can be re-routed around the brain. Unless the reticular formation arouses one to attend, data can be missed.
3. See the chapter in this book, "Don't Apologize!" Frequently, when told to seek forgiveness, counselees will substitute apology instead. But, as that chapter makes clear, the two are essentially distinct. See also, *infra.*
4. I say usually, because (in such matters) it is possible to stumble upon something equally as good or better. But any substitute for God's ways, in the end, will *always* fail (although at times it takes a while to discover this).

presence, "My husband said that a cup or so every morning won't hurt me." She complains about her condition continually, but she won't follow the doctor's directions. Physicians, who are aware of and concerned about this perverse, sinful tendency of patients not to follow directions, do three things that it also might be helpful for counselors to do:

1. They spell out directions very clearly. A counselor ought to do the same, writing out assignments in detail and going over them with his counselees. At points he will find it necessary to add words like these—DO EXACTLY WHAT THIS SAYS! NO DEVIATIONS.

2. They check up on the patient to make sure that their directions were followed. Counselors who give assignments, but fail to check up on how they were carried out, are kidding themselves (usually the early part of each session is devoted to checking out homework *in detail:* "Tell me, step by step, what you did and what happened").

3. They warn (like the Toyota mechanic) about the possible serious consequences of failing to follow directions. The Bible motivates by positive and negative means: promise and warning (cf. my discussion of this in *Matters of Concern,* pp. 28-31).

Now, let's take an example. Suppose you have told a counselee to ask God for forgiveness for a particular sin and then go to the person he has wronged by it and seek his (or her) forgiveness as well. The counselee agrees. All looks well. When he returns for the next session, he reports that he has done so. (You fail to check out the exact particulars of what he said and did.) Pleased, you go on to other matters. Then, at the next session, the counselee announces that "this business of seeking a brother's forgiveness hasn't done any good." Things, he indicates, aren't any better; in fact, they seem worse. He says, "I'm sorry I took your advice."

There can, of course, be many other dimensions to such a problem (failure on the part of the offended party to forgive, or to live up to his promise of forgiveness. But, for the sake of simplicity in making the point, let's leave these possibilities aside for this discussion[5]). But let us say that this is what happened:

Your counselee heard your advice. However, he "translated" your words (even when written, this can happen), "ask forgiveness" into "make up with" or "tell him you're sorry" or "apologize." That isn't what you *said*, and it isn't what you *intended*, but it is what (in his sinful perversity) he *did*.

What he did was *partial*. He went to the offended party as you directed, but it was also *perverted:* he did something qualitatively different. He did not follow directions. He said, "I'm sorry," instead of "I've sinned; will you forgive me?"

Now, there could be any number of reasons why he fulfilled the assignment in this way. Take two:

(1) It could be his pattern to "do things his own way."

(2) He could genuinely not have known the difference.

Let us consider (2) more closely.

In this case, the counselor also bears some responsibility. Counselors ought to know about such perversions of biblical action; they should know that people substitute apologies for seeking forgiveness. And, therefore, they should spell out exactly what asking for forgiveness entails. In fact, they should anticipate such a possible "translation" and guard against it by clearly distinguishing the two things when giving the assignment. Because so few persons recognize the difference, and because most people persist in confounding forgiveness and apology, of necessity good counseling involves spelling out *in detail* what is and (with equal clarity) what is *not* meant by the assignment. And, it would be well to warn against substituting the one for the other. He might explain,

"Seeking forgiveness and saying 'I'm sorry' are two entirely different ways to handle the same situation. One is God's way; the other man's substitute. The former stems from repentance (leading to confession—an admission of sin—and to the granting of pardon); the other may stem from sorrow (often, as in Esau's case, men-

---

5. But not, however, in a genuine counseling context if the other party can be brought into the counseling session as well.

13

tioned in Hebrews 12:15-17, sorrow arises over the *consequences* of sin, rather than the fact of sin as an offense against God and others, and his inability to reverse them). The two differ radically. An apology is no more than a statement about one's feelings: 'I'm sorry.' It is non-specific—is he sorry about what happened to himself or to others? Does he recognize the fact that he has sinned, first and foremost against God? What do the words mean?

"Because they are non-specific, the words of apology elicit some non-commital response (if any is forthcoming at all). Why shouldn't they? They are vague, and (indeed) ask for no commitment from him. Having made an apology, one may *assume* that the matter is closed. The truth is that it is not. Neither party has committed himself to closing the question; nothing has been done about the past act or about their future relationship. This leaves all options open.

"In contrast, asking for forgiveness is quite specific, when done biblically. Say to the one you wronged, 'I have sinned against God and against you [Luke 15:18]. I have confessed my sin to God [if you have], and I know He has forgiven me; now I ask you to do the same. Will you?' Such a statement is specific. By it you recognize the serious nature of what you have done—it is sin, against both God and him. Secondly, it asks for a concrete response on the part of the one that you wronged (don't settle for a non-committal reply like 'Forget it.' Say, 'No, this was sin. That requires forgiveness. I want to set the matter to rest; will you forgive me?'

"Sometimes the person wronged is willing to settle for less so that he can go on holding the offense against you. If he dodges an answer, or refuses to forgive, remind him of Luke 17:3-10. If he still refuses, Matthew 18:15ff. comes into play (with another believer).[6] He must say either 'yes' or 'no.' You must know the answer.

---

6. In seeking forgiveness from an unbeliever follow Rom. 12:18 (for a thorough discussion of this, see my book, *How to Overcome Evil*).

"When you go to another, the object isn't merely to express your feelings—even of regret. You must go (as the Scriptures make clear) to be reconciled to him. The substitute, 'I'm sorry,' does nothing about the *relationship;* the biblical way opens the door on a new beginning.

"And, one more thing—if either you or the person to whom you go doesn't understand what forgiveness is, and, therefore, what the granting of forgiveness entails, let me tell you plainly. Then you can explain to him what you have in mind. Forgiveness is a *promise.* When God forgave you in Christ, He promised not to 'remember your sins and iniquities against you any more.' The one who asks for forgiveness also asks for *that;* the one granting forgiveness promises *that*—and nothing less. This promise is three-fold in his case:

(1) 'I won't bring the matter up to you again'
(2) 'I won't bring it up to others'
(3) 'I won't bring it up to myself' (i.e., allow myself to sit and brood over it in self-pity).

Asking and granting forgiveness implies future effort to work for a new, biblical relationship. When God reconciled us to Himself, He didn't leave the matter with forgiveness. Once the sin was forgiven, He insisted on building a new, proper relationship with us (cf. Eph. 4:17).[7] Now, what do you think of this? Is it clear? Do you have any questions?"

Some such presentation of the assignment must be given (whatever the subject may be). By going into it in some detail (you may even want to *read* this to a counselee at times) you will forestall all sorts of problems. By giving an opportunity for feedback at the close, often you can discover whether the counselee understands, believes, intends to follow directions, etc. His response usually will lead to further clarification of the issues.

In spite of such specific directions, warnings, etc., some counselees

---

7. On this, see my *Matters of Concern,* pp. 36ff., where I discuss how reconciliation must lead to a new relationship.

will persist in "doing it their own way" with the usual consequences. When they come to you complaining about the need for a $200-plus repair job on their relationship, they must be told—in no uncertain terms—who failed.[8] How do you do this?

Fundamentally, there is but one thing to do (a variety of approaches may be used, however): gather complete, exact data about what the counselee did/said and did not do/say. Many counselors settle for arguing about incomplete, inexact data; they do not probe deeply for facts. After all, if what you told him truly is biblical (and now we assume it was), then the counselee is charging that God has failed, that His Word isn't trustworthy. This is serious and cannot be handled like an egg, "once over, lightly."

Ask questions: "How long did you do it? What was the tone of your voice when you said that?" etc. You may have to say, "Tell me specifically, in detail, step by step, what you did and said; what he did and said in response. First, you went to him—where? Under what circumstances? Were others present? Did you make an appointment? . . ." and so it must go (on and on at times). When you require facts, you will soon discover what is at the bottom of his failure. More often than not—as you might expect—there it is, an ersatz oil filter!

When you get hold of that filter, you can show him plainly—explain what went wrong and begin to deal with what, perhaps, is an equally serious (or even more serious) problem—this pattern of doing things another way.

Well, I've told you. I've advised you to do several things. But I am certain that some of you—even you Christian counselors—will say, "Well, yeah, maybe so . . . but I think there's another way to do it."

---

8. Of course, if the counselor also failed in any way—perhaps in not becoming specific enough—he should confess this and seek forgiveness from the counselee, thus becoming a model for him.

3

Stress—A Christian Approach

Let's talk a bit about stress. Since Hans Selye's studies, stress has been in the news. What do Christians have to say about the issue? The word is used in several ways by various people to denote different things. Therefore, it is essential, at the outset, to define the term as I shall be using it in this chapter.

Popularly, the word stress is used as a synonym for what I shall call *pressure*. By pressure I mean force exerted upon an individual's body (or some part of it). This force may be located either without or within the individual himself. In this chapter I shall not use the word stress in that sense. Whenever referring to such force, I shall always use the word *pressure*.

More technically, the word *stress* refers to debilitating bodily responses to these inner and outer pressures. It is a response in which various normal bodily reactions are (1) maintained for too long a period of time, and/or (2) heightened to a more-than-optimal level. Stress, then, refers to any harmful, self-induced strain upon the body or upon various parts of or organs in it.

I have distinguished between these two terms in order to set forth the biblical viewpoint on stress and pressure more clearly. Some such distinction (use whatever terms you prefer) is necessary in order not to confound things that the Bible separates (as some, in speaking of this subject, have done). Pressures from without (or even at times from within) may not be avoidable; stress (since it is part of an inner, learned response) always is.

It is most important for counselors to recognize this point. If stress

17

is (as many think) unavoidable, then three things follow:

1. The individual undergoing stress is not responsible for it.
2. He is a victim of what others (or circumstances) have done to him.
3. In most instances he can do nothing to alleviate it.[1]

Moreover, it is not at all helpful to speak of *stressors* (as if persons could automatically turn on stress in another by their presence, words or actions). Neither persons nor situations can do anything of the sort. They may *exert pressure,* but not *cause stress.* To speak of stressful situations is, therefore, equally bad. Stress, like tension, is in *persons;* not in circumstances. It is fine for authors and poets to rhapsodize about tension "in the air" or "between" people, but it is wrong for counselors to do so. Tension is always in muscles. Stress is always an electro-chemical response in a person that (like tension) is subject to his control by (1) developing and making biblical interpretation and (2) responses to persons or situations that exert pressure. According to some theorists, stressors are persons who always elicit a stress response in the counselee. While it is true that such a response may *regularly* occur, the reason lies in the counselee himself, not in the so-called stressor. The word stressor ought, therefore, to be scrapped because attention ought to be focused primarily on the changeable habitual response pattern of the counselee, and only secondarily upon the source of pressure.

That fact is significant because it indicates that the counselee, far from being a helpless victim, controlled by the whims of others and the winds of circumstances, is responsible for the stress that he (alone) places upon his body.

Stress, then, is the result of habitual, sinful responses. In counseling it is important to make this clear to counselees. They must be given hope by recognizing that stress is sin. Jesus Christ came to deal with

---

1. I wish to make it clear that I am not including bodily injury or illness, which may cause bodily strain (one system breaking down can place great pressure on another), in this analysis. Sometimes nothing *can* be done about such bodily strain because medical science has no answer to it.

sin. By the Spirit's power, working through His Word, these responses can be exchanged for non-stressful, biblical ones. And the counselee must be held responsible for availing himself of all God's resources for doing so. Stress, as I have defined it, then, is the counselee's own sinful, body-harming response to pressure.

Thus far I have spoken almost entirely of outer pressures. There are inner pressures too. These are *generated* within the counselee by the counselee himself. A sense of guilt arising from unconfessed, unforgiven sin may lead to bad bodily feelings triggered by conscience (the capacity for self-evaluation according to a value standard). Anger, worry and fear (for the wrong reasons, in the wrong intensity, unrelieved by the proper biblical resolution of matters) are others.

In one sense, almost all outer pressures also are inner. Outer pressures do not truly become such (unless they are physical) until (or unless) they are *interpreted* by the counselee as pressures. If a sneer is taken as a smile of approval, it is not very likely to be taken as an occasion for a stressful response. Often, seeing events more biblically, trusting God for his explanation of them, or learning that there is a proper biblical response to them, alleviates the pressure. The outer non-physical event itself really has no power to elicit a stress response. Another's sin cannot make me sin. I won't respond that way unless I am willing to do so. Otherwise, Jesus Himself would have sinned; it would have been inevitable. He would have sinfully injured His body by sinful stress reactions. The fact is—as we know—He did not. We confuse the issue because we look at sinners (even redeemed ones) who so often do respond sinfully—then declare that a pressure ➤ stress response is inevitable. Referring to Jesus makes the distinction I have maintained crystal clear.

Regardless of where the pressure that brings a necessity for response originates—within or without—the counselee must not be viewed as a helpless victim, trapped in its web. The Scriptures teach the counselee how he is to interpret and respond to trials, persecution and other hard times as a Christian. They explain what he is to do about guilt. If he injures his body by responses that set loose harmful chemical and muscular states, that is his fault. If he had followed the Bible, stress wouldn't have occurred. He cannot blame stress on pressure; ultimately, to do so is to blame God, Who sovereignly controls both circumstances and persons.

Now, it is unnecessary for the counselee to understand fully how resentment (e.g.) leads to colitis for him to stop putting stress upon his colon. All he needs to know is that the Bible forbids resentment and that it charts another course of action for the Christian in the handling of his anger (cf. Eph. 4:26-32,[2] where the believer is told not to let the sun go down on his anger, and where he is told how to respond by building the other up with his words, while he destroys the problem that has arisen). If he follows this and other biblical directives pertaining to anger and the responses to other pressure-type situations, stress will not occur.

Whether or not the counselor elects to explain something of the physiological dynamic involved, he must always make it plain that (in the end) the *major* reason for avoiding resentment is *not to avoid stress,* but to please God by obedience. That is why a simple believer, who lives in a manner pleasing to God, can live a stress-free life, purely by studying and following the Bible (cf. Ps. 119:98-100). The one who makes glorifying God his constant goal truly finds that he does *enjoy* Him as well!

Surely the Apostle Paul (not to speak of Jesus Himself) was under unbelievable pressures (cf. II Cor. 4:8, 9, 16, 17; 6:4-10; 11:23-29). Those passages, if they indicate anything, show that he should have had colitis, ulcer, heart problems, etc., if the current pressure = stress view were true. Yet, he had none of these difficulties because even though undergoing greater pressures than any counselee you will encounter, he did not subject his body to stress through sinful interpretations and responses to these pressures. That is why he could go on serving Christ under such trial. Like Christ, Who did not get ulcers on the cross because He prayed for those who were condemning Him to death, Paul handled wrongdoing toward himself rightly (cf. Phil. 1, etc.).

---

2. See *The Christian Counselor's Manual* for more on this.

Paul's case vividly illustrates the falsity of the modern view symbolized by the simple equation

$$\text{Pressure} \longrightarrow \text{Stress}$$

This is too simplistic a view. A true biblical picture looks like this:

$$\text{Pressure} + \text{sinful response} \longrightarrow \text{Stress}$$
$$\text{Pressure} + \text{righteous response} \longrightarrow \text{Peace}$$

The difference between the two constructions is the difference between responsibility and irresponsibility, the difference between hope and despair, the difference between health and sickness. Christian counselors will be well advised to maintain a sharp distinction.

4

Drugs and Counseling

Of course there are other types of medicine (e.g., medicines to fight infection, inflammation, etc.); but I'm not thinking about those in this chapter. Rather, what I have in mind are the two types of drugs given to persons who are involved in the sort of behavioral problems that also lead to counseling. Questions often are raised by counselees about these. Counselors must grapple with the effects of drugs on counselees, and (in general) there are a number of reasons why a Christian counselor ought to take a clear-cut position about them.

Probably the most convenient way for laymen to think about such drugs is to divide them into two categories. These are:

1. Drugs that supplement bodily chemicals.
2. Drugs that inhibit bodily functions.

Drugs of the first category, like insulin, do for the body what it ought to do for itself, but (for one reason or another) doesn't. They meet *a genuine bodily lack,* a need. Such drugs do not interfere with normal bodily functions, but assist them and make them possible.

Drugs of the second category include the tranquilizers and other drugs that are given to *inhibit* certain normal bodily functions. In other words, *these drugs have an opposite purpose and function.* The use of such drugs is

1. Highly questionable in most instances.
2. If appropriate at all, only for a very brief, temporary period (e.g., to calm a counselee in a suicidal or hysterical state).
3. Never to be used when counseling ought to be given instead;

cannot be substituted for changes of behavior that ought to be effected by the Spirit of God through the ministry of His Word.

These rough guidelines may be of help to Christian counselors who (in a variety of situations) may have to deal with such questions. While counselors may not prescribe drugs, they may

1. Refuse to counsel when they find that because of its side effects they are talking to the pill more than to the person.
2. Call the prescribing physician (with the counselee's permission) and request that the drug be eliminated.
3. Encourage the counselee to assume more personal responsibility for behavior change, and urge him to face rather than run from problems (into drugs), leading to speedy disuse of drugs of the second sort.

Drugs of the second category often create new problems for those who take them, some of which are equally as serious (from the counselor's viewpoint) as the problem they are designed to relieve. Actually, they do not solve problems; they only mask them.

For helpful, further suggestions, each pastor should develop a close working alliance with a physician who recognizes the importance of not over-prescribing drugs. From this alliance may come various benefits, one of which will be a better understanding of drugs that it is impossible to include in this broad summary.

5

The Practicality of the Sermon on the Mount

One fact that I have insisted on over the years (and have worked hard to rectify) is that conservative churches have been strong on the *what-to* (in both preaching and counseling—i.e., where they have done biblical counseling at all), but weak on the *how-to*.

I

In counseling I have discovered that many counselees are in serious trouble because, while they know *what* the Lord requires of them, they do not know *how* to go about meeting these requirements—no one ever told them. Indeed, many don't even know where to begin. Again and again in counseling sessions the breakthrough comes when I begin to apply known scriptural truths practically (concretely directing the counselee in the ways and means of kneading biblical principles into the dough of his life). That's when he comes alive and things begin to happen. Before, he knew what to do (at least generally, though sometimes this needs sharpening too); this he had been taught again and again (in Sunday School, from the pulpit, in Christian books). And usually I find that he has tried, only to fail again and again. Soon (characteristically) he gives up, saying, "Well, maybe Paul can do it, but I'm not Paul." This failure syndrome is widespread in the church.

The answer to the problem—as I have taught in all my books—is to begin to include the *how-to* in all counseling. When I caught on to this and began to focus on this in my counseling practice, I also began to see a tremendous difference in counseling results. If my past 14 years of counseling experience has demonstrated anything, it has pointed out the utter need for creative practicality in the *use* of the Scriptures.

Now, as I said, I have hammered away at this point, given many examples of what I mean and have taught others also how to use the Scriptures practically (that doesn't exclude exegesis and theology, but rather seeks to achieve individual applications of both). But, as I scan my books, I notice that I have largely *assumed* that this was a biblical emphasis; I have not adequately supported that assumption from the Scriptures themselves. And, in question-and-answer periods this has been pointed out by various questions from time to time. So here I shall make one initial thrust that—in and of itself (I believe)—should establish this practice as biblical.

If, over the years, any unit of biblical material has been thought of as "idealistic" or "impractical" by those who do not believe or do not understand (or are unsympathetic with) its teachings, it has been the Sermon on the Mount. I propose, therefore, to examine this sermon (as it appears in the Gospel according to Matthew) to show (1) that the charge of impractical idealism cannot be sustained and (2) that the Scriptures clearly demonstrate that (in His preaching) Jesus was concerned equally with the *what-to* and the *how-to*. The Sermon on the Mount, I think you will agree (when I am through), is eminently practical. Moreover, along the way, I hope to discover some of the how-to for the development and use of how-to. So let us begin.

II

The first section of the Sermon on the Mount (Matt. 5:1-20) is introductory; it sets the stage for what follows. One would not expect much application in the introduction to a sermon. The beatitudes (which have very practical implications for life—someone has quipped, "The beatitudes are the attitudes we ought to be at"—but these are not spelled out practically) give an exciting profile of what God's people may (indeed *must*) become. Here, in this list, are both their ideals and their hope. Then, in summarizing the influence

25

that Christians like this may bear, Jesus says they must be salt (a preserving influence) and light (an illuminating, guiding influence). All these ideals are possible and may be realized, not by overthrowing the O.T. principles of living (vv. 17-19) but (unlike the scribes and Pharisees) by properly interpreting, applying and living according to those commandments in all their fulness (v. 20). This fulness would be described by Jesus in the sermon that follows and demonstrated by Him in the life He would live and the death He would die.

The phrase, "You have heard . . . but I say," refers not to the O.T. Scriptures—as though Jesus were abrogating God's principles of living taught there—but to the false scribal interpretations *and applications* (He takes up *both*[1] and, therefore, counters *both* with correct alternatives.) In the sections that follow, Jesus shows how to *interpret* and to *apply* the Scriptures properly. Naturally, He makes concrete, practical, *how-to* type applications in doing so. Even the conclusion to the sermon fits this analysis; it too is practical in emphasis: The Christian's righteousness will exceed the righteousness of the scribes and Pharisees when he learns *both* to *hear* and to *do* all Jesus commands.

N.B., Jesus lays emphasis upon *both* hearing and doing; He sees no place for truth unapplied and unappropriated. The what-to is not enough (in some ways, that was the Pharisee's problem: he knew the what-to, but he either failed to work it out in daily living, or did so in a perverted way); it must issue in practical Christian living.

Following the introduction, Jesus becomes practical and specific. First He takes up the sixth commandment, the one that prohibits murder (v. 21). The scribes had restricted its application to the limited circumstance of actual homicide. But Jesus makes it clear that the commandment is broad; He shows too that it has an inner application as well. Therefore, it includes unrighteous anger, and the expression of such anger in words. For instance, two Christians must never allow any matter to separate them because of anger.

---

1. Most commentators have stressed the interpretations alone. The two can be distinguished but, of course, cannot be separated; the one supported the other.

Bitterness and resentment may not come between them; they must be reconciled.

"But what happens when, in this world of sin, they do allow such things to come between them?" someone might ask. Jesus anticipates the situation, and (in very practical *how-to*—here even step-by-step—terms) He tells us *how to* handle the situation (vv. 23, 24). The practical how-to comes in the form of a procedure growing out of the priority of reconciliation. Clearly verses 23 and 24 are how-to verses.[2]

Next, Jesus makes a second application of the sixth commandment. Once again He shows exactly how it may be applied, this time, when dealing with an unbeliever. In a pending court trial, it is better not to let your anger keep you from doing the sensible thing—settling out of court, as quickly as possible. Otherwise, you may be sorry.

So, as Jesus discusses the sixth commandment, we note that He offers two case studies and recommends specific, concrete action, often in the form of steps ("First . . . then"). These are important principles for counselors to understand and follow.

But that is just the beginning. Next, He turns to the seventh commandment (vv. 27-30). Again, after broadening the commandment beyond the mere outward act to include the heart, He turns to how-to (vv. 29, 30). If one must not look on a woman lustfully, then (the question arises) *how* can he avoid doing so? He gives a concrete answer: by putting impediments in his way. Whatever member of the body has been offending (even a *right* eye, *right* hand, *right* foot——*right*, indicating the most important), it must be removed. Jesus never intended this to be understood literally. His point was, as mutilation would make it difficult to perform an act again, so whatever led to adultery (or any other sin) of the heart similarly must be removed. The truly repentant believer does not want to offend again, so (and this is the *how-to*) he will do all he can to make it difficult to fall into the same sin again.[3]

---

2. Cf. Matt. 18:15ff.; Luke 17:3ff. for other step-by-step how-to directions about the same matter.
3. For more on this, in detail, see my *Christian Counselor's Manual*, ch. 19.

In verses 31 and 32, Jesus takes up another false interpretation that (again) leads to sinful action. Deuteronomy 24 was not intended to allow or institute divorce, but only to regulate it. In this case, the Pharisees had broadened a narrow O.T. passage to make it teach things that it was not designed to say. So, Jesus narrowed it once again to the correct interpretation (I cannot treat the many ramifications of the divorce/remarriage question here. I have tapes[4] available on the question and am writing a book on the subject). In the process, Christ clarifies the biblical position on divorce, the exception to it (among believers) and the results of violating the biblical position by misusing the Scriptures for one's own purposes. There is no *how-to* here, because the discussion is (essentially) negative; but there is plenty of how *not* to!

Turning to the next passage (vv. 33-37), Jesus tightens up another commandment that was being misused by the Jews. Their preoccupation was with the exact formula of oath-taking. By cleverly worded vows and oaths they could seem to swear when they didn't do so at all—or at least that's what *they* thought! Christ was concerned about honesty—being a man of one's word. One's reputation for honesty should be so stainless that his word alone is sufficient (he need not swear).[5] But the important fact, for our purposes, is the clear-cut how-to that Jesus gives. He teaches explicitly that one must solve the question of oaths *beforehand,* not afterward (v. 37—He must always mean yes when he says "yes" and no when he says "no"). Christians must stop playing word games altogether (vv. 34ff.). Simply, clearly, say yes or no and mean it. That is long-term, sweeping, but explicit how-to. It sliced through all the confusion, arguments and sophistry. No casuistry was needed.

In verse 38, another issue is raised. The Christian's personal ethic must be distinguished from civil punishment (Paul picks up on this

4. Available from Christian Study Services, 1790 E. Willow Grove Ave., Laverock, Pa. 19118.

5. On this passage (and the entire sermon) see John R. Stott's excellent book, *The Christian Counter Culture* (Downer's Grove, Ill.: InterVarsity Press, 1978).

in Romans 12 and 13). As individuals, we must learn to respond with love, overcoming evil with good (for a full discussion of this see my *How to Overcome Evil*). Verses 39-42 are *how-to* verses—each explains *how* God wants Christians to handle pressure and persecution rather than retaliate. To help, again Jesus illustrates the how-to principles by cases that clearly might apply to actual situations that any one of them might face.

In verses 43-48, Jesus continues this basic theme: a Christian must *love* his enemies. But, unlike many modern preachers, Christ didn't leave the concept of love hanging in thin air—undefined and amorphous. Rather, He was quite specific: love focuses on the other person; not on one's self. Therefore (note the specific how-to) a Christian must pray for his enemies. That concrete proposal Paul developed (as we must develop all such suggestions) in Romans 12:14ff.

And so the sermon continues. There is no let-up on the practicality of the material confronted in chapter 6. Here, the general principle is set forth: Don't do righteousness for the approval of others, or that is *all* you will get for your efforts. Jesus cites four areas of abuse (note how He works a principle into a number of practical situations):

1. Giving charity for personal acclaim (vv. 2-4);
2. Praying like the hypocrites (vv. 5, 6);
3. Praying like the pagans (vv. 7-15);
4. Fasting to exhibit humility to others (vv. 16-18).

To each of these four areas, Jesus appends some how-to advice that (if followed) will keep the Christian from falling into the traps just mentioned. Here it is:

Verse 3—Do your giving anonymously.

Verse 6—Pray regularly in a private place.

Verses 9-13—Pray briefly and to the point, listing distinct items in sequence, ridding prayer of all unnecessary repetition.

Verses 17, 18—Fasting before God alone.

Indeed, as you can see, even the so-called Lord's prayer was given (at this place) in order to show *how to* pray (cf. v. 9a). It is a how-to model.

The next section of the sermon (vv. 22-34) covers the inter-related sins of avarice and anxiety. The answer to avoiding these Siamese twins is stated in very practical terms (vv. 33, 34):

1. Set your priorities properly (v. 33);
2. Focus your efforts and concern on solving today's (not to-morrow's) problems (v. 34).[6]

Chapter 7 continues along the same lines. What to do about judging is the theme of the first five verses in this chapter. Jesus not only sounds a warning against sinful forms of judging, but He lays out a concrete how-to procedure that (1) will prevent one from sinful judging and (2) will help him to judge righteously (v. 5). In modern terms, the how-to principle may be stated this way: Put the lid on your own garbage can before complaining about the odor from someone else's.

Though this discussion has been brief and summary, I think it is perfectly clear by this point that Christ was concerned about how-to as well as what-to. Without detailing the rest, notice how-to instructions (continuing throughout chapter 7) in verse 7 (ask if you want something), verse 12 (treat others as you'd want them to treat you), and verse 16 (you can discover false prophets by observing the fruit of their teaching in lives—theirs and those of their disciples). Then, to cap off the whole sermon, Jesus insists on *doing* what He has said, not merely hearing it. But to know how is not the same as to show how. Jesus recognized this, and throughout the sermon insisted on *showing* how.

Now, in conclusion, let's draw together a few principles that will help us to understand *how to* use *how-to.*

1. Jesus gave specific instances of what He taught; He used case studies. He didn't merely state principles abstractly as so many do today. You can actually picture (in your mind's eye) the

---

6. Verse 34 has been unpacked in a pamphlet, *What to Do About Worry;* verse 33 could (likewise) be treated much more fully.

man laying down his gift on the altar, getting up, leaving, looking for his brother, etc.

2. Jesus illustrated principles so they would be clear and memorable. Once having heard it, who could ever forget the splinter and the board of Matthew 7, or the principle it illustrates?

3. When giving a specific case (plucking out the eye that adulterously looks on a woman in lust), Jesus generalized (to the hand, and elsewhere to the foot) as well. He thereby extended the principle of making it difficult for one to sin again to all sorts of situations.

4. Jesus even gave actual models to follow (cf. the Lord's prayer).

Let us be thankful for the practicality of the Sermon on the Mount. Jesus showed us the importance of such practicality in Christian instruction. We too, in the ministry of the Word (in preaching and in counseling), must do the same.

6
Don't Apologize!

It is time to say it clearly—so that no one may misunderstand: the Bible nowhere advises or allows (and certainly doesn't command) apology.

Yet, in spite of this fact, Christians (and even Christian counselors) somehow seem to be addicted to apologizing and advising counselees to "go apologize" to others whom they have wronged. To all such, I have one piece of advice: Stop it!

"Well, what on earth is wrong with apologies?"

Fundamentally, two things.

I

An apology is an inadequate, humanistic substitute for the real thing. Nowhere do the Scriptures require, or even encourage, apologizing. To say "I'm sorry" is a human dodge for doing what God has commanded. And (as we shall see) since it is man's substitute for God's requirement (and has all but replaced that requirement), it has caused a great number of problems in the church. By replacing the biblical requirement for dealing with estrangement, it has allowed estrangement in the church to continue unchecked.

"What is this biblical requirement that has been replaced?"

Forgiveness.

"Forgiveness?"

Yes. I shall not now develop this point by discussing the numerous passages that speak of Christian forgiveness. Instead, I shall simply refer you to other treaments of the subject.[1]

---

1. See *The Christian Counselor's Manual,* pp. 63-70, 88, 361; *Christian Living in the Home,* ch. 3.

As long as Christians continue to say to those they have wronged, "I'm sorry" (or words to this effect), instead of "I sinned; will you forgive me?" and as long as they receive the natural response, "Oh, that's all right" (or something similar), the real solutions to the many difficulties that could have been reached through forgiveness will continue to be by-passed. The church will labor under the burden of resentments and bitterness on the part of its members.

"Why do you say that?" you may wonder. Let me explain; and that explanation leads to a second point—apology is wrong, not only because it is man's inadequate substitute for God's revealed method of righting sour interpersonal relationships, but (as such),

II

apology elicits an inadequate response. When one asks, "Will you forgive me?" he has punted; the ball has changed hands, and a response is now required of the one addressed. The onus of responsibility has shifted from the one who did the wrong to the one who was wronged. Both parties, therefore, are required to put the matter in the past. And, the proper response (Luke 17:3) is, "Yes, I will." Like God's forgiveness ("Your sins and iniquities I will remember against you no more"), human forgiveness is a *promise* that is *made* and *kept*.

When one person says, "I forgive you," to another, he promises:
1. "I'll not bring this matter up to you again"
2. "I'll not bring it up to others"
3. "I'll not bring it up to myself (i.e., dwell on it in my mind) "

The response, "Yes, I'll forgive you," then, is a promise that entails quite a commitment—one to which the forgiven brother (and God) may hold him, and one that (if kept) will lead to forgetting the wrong (not forgive and forget, but forgive to forget) and reestablishing a new, good relationship between the parties involved. So, an apology is an inadequate substitute because (a) it asks for no such commitment, and (b) gets none.

An apology keeps the ball in one's own possession. The other party is required to do nothing about it (and usually doesn't). To

33

say "I'm sorry" is, you see, nothing more than an expression of one's own feelings. To say, "I have wronged you," and then to ask, "Will you forgive me?" is quite another thing.

Therefore, counselors (in advising counselees[2]) must be quite clear about this matter. When they are, and when a proper understanding of this matter once again begins to permeate the Christian church, many of the current difficulties we are experiencing will disappear. Let's do our part in hastening that day.

---

2. See an earlier, spelled-out explanation of how to do this in the article entitled, "Failure in Counseling."

7

Presuppositions and Counseling

All counseling systems rest upon presuppositions. For instance, Freudianism (as one among many assumptions) presupposes that human beings are the product of evolutionary development. It also presupposes that human beings behave as they do because of their unconscious. Rogerianism presupposes that (at the core of his being) man is basically good. It also presupposes that he is filled with untapped potential and solutions to all sorts of problems. Skinnerianism presupposes that man is nothing more than an animal. It also presupposes that by changing the contingencies in his environment, man's behavior can be manipulated. These are only a few of the presuppositions (or basic ideas) that govern and condition all the research (it is *not* objective), practices and development of methods and techniques within these systems. Everything in a consistently framed system grows out of and depends upon its presuppositions.

So does biblical counseling depend upon its presuppositions.

In order to think about this matter more clearly, I have listed (not exhaustively, but suggestively, in random order) what (in my opinion) are some of the presuppositions that are foundational to biblical counseling. Read carefully the 25 presuppositions that follow and see if you agree with them.

1. There is such a thing as peculiarly *Christian* counseling.
2. Not all counseling done by Christians is Christian counseling.
3. The Bible is the sufficient source for the principles needed to do Christian counseling.

4. God is the sovereign Creator and Sustainer of the universe.
5. Counseling depends ultimately upon the work of God's Spirit.
6. Man was created in God's image as a responsible being.
7. Human thought and behavior is moral.
8. Man is a sinful being, guilty and corrupt as the result of the fall.
9. Man's corrupt nature leads to sinful behavior and behavior patterns.
10. Sin results in misery.
11. Unregenerate persons cannot be changed by counseling in a way that pleases God.
12. Regeneration by the Spirit is a prerequisite for biblical change and obedience.
13. Problems of regenerate persons can be solved God's way by God's power.
14. God requires and equips His officers In the church to counsel as a life calling.
15. God requires and equips all believers to counsel.
16. The church must become involved in counseling.
17. Church discipline is an important factor in biblical counseling.
18. Methodology must grow out of biblical principles and practices.
19. Non-Christian content or methods may not be eclectically incorporated into a Christian system.
20. Counselors should expect and see results from Christian counseling.
21. Counselors must study the Scriptures telically.
22. True counseling is a ministry of the Word leading to sanctification.
23. Unbelievers must be evangelized before they can be counseled.
24. Problems with an organic base also should be handled medically.
25. The Scriptures set forth the principles for human living that were demonstrated in the life of Christ.

Now, as I said, this list of presuppositions is not exhaustive (indeed,

I arbitrarily cut off the list at the number 25 so that it would not become unmanageable). But every presupposition is important.

Something of the importance of holding correct presuppositions, and of avoiding falseness, is plainly pointed out by Paul in Galatians 4:9:

> But now that you know God (or rather, that you are known by God), how can you turn back to those weak and pitiful presuppositions? Do you want to be enslaved by them once again?[1] (The New Testament in Everyday English).

Here Paul makes it clear that false presuppositions enslave. One's thinking and actions grow out of his presuppositions, as we have seen. He is bound to his presuppositions. How important, then, it is to have biblical presuppositions on which to found one's life and life work! Whoever is "bound" to God's presuppositions is free indeed.

Some (perhaps many) who read will have little or no difficulty with all (or most) of the 25 presuppositions. Others will find snags all along the way. If you are among the latter, I urge you to study the Scriptures carefully to see whether these things are so (but as you do so, carefully examine the presuppositions that you bring to my list and to the Scriptures).

Presuppositions are of great importance (as I said) because they govern all that we do in counseling (as elsewhere). Therefore, it is important to become aware of our presuppositions. Reading the list may help you to do so. Perhaps you would find it helpful to write up your own list of 25 presuppositions to contrast, amplify or supplement mine. At any rate, becoming aware of presuppositions is vital to any serious thought and practice in counseling.

---

1. Hendriksen's arguments for the interpretation of *stoichea* as basic (or elementary) principles (= presuppositions) are convincing. The references to angels or elementary spirits are all late and specialized.

8

Getting Organized

Recently, in speaking with a pastor who is unsuccessfully attempting to counsel a couple who have separated (and who give clear evidence of many irregularities and erratic tendencies in their lives) I was struck afresh by the fact that many (perhaps most) pastors do not structure their counseling adequately. Clearly, as our conversation continued, it became apparent that much of his failure stems from this lack.

Instead of setting formal times and places for counseling on a regular basis, I find that many pastors counsel in a very spotty way—whenever they happen to think of it, whenever there is pressure to do so, whenever they are faced with some pending calamity or whenever the spirit (not the Spirit) moves them. And, they will counsel anywhere, whether the conditions are optimal or not (even when there is no emergency to do so).

No wonder, then, that all too few counselees are helped by this hit-or-miss approach. Often, biblical counseling gets a bad press from this sloppy imitation of it. Such shoddy counseling procedures are deplorable (just as bad as carelessly prepared sermons) and must be corrected. Pastor, if these hard words apply to you—then it is time for you to get organized!

Most counselees (whatever their other difficulties may be) need discipline in many areas of their lives. Even if lack of discipline is not the central problem, accompanying it is the need for order, regularity and persistence—in short, order and discipline. Without it, other problems cannot be solved; order and discipline are preconditions for successful counseling. When the counselor not only fails to demand

38

discipline of his counselees, but also fails to structure orderly conditions for change and, himself, lacks discipline, he thereby inhibits and impedes, rather than furthers, his counseling goals. His own modeling can defeat all that he says.

Why are order and regularity important? Because, among other things, no counseling (as I said) can take place where disorder and confusion prevail. In attempting to put off old sinful behavior patterns and put on new ones, discipline is of the essence (see my booklet, *Godliness through Discipline;* cf. II Tim. 4:7). Two of the basic elements of discipline are order and regularity. Success in replacing old patterns with biblical ones greatly depends upon these two elements. The counseling climate and structure must provide for discipline.

Man was made in God's image. God is "not a God of confusion"; He is a God of orderliness (cf. I Cor. 14:33). On the basis of that fact, Paul ordered the Corinthian church to do everything "decently and in order." But the principle that, because He is not a God of confusion, He demands order, is broader than the worship context to which it was applied. The principle itself is stated without such limit; it has a place in all the work we try to do for Him. He will not have us in confusion in His Name.

To reflect God's ways in our activities, we must be willing to be orderly in *our* affairs. God planned His work, then worked His plan. Christ came "in the fulness of time"—i.e.. right on schedule. He often said words like, "My hour hasn't yet come"; when it did, He noted that fact too. He was conducting His ministry according to a divine timetable. Orderly sequence, planning and scheduling obviously are all elements of the amazing ministry of Christ. Our ministries too must reflect these qualities.

Now, of course (in necessity, on occasions of rare opportunity, etc.) one could counsel anywhere, at any time—we have often said, "We could counsel on a subway." At one point I had to use my VW Microbus as a counseling office. There also must be flexibility (*our* programming isn't divine!); our schedules must not be chiseled in stone. But surely to depart from a well-thought-through schedule

39

ought to be the exception, not the rule. Unfortunately, in some cases, the opposite is true.

When a counselor's approach to counseling, then, is spotty, unstructured, irregular and doesn't follow a prayerfully constructed schedule, he simply shouldn't expect consistently good results. Indeed (unwittingly) he is programming his counseling, even though he doesn't know it—for failure. You cannot overcome the disorderly patterns of others' lives by more of the same. If you have problems saying "no," refusing to counsel under less than optimal conditions (when they are available), etc., read my suggestions about these matters in *Matters of Concern,* pp. 83, 84.

I suggest, therefore, that you chalk out certain hours for counseling. They can be largely afternoon hours. (Men take off from work to see other counselors, physicians, dentists, lawyers, etc.; they will do the same for you.[1] What you offer is a service equally as important as any of these, to say the least.) Then, set up weekly sessions for each counseling case. (A full course of life occurs every seven days. About that much time, therefore, is needed to work biblical principles and practices discussed in the session into all aspects of life.)

So, pastor, let me ask you—have your counseling practices been orderly? If not, then it is time for you to get organized, don't you think?

---

1. Regularly, pastors complain, "I don't charge money like a counseling center does, so my people aren't as motivated as theirs." That is wrong. Time *is* money. Proper appreciation for time (yours and the counselee's) can solve all such problems. Why should your family be penalized by your absence every evening for counseling to accommodate others merely so they can make more money. Think through *everyone's* priorities, including your own; be sure they are God's.

9
Using the P.D.I.

In nouthetic counseling circles, the P.D.I. (Personal Data Inventory) has been used for some ten years or more (a copy is reproduced at the end of this article). During that time, it has proven very helpful. Its use has been explained to those who have studied at C.C.E.F. and at the training centers in this country that are associated with N.A.N.C.[1] But many other persons who have become involved in biblical counseling also have become familiar with it. As a result, from time to time, I have been asked to explain its use. I shall do so in this article. N.A.N.C. training centers may find it very helpful to assign the reading of this article to new trainees. First, I shall say a few general words about the P.D.I., then I shall simply move through the form, in order, commenting on various uses and the possible interpretations of responses in each.

First, then, let me suggest that you *always* use a P.D.I. in *every* counseling case. You may ask, "Do you really think I should? For instance, should I have every member of my congregation fill one out? I already know all these things about them." The answer is yes and no. Probably you will do well to have page 3 (the pink page) filled out by *everyone*. But, in such cases, it would be well for *you* (as pastor) to fill in all the data you can on the first two (yellow) pages, from your own records and personal knowledge. As you do, you

---

1. CCEF = The Christian Counseling and Educational Foundation, 1790 E. Willow Grove Ave., Laverock, Pa. 19118 (P.D.I. forms may be purchased at this address). NANC = The National Association of Nouthetic Counselors, 100 Doncaster Dr., Lafayette, Ind. 47905.

will discover that *in most cases* you actually have far less information than at first you may have supposed. Try it; you'll be astounded that you were going to counsel with so little knowledge about essential data. I think, therefore, it won't be long before you will begin to use the P.D.I. with everyone—including your members.

In instances where you begin to counsel persons totally unknown to you, you will discover that the P.D.I. uncovers much valuable data quickly. I recommend that you use it more frequently and more fully than (at first) you may be inclined to.[2]

Who fills out the P.D.I.? In most cases, the counselee should arrive at least a half hour prior to the first counseling session. The church secretary then hands the P.D.I. to the counselee(s)—one to each counselee—and tells him (them) to fill it out. When this has been accomplished, the secretary brings the completed form(s) to the pastor, who goes over it privately. Five minutes of consideration of the form by the pastor ought to prepare him for the interview.

The counselor makes notes (question marks, checks, underlines, exclamation points, etc.) on the P.D.I. as he considers it (the P.D.I. is his property, and he retains it, along with weekly records and other data, in his manila file on the counselee). Usually, notes are made with a red felt-tip pen so that, when needed, he can spot these readily in the sessions that follow. At the top of page 1, if there is a husband and wife, he marks down a large "H" or "W." This enables him to quickly note which P.D.I. belongs to which counselee. Because he must often locate material quickly during discussions that follow, such notations really help. Sometimes he also copies notes from the P.D.I. onto the agenda column of the W.C.R. (Weekly Counseling Record[3]).

Items that the counselor marks on the P.D.I. (or places in the

---

2. Sometimes the easiest way to ask a counselee a potentially embarrassing question (especially a member of your church) is through a written form (obviously, a printed sheet was not designed particularly for some one individual). Some of these questions might never be asked (or the data gathered) otherwise. Use of the form indicates concern for thoroughness; most members appreciate that.

3. Available also at address given in footnote 1, *supra*.

W.C.R.) are quite varied. They may include such matters as, "Why did the Dr. prescribe that drug?" "Check out this emotional upset," "Should I phone the physician about this?" "This sounds important," "Vague," "What was the reason for the arrest?" etc. Usually, the counselor will work out his own abbreviations for such notes (e.g., "Why drg?" "Phys?" "Imp?" "?" "reason?"). The notations that he makes will form the basis for further inquiry and discussion.

Now, let us look at the P.D.I. itself.

Under *Identification Data,* everything is rather straightforward. If any of the data are omitted, check these omissions with a red pen and (early in the first session) find out why. In *some* cases *failure to include data* (here or elsewhere) *could be significant.* Ask later about it.

Clearly, check marks by the counselee in the separated or divorced blanks call attention to themselves immediately. Underline them, and discuss these matters early in counseling (especially when the dates given are quite recent). Other checks in the widowed, single, going steady blanks could be of importance (and may figure significantly at a later point), but *usually* don't call for immediate discussion.

Answers to the questions concerning *education* can be informative. If, for instance, the wife is a college graduate and the husband didn't complete high school, one *possible* source of difficulty (to be explored) immediately comes to mind. If, in addition to other parallel data, you discover that the counselee dropped out of high school in his senior year, that fact may be profitable to investigate. It could indicate the first evidence of a life pattern of quitting when the going gets tough.

Information on who referred the counselee also can be helpful in any number of ways. Perhaps this person himself can help. At some point you may wish to ask the counselee's permission to invite this party to a session to disclose certain data. You may wish to call him/her during a session for information about some point, or to seek his/her assistance in a project that the counselee may undertake in his homework.

These uses of identification data are only suggestions, of

course, but they serve to show you how much you can learn from seemingly "standard" information. Begin to discover for yourself how much more is revealed by such simple responses.

Now, let us turn to *Health Information*. Obviously, answers that indicate that the counselee's health is declining (or those substituted under "other") require investigation. Large losses (or gains) in weight may indicate either physical problems or significant emotional turmoil. Past illnesses (e.g., a coma), handicaps (e.g., a club foot), or injuries (e.g., a concussion) can be of significance in understanding a counselee's problem. Pursue carefully any that *may* seem to link up. Send for medical reports, phone a physician for an evaluation, etc. CCEF starter kits for counselors[4] contain a *Release of Information Form* that the counselees may sign to obtain data from a physician. The simplest way to get this is to ask the counselee to ask his physician to send you a report.

The date of the counselee's last medical examination can be important. Reports of recent examinations are often *very* helpful. Be sure to send the counselee for an examination when you feel there is any possibility that there is organic dysfunction behind certain behaviors, unless he has just been examined *for the problem under consideration* and the report is negative (be sure you *see* the report; for various reasons, counselees may misread, misunderstand or, at times, falsify reports).

Naturally any mood-changing drugs that the counselee is taking may be of importance to counseling. You may be talking to the pill rather than to the person if you are not careful about this question. A normal response (apart from drugs) may be brighter, exhibiting more concern, or less anxiety. See the chapter in this volume, "Drugs and Counseling" for further information (or my larger chapter on drugs in *The Big Umbrella,* where I have tried to set forth some guidelines for helping persons who depend on drugs).

You will want to obtain last year's P.D.R. (Physician's Desk Reference) from your physician so that you can look up the effects of

---

4. Available at the Laverock address.

drugs on your counselees. Side effects of some drugs affect counselees quite dramatically. There have been times when counselors have noted these and have had the counselee notify the prescribing physician about the fact.

The question about "severe emotional upsets" often elicits very important data. Investigate the data very closely. Frequently, the counselee will indicate events (or patterns) here that can lead quickly to the heart of some difficulty. Pursue the data given here fully enough to discover the nature of these upsets and whether they recur according to some pattern.

A *yes* response to the question on arrest (which seems out of place here, but isn't—we get honest answers by including it here) can be of significance. By asking "When?" you (as I once did) may receive this retort, "My wife had me locked up last week." Clearly, this reply has put you onto something right away.

There is little that I need to say about the *Religious Background* section; to Christian counselors, the value of such data is great. The *exact* wording used is important because it is designed to cover (and uncover) all sorts of facts from all sorts of persons. A *tentative* evaluation of the counselee's faith and life may be gained by a careful reading of his responses. But this evaluation should never be absolutized; it must be subject to re-evaluation at any time. The last question about "recent changes" often brings out important facts. Learn to ask for further details regarding answers given here.

We now turn to page 2 and *Personality Information*. The first two questions about previous counseling are *very* important. If the counselee indicates that he has had counseling before, you will want to know (1) with whom and to what extent, (2) whether failures have destroyed his hope (look especially for this where he has been to many counselors),[5] and whether his mind has been filled with erroneous concepts and/or excuses derived from previous counseling

---

5. If this is the case, see *The Manual* (on hope) for how to generate hope again.

(listen for psychiatric or psychological jargon in his descriptions of his problem). *In all cases,* try to discover:

(1) What was attempted or done in previous counseling (sometimes new problems grow from counseling).

(2) What the counselee was taught (and believed) about himself, his problems, others, life, etc.

(3) What the counselee did about any advice that he was given.

(4) What the outcome was.

(5) What the counselee's present evaluation of previous counseling is.

From a *discussion* of these data, you will often learn much about a counselee himself, as well as something about his life problems. Don't miss either angle.

The words to underline and circle help you to discover the present (note the word "now") state of the counselee. If she circles nervous, impulsive, moody, often-blue, introvert, self-conscious, lonely, sensitive, you can almost count on meeting a depressed woman (or one on the depression skids, traveling fast) in a few minutes when she comes through your door. The same circles, however, may (in fewer instances) indicate heavy medication, grief, etc. I will not try to open up all of the possibilities that various combinations of marked words *may* indicate (note: always read these answers in relationship to others in the P.D.I.). Instead, I suggest that you try out the list on yourself, your friends and counselees. From their responses, and what you know of them, begin discovering which combinations *usually* (not always) indicate what. You will want to develop your own reference chart. You'll learn more from this than if I were to tell you how various combinations may indicate certain trends (and you'll enjoy doing so). One last note on this section—Answers to "other ...." will be infrequent. Ones given usually are highly significant.

The next series of questions, extending from, "Have you ever felt people were watching you?" to "Do you have problems sleeping?" are there to uncover possible perceptual problems. A series of yes answers, particularly yes answers about hallucinations and sleep loss, may be of great importance. Some persons seem to suffer from perceptual problems due to drugs, sleep loss or chemical imbalances and malfunctions within their systems. Effects upon perception (seeing, hearing, smelling, tasting, touching, perceiving depth) may occur in almost any combination and intensity. The counselor should look for

(1) Multiple responses (sleep loss and hallucinations, etc.). If there are a number of such problems, he has stronger reason to suspect perceptual difficulty.

(2) Misunderstood responses (an attractive woman may have problems with people watching her—not from perceptual difficulty but because of her beauty.

Perceptual problems can cause great difficulty; it is hard to live with them. Yet some causes are quickly remedied by (1) sleep, (2) removing toxic substances from the environment, (3) massive vitamin therapy, etc. In cases where there seems to be difficulty unrelated to drugs or sleep loss, a further question-and-answer test may be used to confirm or deny the suspicions that grow out of these sample questions. This is the H.O.D. (or Hoffer-Osmond diagnostic test) mentioned in *Competent to Counsel,* pages 37ff.

Turning now to *Marriage and Family Information,* we discover that the P.D.I. asks what seems to be largely routine, clear-cut questions. That is true, but there are some uses of answers that may not immediately be as apparent as the questions that evoked them. Let me mention a couple of these (you'll soon discover others) to give you some idea of what I have in mind.

Occupations, for instance, often are areas of concern and pressure (gobbling up a husband's time, difficulties at work brought home, misery from failure to find an occupation that matches one's gifts, working at a job that one's spouse disapproves, etc.).

The response that a couple has filed for a divorce or has been separated on previous occasions, shows immediately that there has been long-standing difficulty in the marriage. Many of those former problems will have never been solved. Troubles may be complex and quite complicated by now (cf. *Matters of Concern,* p. 20, for help in sorting things out). Find out the occasions for those previous difficulties, what they led to and how they are related to the present problem (directly—"same old thing again"; indirectly—"before it was his mother; now *he's* acting just like her").

When the wife's age is greater than her husband's (especially if there is a large gap), it is possible (but not *necessarily* so) that she married him as a last resort. Look for bitterness and resentment in either or both parties. Very short engagements *may* indicate poor reasons for marriage in the first place (explore this); or very long engagements *may* indicate indecision, or other problems.

Many children, spaced closely together, *in some cases* also may cause problems—look for resentment. Previous marriages (especially investigate the thorny problem of integrating children from them— occasions when this has been done well are rare) often cause difficulty. Wrong patterns, expectations, fears, and odious comparisons, developed in a former marriage may (unnecessarily) be carried over to the present one. Indeed, it is likely that this has happened (look into it).

Where the counselee was in the lineup of siblings (how many older/ younger brothers/sisters he had) often has significance ("Dad had nothing for me, but after I left home his financial picture improved and the other kids cashed in; I resent it").

Now, we turn to the pink sheet (the colors are mildly motivational). The five questions here allow the counselee to tell his/her own story in his/her own way. No one could structure beforehand all the questions that might cover all situations that occur among counselees. Hence this page (it also allows for some duplication that invites comparison with previous answers. Significant contradictions should be probed).

In these answers, you may learn a lot not only from the data given but also from *how* it is given. Does the language—grammar, vocabulary and sentence structure—indicate good or poor communicative skill? Wisdom? Foolishness? Poor communication skills often point to misunderstandings, etc. Circle (in red) nasty, harsh words (to be referred to later when discussing communication). Other attitudes often emerge too (hesitation, over-qualification, etc.). In answer to questions 1-3 a teenager wrote:

Q. 1.—What is your problem?
A.—Nothing.
Q. 2.—What have you done about it?
A.—Nothing.
Q. 3.—What do you want me to do about it?
A.—Same thing.

At least two facts were apparent:

1. He didn't want to be there and had no hope;
2. He had a sense of humor (note the switch in answer to no. 3). It was through humor that he was reached, and eventually given hope and helped.

When two or more parties come for counseling, it is interesting to compare and contrast the answers that they give to questions 1-3. Some obvious problems emerge instantly when you see quite diverse understandings of the same difficulty (or its causes). That, itself, may be *one* problem (or the *basic* one at times).

The answer to question 1 tells you how the counselee sees his difficulty, and on what level (symptomatic or causal). The precision (or the lack of precision) with which he describes it also can be revealing. If he knows and can state clearly what his problem is (and is not deceiving himself), then you need not waste time trying to discover it or explain it. (Be sure his understanding is correct—find out how he arrived at this interpretation. Confidence and clarity don't always flow from correctness.) If the counselee's words are fuzzy (on the other hand), you will have to help him sharpen his focus. The difficulty may lie in his ability to express himself, in his understanding of his problem, or in both of these areas. Check out *both*.

After all supplementary information about answers on the first sheet has been gathered by orally asking questions growing out of written responses, the best place to begin talking is with question 1. I usually read it out loud (for him and any other counselee present) and then say, " Can you tell me something more about. . . ." or "When did you first discover. . . ." or some similar question that grows out of the written response.

I have discussed this before,[6] but let me here remind you briefly that answers to question 1 can be given on any one of three levels:

1. The level of *irritation*. This is what irritated the counselee or others (or both) enough to motivate him to come (e.g., "I've been depressed for over three weeks"). Of course, his interpretation (what he *took* an event, or series of events, to mean or be) may be wrong. Indeed, his interpretation of the problem may be correct, partially correct or wrong (e.g., he may see an event as a crisis, even though it isn't.[7] But so long as he perceives it to be so, he will react to it in that way). People who settle for solving problems at the irritation level often care only for (symptomatic) relief. Such persons usually settle for drugs, etc.

2. The level of the *causal event*. Here, you read answers like, "I was fired from my job for lying." The counselee may see this as the basic problem, when (actually) it may be the culminating result of other, more basic problems. Don't settle for this if there is more. On the other hand, don't invent problems that don't exist.

3. The level of the *underlying* pattern. The particular causal event ("I blew up at her") may be but the latest in a long series of such outbursts under similar circumstances. To seek forgiveness, therefore, is proper but inadequate. The counselee's habitual response pattern itself must be exchanged for a biblical one. Otherwise, the problem will continue to crop up in the future. Much more could be said about question 1, but probably that is enough to remind the regular reader of nouthetic counseling books about the things that have been said elsewhere.

Question 2 yields much helpful information. Look especially for:

a. Right things done in wrong ways.

---

6. The *Manual*, pp. 274ff.
7. *Lectures*, pp. 107ff., where imaginary crises are discussed.

b. Wrong things done, thought to be right.
c. Right things partially done.
d. Complicating problems, growing out of previous wrong actions.
e. Continuing erroneous efforts.

Usually, the discovery of complicating problems is the most valuable fact that you will have to uncover in answer to this question. With that I shall leave it.

Question 3 is important. This *agenda* question lets the counselor know (1) whether he and the counselee have the same objectives. When they differ, agendas must be renegotiated until they both agree—with the Scriptures ("It isn't enough to want your wife back, Joe; you must want to change because God says so—whether Phyllis returns or not"); (2) whether the counselee has hope (if not, you must help him to generate biblical hope—cf. *The Manual* on hope). Without understanding these facts, counselors often will spin their wheels, getting nowhere, and failing to understand why.

Question 4, in itself, usually is fairly unproductive, but sometimes may yield interesting information. In comparing and contrasting the answers here with the words circled on the previous page, you may discover interesting inconsistencies that are profitable to explore (don't try to do all this right away, however; put such items on your agenda for later). Usually, the way that one sees himself *basically* (not necessarily as he is *now*) will be described in this question.

Because no questionnaire can foresee all situations, question 5 has been included. Often very valuable data will be picked up by this question. Always *pay close attention to* whatever is included in this answer. More often than not, it contains clues (sign pointers) to the basic problem.

Hopefully, this discussion of the P.D.I. will be useful in encouraging its use (leading to more productive counseling), and its *proper* use. Careful, thoughtful study of answers to the questions on the P.D.I. may speed up counseling by getting to the heart of issues from the outset. The P.D.I. cannot do everything; do not depend solely upon it. But for whatever value it may have, may it help you to be a more faithful counselor for the Lord Jesus Christ.

51

PERSONAL DATA INVENTORY

IDENTIFICATION DATA:

Name _____ Phone _____

Address _____

Occupation _____ Bus. Phone _____

Sex ____ Birth Date _____ Age _____

Marital Status: Single____ Going Steady____ Married____

Separated____ Divorced____ Widowed____

Education (last year completed): _____ (grade)

Other training (list type and years) _____

_____

Referred here by _____

Address _____

HEALTH INFORMATION:

Rate your health (check): Very Good____ Good____ Average____

Declining____ Other____

Weight changes recently: Lost_____ Gained_____

List all important present or past illnesses or injuries or handicaps:

_____

Date of last medical examination _____

Report: _____

_____

Your physician _____

Address _____

Are you presently taking medication? Yes____ No____

What _____

Have you ever been arrested? Yes____ No____

State circumstances: _____

_____

Are you willing to sign a release of information form so that your counselor may write for social, psychiatric, or medical report? Yes_____ No_____

RELIGIOUS BACKGROUND:

Denominational preference : _____

Member _____

Church attendance per month (circle): 0 1 2 3 4 5 6 7 8 9 10+ Baptized? Yes_____ No_____

Church attended in childhood _____

Religious background of spouse (if married) _____

Do you consider yourself a religious person? Yes_____ No_____ Uncertain_____

Do you believe in God? Yes_____ No_____ Uncertain_____

Do you pray to God? Never_____ Occasionally_____ Often_____

Are you saved? Yes_____ No_____ Not sure what you mean_____

How frequently do you read the Bible? Never_____ Occasionally_____ Often_____ Do you have regular family devotions? Yes_____ No_____

Explain recent changes in your religious life, if any _____
_____

MARRIAGE AND FAMILY INFORMATION:

Name of spouse _____

Address _____

Phone _____ Occupation _____

Business phone _____ Your spouse's age _____

Education (in years)_____ Religion _____

Is spouse willing to come for counseling? Yes_____ No_____ Uncertain_____ Have you ever been separated? Yes_____ No_____

When? from_____ to_____

Has either of you ever filed for divorce? Yes_____ No_____

When? _____

Date of marriage _____

Your ages when married: Husband_____ Wife_____

How long did you know your spouse before marriage? _____

Length of steady dating with spouse _____

Length of engagement _____

Give brief information about any previous marriages: _____

Information about children:

PM*	Name	Age	Sex	Living Yes No	Education in years	Marital status

*Check this column if child is by previous marriage

If you were reared by anyone other than your parents, briefly explain: _____

How many older brothers_____ sisters_____ do you have?

How many younger brothers_____ sisters_____ do you have?

Have there been any deaths in the family during the last year?

Yes____ No____ Who and when: _____

PERSONALITY INFORMATION:

Have you used drugs for other than medical purposes?

Yes____ No____ What? _____

Have you ever had a severe emotional upset? Yes____ No____

Explain _____

Have you ever had any psychotherapy or counseling before?
Yes_____ No_____ If yes, list counselor or therapist and dates:

_____

_____

_____

What was the outcome? _____

_____

Circle any of the following words that best describe you now:
active ambitious self-confident persistent nervous hardworking
impatient impulsive moody often-blue excitable imaginative
calm serious easy-going shy good-natured introvert extrovert
likable leader quiet hard-boiled submissive self-conscious
lonely sensitive other _____
Have you ever felt people were watching you? Yes_____ No_____
Do people's faces ever seem distorted? Yes_____ No_____
Do you ever have difficulty distinguishing faces? Yes_____ No_____
Do colors ever seem too bright? _____ Too dull? _____
Are you sometimes unable to judge distance? Yes_____ No_____
Have you ever had hallucinations? Yes_____ No_____
Is your hearing exceptionally good? Yes_____ No_____
Do you have problems sleeping? Yes_____ No_____
How many hours of sleep do you average each night? _____

BRIEFLY ANSWER THE FOLLOWING QUESTIONS:

1. What is your problem? (What brings you here?)

2. What have you done about it?

3. What do you want us to do? (What are your expectations in coming here?)

4. What brings you here at this time?

5. Is there any other information we should know?

10

Flexibility in Counseling

One of the problems that many counselors discover early in the counseling enterprise is that no two cases are exactly alike. In general (at bottom, of course) there is only a certain number of fundamental principles and categories that fit all cases (I have discussed this in my pamphlet, *Christ and Your Problems;* but I also said that each situation—in its secondary features—is unique).

I

People who think that they can develop a system, complete with steps and procedures, that neatly fits each and every counseling case will be sadly disappointed in the results of such counseling. The danger of cramming everyone into the same mold doesn't occur only in the over-systematizing attempts of Christians (in my opinion, Chas. Solomon's Spirituotherapy is a good example of this sort of approach) but applies equally as well to reductionist systems like Freudianism, Skinnerianism and Rogerianism. In all of these, people's problems are analyzed and handled according to preconceived human notions of what is wrong (and what to do about that). They do not allow the problem itself to inform the counselor. Instead, the system is pressed down upon the case like a cookie-cutter, and all the facts and data left over are disposed of discreetly (and thereafter ignored). Thus, all problems may be traced back to poor socialization, aggression and sex, to untapped potential in the counselee or to faulty environmental conditioning—depending on whether one's orientation is Freudian, Rogerian or Skinnerian.

"I can see that, but don't Christians do the same thing?"

Yes and no. By that I mean (first) that Christians see *one* human cause behind problems—Adam's sin. This sin brought God's judgment upon man and his environment.

"Well, there you are."

Yes, but where are we? Think for a moment, about which system allows for more flexibility. Is it the one that goes back—all the way back—to Adam's sin, as the overarching general cause, or one that finds the source of human problems in some later, secondary, more limited factor? Frankly, I am tired of reading snide remarks by some Christians (and by non-Christians about Christians) to the effect that biblical counseling is inflexible because it sees sin in everything. This is said (knowingly) as if it were obvious that, by acknowledging the Bible's teaching that all men are born corrupt and guilty because of original sin, one limits his ability to counsel. Let me protest loudly, "Not so!"

No one, and I say this advisedly, *no one* limits counseling less than the one who takes human problems back to their beginning.[1] It is those who stop at some point short of this who will limit counseling. They not only limit themselves to a truncated view of man in which all the important data about his creation, fall and the redemption in Christ are ignored, but (as a result) limit their analysis of the human predicament to partial and misunderstood factors. To find the etiology of the human problems that counselors attempt to solve in some less general, later source distorts the picture by limiting it. When a theoretician sees human misery stemming from only one source of human life—the relationship to parents, to authority figures, to the environment, to himself, etc.—he sees reality only in the most limited (and therefore) inflexible way. On the other hand, to find Adam's sin at the fountainhead of human misery is to open *all the possibilities* of examining the place of these resulting effect-cause-effect elements that flow out of Adam's sin. This means that Christians too can see

---

1. Of course, I might go back further to discuss God's sovereignty in the matter, but I am doing this in another book soon to be published. Since going back to Adam's sin takes the Christian back further than any other system, my point is sustained without going still further.

58

difficulties coming from bad human relationships in all dimensions. But because they see man's difficulty ultimately as the result of a bad relationship to God, they see all these factors as secondary. And they interpret the problem much more *broadly*. Christians will see poor socialization, development of human potential and environmental influence quite differently than Freud, Rogers or Skinner. They will see these as derived, complicating problems; not as basic ones. And, because they see them as deriving their power in man's life from Adam's sin and God's judgment, they will interpret them quite differently; much more broadly. So, it is not the Christian who has narrowed the possibilities; that charge must be laid on the desks of those who fail to acknowledge God's basic problem-solution pattern found in the creation-fall-redemption theme of the Scriptures. A truncated outlook on life is not chargeable to the Christian who has a world view that stretches from eternity past to eternity future. Others *must* (from the denial of the biblical data) absolutize some one factor in human life further on down the chain of events as the cause of problems (and therefore point to a limited solution to them). A wrong analysis (growing out of too limited a view of man's problem) leads to wrong solutions (far less than the larger solution in Christ).

Anyone who limits his understanding of the human predicament by rejecting the biblical analysis is far off base. It is time for this to be said, *widely,* and time for Christians who (ironically, in the name of a "broader" or "enlarged" view) restrict their own counseling by adopting non-Christian presuppositions and methods to hear it too. Christian, burst the bands of non-Christian counseling theory and practice and enter into the full liberty that is in Christ.

II

Christians have a large Bible, and they must learn to exercise all the freedom that their Bible allows. Biblical principles cover *all* of life; they cut a very wide swath. They speak of all the tragedies that develop in divine/human and human/human relationships. All of

59

life in principle (and much in practical example[2]) comes under their purview. Parental and peer influence, child discipline, marriage and family goals and roles, business and work ethic, government, personal ethics, sex, worship—all these—and much more—are subjects discussed in the Scriptures (but differently than anywhere else). How can a Christian, then, help but become a broadly based, widely ranging counselor when his interests are as broad as the Bible?

To limit Christian counseling to some narrow set of rules (or steps) that one has improperly abstracted (and absolutized) from the Bible—as if this were all that God has to say about human living (e.g., "all you have to do is get out of the way and let Christ live His life through you") is to make a travesty out of the true breadth and scope of biblical change.

In another book (soon to be published) I have discussed the wealth of biblical terms that are used to describe the act and the results of human sin. In that place, I consider seventeen distinct words (and that study isn't exhaustive!). True understanding of man's problems and God's solutions, then, is not quite so simple or so limited as some may think (or may misrepresent me as thinking—this is done all the time). The Bible acknowledges the fact that sin was a *great* tragedy; it has an effect on the total man and the totality of his created environment. To fasten counseling to but one (or even two) of these numerous baneful effects (as the cause) is to err by limiting what God has exposed as a vastly larger problem. Sin is the universal, yes; but its effects are numerous and varied.

Therefore, in his analysis of counselee problems, in the solutions that he proposes to them, in the approaches that he takes, the Christian counselor may (must) range throughout the length and breadth of the Bible. It is not enough (1) to isolate one or two biblical passages (or truths) in any exclusive way, or (2) to develop one's own *closed* system from them. To do so, inevitably, is to ignore much that the Scriptures say and teach.

One's systematizing of biblical materials on counseling, of necessity, must be growing and open ended. Qualifying terms ("largely,"

2. Cf. Phil. 4:9.

"often," "sometimes," "most," "many," etc.) will appear regularly in much of the writing of those who undertake to systematize the biblical data (I am continually astounded at the way some critics seem to fail to recognize carefully worded qualifications when making their comments). New explorations into the hinterlands of Scripture will continue to be made. Calls for help must be issued. One could study the Bible a lifetime and not begin to exhaust it. That is why his system must be constructed with flexibility. It must be able to admit and assimilate new scriptural discoveries. Counselors will achieve this by *absolutizing only that which the Bible itself absolutizes* (e.g., "You shall not commit adultery").

III

Flexibility of system, therefore, means being as flexible as the Scriptures. Jesus dealt with no two persons in exactly the same way (study His approaches to persons in the Gospel of John.) Counselors, too, must learn to allow their thoughts and plans to flow into varying situations with all the variety and breadth that the Bible affords them.

It certainly would be a tragedy of the first water if someone were to systematize nouthetic counseling too soon and so tightly (narrowly) as to belie its commitment to all of the expansive vistas of the Word. God forbid this to happen!

Rather, let biblical counselors never shut the door to any new truth from the Scriptures. Let us keep our options open to all God has to say. Nouthetic counseling, to be truly biblical, must always be closed to non-Christian thought, but always open to the Bible. Therefore, it must *never* become a closed system.

True to this fact, each counselor ought to expect to discover new facts about counseling all the time—no matter how small some may be. Let him not fear new material—it will never upset what he *truly* holds in accordance with the Scriptures, since the Bible never contradicts itself. Biblical counseling never becomes pat, cut-and-dried, dull; it is always an adventure. Biblical counseling is flexible— and, therefore, exciting!

61

11

Adaptability in Counseling

Closely connected with the notion of inflexibility (see the previous chapter in this book) is the problem of task-oriented counselors who are more wrapped up in the process of counseling than in helping people.

Take a parallel: Who hasn't sat in a Sunday School class under a teacher whose one goal was to "cover the material" during the allotted time? He will bypass vital questions and concerns, ignore comments, etc., to reach his one-and-only major goal. He will skim important passages, rush through doctrinal complexities, hurdle living issues, all in his mad dash to get to the end of the lesson before the bell rings. He covers the ground all right, but also covers up the truth! Such "teachers" really think little about the people in front of them. They are engaged in an activity labelled "teaching," but that actually would be more accurately called *reaching*. They care only about reaching some arbitrarily chosen point by a specified time. When they do so, they are happy and cut another notch on their Bibles.

Some counselors view their work similarly: There are certain things to be done by a certain session. They will plow ahead at all cost (usually a rather great one), making sure that they get everything done on time. But counseling rarely proceeds uninterruptedly according to schedule. People who have learned to do everything that way will not make good counselors until they relearn biblical adaptability.

While there must be planning, order, direction and even (tentative) scheduling, these all must be adaptable. For instance, one simply may not barrel ahead toward his next counseling goal, giving new home-

62

work, when the previous week's homework is yet incomplete. Better to stick to what has been assigned already, discover what got in the way, lay plans for getting it done this time, and reassigning it (perhaps with *one* small, new assignment).

"But this sets counseling back a week!"

Yes, but going on may set it back permanently! If you don't take the time when it is needed, you will allow problems to pile up and defeat you.

When the counselee's agenda differs from the counselor's in any significant way, it is far better to spend one or two weeks (if need be) to discuss this and reach a biblical agreement. Plunging ahead on two different tracks may mean moving fast—but in two different directions!

What I am calling for is genuine adaptability in counseling. But of what does adaptability consist? Quite contrary to what some fear, the first, and most basic element, in true adaptability is order and structure. I have known people who, when I speak of adaptability, shudder because they think immediately of confusion and chaos. Exactly the opposite is the case. The disorganized person, with *no goals,* doesn't know how to bring about desired results because he has no plan or program for doing so. He may be unpredictable, but he is not adaptive. *There must be a plan to be adaptive.*

It is only when both his long and short range goals and objectives are clear (when a counselor knows basically where he wants to go and how to get there) that he can adapt those ways and means to changing and unpredictable circumstances that occur in God's providence. Counselors, to be biblical, must allow for God's surprises!

In other words, to be adaptive, one must have something to adapt! The two Latin words behind our compound word *adapt* say it all; they are "fit to." We *fit* our counseling plans *to* unknown and unexpected turns of events when we adapt. An adaptive counselor is always busy fitting things to providential events.

But there is also a second essential ingredient in adaptability: *willingness to bend.* Some counselors fail, not from lack of basic ability, but from *unwillingness.* This quality is important. Bending is not always pleasant. When one has put together a shiny, nice, airtight plan, it isn't always easy to scrap it (or radically modify it). Sometimes, like the teacher mentioned above, the counselor finds it hard to adapt his schedule. Some counselors are so enamored with their plans and programs, that they won't bend. But it doesn't matter how good the program is on paper, if it doesn't *fit to* a changed situation, or if the counselee isn't moving at the pace proposed, the program (in the end) is really worthless. The only way to save all the work that went into it, and at the same time to truly help the counselee, is to *adapt* it.

I must distinguish between *adaptation* and *accommodation;* there is no real similarity between the two. Indeed, they must be viewed as processes that are antithetical to one another. The former takes place *always within the boundaries of biblical principle;* the latter does not. Adaptation is fitting *that which is essentially the same* to *a changing situation;* accommodation is *reshaping* one's views, etc., to fit the situation (which itself may not have changed at all).

Christian counselors must not accommodate biblical truths and requirements to the counselee's sinful life or desires. While a counselor *himself* may have to bend (in ways often inconvenient and unpleasant to him), he may not accommodate God's Word. His timetable may have to be rewritten, but he must still insist on repentance and forgiveness. When, in a case like that, where repentance is necessary as a foundation for all that follows, the counselor dare not move on until repentance takes place (to do otherwise would be to compromise the absoluteness of God's requirement.) But he must not *force* repentance either (people who do so, often have a Bible-notching mentality and do not adjust their own schedules well). Adaptation, in a case like this, means willingness to wait.

Take another situation. A counselee finds it more difficult to curb his anger than he ought to, given the amount of time and effort expended on the problem. Adaptability says, "Well, by now I had planned to be well on my way to doing X, Y and Z. Here I am, stuck with this problem. Is it a problem that must be solved before moving to something else? In some cases it is (so you wait and work); in

64

some cases it isn't. What I'll do, then, is rearrange items I intended to handle in sequence so that *while continuing to work on anger,* I shall begin also to work on X and perhaps even Y." The *order* of the plan has been adapted; the *goals* have not. Accommodation would bypass the anger question and go on to something else, thereby indicating (wittingly or unwittingly) that God's requirements about anger (and who knows what else) are negotiable.

The fundamental difference, then, between adaptation and accommodation is clear: The former tailors human plans so as to accomplish God's desires; the latter ignores God's requirements in order to satisfy human desires.

A counselor who has never learned how to adapt will fail continually.

"But, how does one learn to be adaptable? They didn't teach that in seminary."

Perhaps they should have; it is an important matter. If I were teaching counselors in a classroom situation, I would do something like this:

1. Choose ten counseling situations from *The Christian Counselor's Casebook.*

2. One by one, through the first five, have students draw up a counseling plan for the next counseling session (or for the remainder of the one sketched in the *Casebook*), setting forth basic goals:

   a. Goals for the session;

   b. Areas for discussion and decision;

   c. Ways and means for achieving these goals in terms of concrete homework assignments.

3. Then, I would have them introduce five possible hindrances (changes, unforeseen developments, etc.) that might arise to impede counseling as projected.

4. And, finally, I would have them lay out five alternative plans (one for each of the five cases) for attaining these goals.

5. Then, I'd have them do the same as homework for the remaining five cases.[1]

In other words, what a counselor needs to learn is that there is more than one biblically legitimate way to enter the same house (try *all* doors, windows, chimney, etc.). Don't adapt goals, but whatever may be changed *without departing from biblical standards* may be adapted.

---

1. Of course these procedures could also be role-played.

12

Reminding

There is a great deal of first-time instruction that must be done by counselors since a number of counselees seem to be utterly ignorant even of many of the basic scriptural principles of living as well as the truths that pertain to particular situations and issues that arise. Since sin tends to draw people away from the study and personal application of the Word, and since Christians have been brainwashed into thinking they must have "psychology for living" and not just the Bible for living (how did Jesus and the church get along with just the Bible for 1900 years?!), it is necessary to do much educating in counseling sessions.

But while that is true, it is not all. There are many things that people know pretty well—the only problem is that they are not doing them.[1] What they need is not further instruction, or, in some cases, not even how-to information (though many desperately need this most of all), but a powerful *reminder*.

That is why Paul urges Titus to *"Remind* them . . ." (Tit. 3:1), and tells Timothy to *"Remind* them about these things. . . ." That is why Peter wrote, "I shall not neglect to *remind* you continually about these things even though you are established in the truth about which I am now writing" (II Pet. 1:12), and continues, saying, "I think it is right as long as I am in this tent to stir you up by *reminding* you" (1:13), and concludes, "I also shall do everything I can to make it possible for you to *remember* these things after my departure" (II Pet. 1:15). The risen Jesus calls upon the church at Sardis to *"Remember* . . . what you have received and heard; keep it and repent" (Rev. 3:3), and He tells the church in Ephesus: *"Remember,* then, the place from which you have fallen; repent and do the deeds

---

1. Cf. Phil. 3:16.

67

that you did at first" (Rev. 2:5).[2]

From these several selected passages it is clear that remembering is an important part of Christian growth, a significant factor in bringing about change and a powerful incentive to live differently. In a variety of situations, therefore, the Christian counselor must call his counselees to remembrance, often even spelling out for them once again *what to remember and how.*

From just these few passages, we may learn something about *what* it is that a Christian must remember, and in what sort of circumstances a counselor may find it important to remind him of these things.

1. Clearly, it is of prime importance that one call to memory truths one has already been taught which he needs to remember, so that he may live by them. The *Lord's* supper is this kind of reminder. Both in. his letter to Titus and in his letters to Timothy, Paul urges the good minister of Jesus Christ to remind the members of Christ's church about Christian teaching, so that they may, by applying this, "learn to engage in good deeds."

2. But that is not all. Especially in the Titus passage, Paul seems to indicate that Christians need to be reminded of the past life from which God graciously redeemed them, both to contrast their present state with it and to urge them to progress beyond it (cf. Tit. 3:3-8). Peter makes this point clearly when he speaks of those who have *"forgotten* the cleansing" of their past sins (II Pet. 1:9; often, the negative side of remembering is stressed; cf. Heb. 13:16). And even when no direct *call to remember* is given (as such), Paul (and others) follow the practice of reminding believers about the past from which they were rescued (cf. Eph. 2:1-3; the whole book of Hebrews is such a reminder). So there is a second reason.

3. In the two Revelation passages quoted above, the reminder is hooked to repentance (incidentally, note how *Christians* are

---

2. See also Deut. 1:29ff.; 6:12ff.; 7:18ff.; 8:2, 11, 14, 18, 19; 9:7, etc.

called to repentance in contrast to some current trends in counseling circles that deny the need to do so). What could better bring repentance than to contrast present sinful living with "what you have received and heard," and (even more powerful, in some ways) "the place from which you have fallen"? In these instances the doctrine not only had been *taught,* the teaching also had been "received" (i.e., understood and accepted as trustworthy and authoritative). Receiving Christian teaching that way involves a plain commitment on the part of the one who receives it to live by it. And if one had once walked in the truth, but left it, he needed to be reminded of his first love and first works.

4. Lastly, but not altogether separated from what has been mentioned already, Peter says that he reminds his readers, even though what he had to say was well established among them as truth (i.e., "received"), in order *to stir them up.* Reminders, appropriately given at the right place and time (that is what distinguishes them from nagging) are powerful motivators. Counselors are always seeking ways to *motivate* counselees; let Peter teach you one (learn also from Paul and the writer of Hebrews. On this, see "Motivation in Hebrews," in *Matters of Concern,* pp. 28ff.). The verb Peter uses, translated "stir up" is a strong one, indicating action that gets results. It is used, for instance, of *awakening* someone from sleep (not just trying to), of a calm sea becoming *aroused* in a storm, etc. Peter reminds his readers in order to wake them up.

But reminders must be of such a sort, given in such a way, at such a time as is appropriate, or they may tend to do the opposite. A time of need (the time that counselors usually come into contact with counselees) is an especially appropriate time for reminders. But even then they must be given helpfully; not in an "I told you so" manner.

All in all, then, reminding can be an extraordinarily effective tool in the hands of counselors. I probably didn't really have to write this chapter to most of you to tell you something new; I just wanted to stir you up by way of reminders!

69

13

A Basic Christian Vocabulary
Compiled by Jay E. Adams

I have discovered that in the field of counseling many persons know more about psychological terms than they know about Christian vocabulary. That is tragic. I have, therefore, determined to do something about this lack.

Every field of learning has its specialized vocabulary. In order to read and understand the literature connected with it and form accurate concepts, you must master the basic vocabulary of the field. From one viewpoint, it is possible to say that a person "knows" his subject in direct proportion to his ability to be at home with its vocabulary. While learning vocabulary meanings does not necessarily mean comprehending, believing or applying to life the ideas behind them, it surely aids. Ideas cannot be *accurately* formed apart from such understanding. And it is difficult to live what you don't understand. Nowhere is it more important to be familiar with terminology than in the greatest of all fields of study—Christianity. And within the broad scope of Christianity, there is great need among Christian counselors for just such an understanding.

The vocabulary is also published separately in pamphlet form for distribution in quantity.*

This list is entirely basic. It is what every Christian should know as a *minimum*. Other words, or fuller explanations of some of these may be looked up in a good Bible dictionary or systematic theology text. A planned study of the terms in this list will help you to become

---

* Copies may be obtained from the publisher or from CCEF (latter's address on page 41).

familiar with these words. Learn a word each day. Look up several verses in your concordance that use the biblical word. Use it in conversation at least three times during the day. Go over all the past words that you have already learned. Knowing these terms will help you to become conversant with the Scriptures and the best Christian literature.

Adoption—One of the figures of speech used to describe the reception of believers into the family of God (Gal. 4:5; Eph. 1:4). It emphasizes especially the fact that men are not naturally born the children of God. All the rights and privileges of sonship pertain to an adopted child.

Advent—A coming or appearance; used of the first (II Pet. 1:16) and second comings of Christ.

Agnostic—Literally, "he who does not know." Agnostics are doubters of two kinds: honest doubters (seekers who are troubled by their agnosticism and who want to know the truth if possible); dishonest doubters (who have stopped searching for truth, concluding that ultimate knowledge is impossible).

Altar—A place of sacrifice. True Christian churches do not have altars today because Calvary was the last sacrifice acceptable to God (cf. Heb. 9–10).

Amen—A response denoting consent or agreement and meaning, literally, "so be it." It may be spoken sincerely, reverently and audibly at the close of prayer (I Cor. 14:16).

Angel—A created spirit (Heb. 1:19) whose name means "messenger" and who is appointed to minister to Christians. Fallen angels are the demons of Scripture (Matt. 25:41). Angels appear in the form of men (Heb. 13:2; Acts 1:10). Humans who die do not become angels, as has been erroneously taught; they are of a separate order of beings (Ps. 8:4-5).

Apocrypha—Uninspired books written during the interval between the writing of the Old and New Testament books. They never were accepted by the Hebrews, Christ, the apostles or the early church. Some of them are wrongly attributed to writers who did not compose them. They contain much interesting history, but also many errors

71

of fact, doctrine, history, and science. It was not until April 8, 1546, that the Roman church declared them to be canonical.

Apologetics—The defense of the Christian faith. The word originally meant a defense made in a law court, and has nothing to do with apologizing.

Apostasy—That state into which those who turn away from the truth enter after they have renounced the faith that they once professed. True Christians never turn apostate. Apostates were not Christians in the first place (I John 2:19; Matt. 7:23).

Apostle—Literally, "one sent forth." The word is used in a general sense of any missionary (cf. Acts 13:3; 14:4, 14), but most frequently in a restricted sense of the twelve men whom Jesus appointed and sent forth to found the church. Their work was foundational (Eph. 2:20; 3:5) and not to be duplicated by others.

Ark—A chest or box. Refers to three things in Scripture: Noah's ark, the boat that looked like a big box; Moses' ark in which he was afloat on the Nile; the ark of the covenant—literally, a box that contained the tables of the Ten Commandments and other valuable items, and was kept in the holy of holies beneath the place where God's presence dwelt.

Assurance—The biblical doctrine that when one is saved, he may *know* it (I John 5:13). God did not want us to guess about our saving relationship to Him.

Atheist—One who does not believe in the existence of God. No person knows enough to be an atheist. He would have to be everywhere at the same time to declare that God is nowhere. If he were, he wouldn't say so—he would be God.

Atonement—The word is used both to denote the satisfaction that is brought about by the death of Christ (issuing in the reconciliation of God and His people), and the death itself which produces the at-one-ment. Christ's atonement was designed for specific persons (John 17:7; Isa. 53:8; Matt. 1:21; etc.). If Christ suffered for the sins of "mankind" in the abstract, He would not be a *personal* Savior and no one could suffer in hell; God would be unjust in exacting the same punishment twice.

Baptism—There are two aspects of baptism. The first is the inward, invisible baptism of the Holy Spirit that occurs at conversion. This is necessary for salvation (Rom. 8:9). The second aspect is outward, visible, water baptism, which symbolizes the inward reality. Water baptism was always performed by sprinkling or pouring, as this alone could adequately symbolize the descent of the Holy Spirit, who is poured out (or shed) upon us. Holy Spirit baptism produces two effects: cleansing (negative) and union with the body of Christ (positive).

Bible—A word that means "book." Since ancient writing paper (papyrus) came from the Mediterranean city of Biblos, the word *biblos* (bible) came to mean "book." The Bible is THE Book. Though written by many authors, God, the Holy Spirit, is the one Author behind them all. Hence, it is rightly viewed as one coherent Book.

Bishop—Literally, "overseer, supervisor or superintendent" (see **Elder**).

Call—There are two calls—the external call (which comes to saved and unsaved alike), i.e., the preaching of the gospel, and the internal (or effectual) call, which is the work of the Holy Spirit in the heart of God's people that regenerates and enables them to believe the gospel. This latter is irresistible.

Calvinism—That scriptural system of theology especially formulated by John Calvin which is founded upon the two basic doctrines of the sovereignty of God and grace.

Christ—The Greek equivalent of the Hebrew word "Messiah," both of which mean the "Anointed One." Jesus was anointed prophet, priest, and king, and this anointing probably took place at His baptism (as there is no other record of an anointing) when the Holy Spirit came upon Him (in John 2:20, 27, the Holy Spirit is called an anointing). The baptism symbolized the anointing of the Holy Spirit (cf. Luke 4:18).

Church—(see **Ecclesiology**).

Commentaries—Volumes supplying background material and interpretations of the verses of various books of the Bible.

73

Concordance—A book containing all (or nearly all) the words of the Bible listed alphabetically, along with every occurrence of them (by verse). It is valuable for word, doctrinal, or topical studies, the determination of the exact location of half-remembered verses, and many other uses.

Conversion—An "about face." When one has been walking the wrong way, God turns him around in the other direction by regeneration, repentance and faith.

Covenant—An agreement between two or more persons, usually sealed by a bloody sacrifice (hence, one literally "cuts" a covenant). The old and new covenants are to be distinguished from the books that contain them (and bear their name). The covenant of grace is God's plan of salvation, in which He saves men in all eras by grace alone.

Creation—To create is to produce something out of nothing (ex nihilo) Men "make" (i.e., use previously existing materials); God alone can create. In creation, matter was brought into existence.

Deacon—Ordained officers of the church of Christ (Acts 6:6), whose basic function is to take over all temporal matters assigned to them by the elders, are called deacons. Their qualifications are found in I Timothy 3:8-12. Their minimum duties are to visit the sick, care for the poor, and comfort those in trial.

Death—(see **Life**). The separation of the soul (or spirit) from the body (II Cor. 5:8; James 2:26). Spiritual death (Eph. 2) is separation from God in this life. The "second death" (Rev. 20) is the separation of the soul and body from God forever.

Demons—Fallen angels. They are capable of possessing the unsaved, and are to be distinguished in such activity from sickness and madness (which, however, they may cause). The recently proven fact of hypnotism (in which the mind of another can influence the words, thoughts, and actions of a subject) has removed most of the old objections and prejudices against the possibility of demon possession. Many modern notions about demons and their activities are unscriptural.

Depravity, total—The Scriptures teach that men are all together

74

sinful, and individually, altogether sinful (Rom. 3:23; 8:7-8; et al.). Every part of human life has been affected by sin, but not as badly as it might be were it not for God's restraining grace.

Devil (or Satan)—These two words mean "slanderer" and "adversary" respectively, and signify something of the activity of this being. The devil is a fallen angel who is the chief opponent of God and His people. He is not to be conceived of as a horrid-looking creature in red tights, with a pointed tail and horns. Rather, as a spirit, he makes his appearance in many forms, even as an angel of *light* (II Cor. 11:14). Neither does he "run" hell, but shall in the last times be committed to eternal punishment there (Matt. 25:41).

Disciple—A "learner" or "pupil." Discipleship is the biblical method for training and consists of teaching by both word and example.

Discipline—Church discipline is the watchful care over members of Christ's church in an attempt to lead them away from sinful beliefs and practices. It indicates regularity and order in the personal life as well.

Doctrine—"Teaching." The summarized teaching of all the verses of the Bible on any subject is the biblical doctrine (or teaching) on that subject.

Ecclesiology—The study of the church. The word "church" is derived from *ecclesia,* which means, "the called out ones." In Scripture, this term is used to denote two things: (1) The invisible church —all those of every era who have been saved throughout all the world. (2) The visible church—local congregations or groups of them in a particular area; i.e., all those who have been baptized into the fellowship of the organized body. All who are in the visible church are not necessarily in the invisible. Membership in the visible church is not essential for salvation, though membership in the invisible church is. The word "church" is never used in the Bible to denote buildings or denominations (the two uses are definitely modern). The word always refers to people.

Eden—"Pleasures." The phrase "the garden of eden," when literally translated, is "the park of pleasures."

Edification—The building up (or strengthening) of fellow Christians in their faith.

Elder—"Old, or mature man." The Greek is "presbyter" (hence the word "presbyterian" or rule by presbyters). See Titus 1:5-9; I Timothy 3:1-7, et al., for functions and qualifications of the office. The Scripture distinguishes between the ruling elder and the teaching-and-ruling elder (I Tim. 5:17). The latter is also called the pastor and teacher (Eph. 4:11). The word "bishop" (overseer) speaks of the work of the elder, whereas "presbyter" speaks of his qualifications. The presbyter and bishop are the same man (and not two different offices); see Titus 1:5, 7.

Elect—The elect is that company of human beings whom God selected from all eternity to be His people. This election is unconditional, based solely upon His own wise purpose, and in no sense dependent upon the merits or faith of the elect (which are the result and not the cause of election). See Romans 11:7, 28; I Thessalonians 1:4; I Timothy 5:21; Romans 9:11ff.

Epistle—A letter.

Eschatology—The study of the last things. The doctrines concerning the second coming of Christ, the resurrection, the judgment and the final state of man.

Eternal security—The scriptural teaching that a man once saved can never be lost (cf. I Pet. 1:3-5; Rom. 8:35-39; John 17:12; 10:28-29; Phil. 1:6; II Tim. 1:12). To teach that a saved man could be lost is to admit that God is not a good Father, Christ's work on the cross can be frustrated by Satan, and that God fails to keep His promises. One continues in the faith by perseverance. God enables true believers to continue.

Evangelism—The presentation of the gospel message for the purpose of leading others to saving faith in Christ. See **Gospel.**

Faith—Trust, dependence, reliance, belief. Saving faith consists of knowledge, assent, and trust. When directed toward an unworthy object, faith becomes gullibility.

Fasting—To abstain from food, either partially or wholly, for the purpose of mourning; to allow time for prayer; in case of national emergencies or prior to undertaking an important task. Biblical fasting must be voluntary and occasional; not stated.

Flesh—Besides its ordinary meaning, this word often has the special biblical meaning of the body habituated to evil (see esp. Rom. 6–8; Gal. 5).

Gehenna—(see **Hades**).

Gifts—Abilities given by God to His people for His service and their edification.

Glorification—The divinely wrought change that takes place in the believer when he dies, whereby he becomes sinless (and especially referring to the resurrection, when he will be made complete in perfection of both body and soul).

Gospel—Literally, "good news." This good news, which must be believed for salvation, consists of two elements: (1) The penal, substitutionary death of Christ for our sins; (2) The bodily resurrection of Christ (cf. I Cor. 15:1, 3, 4).

Grace—The unmerited favor of God shown toward men. The unearned love and mercy God shows toward persons who deserve the opposite. *Common grace* is the good which God does for believers and unbelievers alike (Matt. 5:45), while *special grace* is the salvation and consequent blessings He dispenses to the elect alone. The word is used also to designate *help* or *aid* that God gives to His children.

Guilt—Culpability before God or man, making one liable to punishment. This word should *never* be confused (as it so often is in counseling circles) with having a sense (or feeling) of guilt.

Hades—Literally, "the unseen world" (i.e., the invisible world; unfortunately translated "hell" in the KJ version). This is the general biblical word for the world of departed spirits. It corresponds to the Hebrew "sheol." Hades is composed of at least two areas: (1) The place of bliss (Abraham's bosom, paradise, heaven). (2) The place of punishment (gehenna, hell, the lake of fire, the place of torment). The word gehenna is properly translated "hell" in the modern sense of the word as the place of eternal punishment.

Heart—The inner life one lives before God and himself. Not equated with feelings (as in our day).

Heaven—There are three heavens (cf. II Cor. 12:1-4). They are: the atmosphere (or air) surrounding the earth, the sky (space, where the stars and planets are located), and the third heaven (where God dwells).

Hell—(see **Hades**).

Heresy—Teaching contrary to the Word of God that denies the way of salvation. The word originally referred to schismatic activity. The two concepts are related.

Holy—The word refers to any person or thing which has been separated, or "set apart" from sin (or regular use) unto God (or special use). In many places, it can mean simply *special*.

Holy Spirit—The third Person of the Trinity. He dwells within every true believer.

Idolatry—The love and worship of any substitute for the true God, whether a physical idol, a person, or a possession (cf. Col. 3:5b).

Impute—To reckon or account, as in Romans 4:6, 11, 22, where righteousness is reckoned to one's account by faith.

Incarnation—The act of Christ becoming a human being by assuming flesh. Christ was true man (in every sense apart from sin) as well as true God.

Inspiration—Literally, that which is "god-breathed." The Scriptures were inspired of God in such a way as to render them inerrant and infallible in language as well as thought. Inspiration refers to the writing, not to the writers.

Intermediate state—The conscious state of the soul (spirit) between death and the final resurrection.

Jehovah—An improper spelling of the Hebrew name for God, which is, literally, Yahveh. Yahveh comes from the verb to be, and means "The One who Is" (cf. Ex. 3:14).

Jesus—Means "Jehovah is salvation." It is the N.T. form of the O.T. name Joshua. It speaks clearly of Christ's mission as Saviour (cf. Matt. 1:12).

Jew—A term derived from "Judah," meaning "one who belongs to the tribe of Judah." This word is used only after the exile and restoration. Judah was the principal tribe to return, but the designation embraces all who returned to the land, whether of Judah or another tribe. In the N.T., Paul broadens its usage still more, as he changes it from a racial to a religious term which includes all true Christians (Rom. 2:28, 29).

Justification—A legal action whereby the believing sinner is forgiven, cleared of all his sins, and accounted righteous on the books of heaven. Justification is by faith alone (Rom. 4).

Law—A term used broadly to refer to the whole Bible, the O.T. Scriptures, and more specifically to the Pentateuch (the first five books of the O.T.), and in its most restricted sense, to the Ten Commandments alone.

Liberalism—That system which, because of disbelief in the inerrancy and infallibility of the Bible, is led to reject the doctrines and teachings contained therein. It is unbelief parading under the name of Christianity. In its more recent form, it attempts to distinguish the Word of God (which is said to be found behind the words of the Bible) from the Bible itself. The Word of God is said to be true and perfect, but the Bible imperfect. Liberalism, in all its forms, always challenges God's Word.

Life—The Bible speaks of three kinds of life (and death, q.v.):

Life (union)		**Death** (separation)
Physical	Body + Soul	Body − Soul
Spiritual	Soul + God	Soul − God
Eternal	Body and Soul + God	Body and Soul − God

Lord's Day—The first day of the week, on which the Christian church is to worship (cf. Rev. 1:10). Whereas the seventh-day Sabbath was a day of total physical rest, the Lord's Day is to be one of total spiritual activity. These elements of the Sabbath and the Lord's Day are not to be confounded.

Love—Constructive good will. The highest gift of God. Not a matter of emotions first, but of giving to another what God commands, out of obedience to Him.

Messiah—(see **Christ**).

Miracle—A powerful work of God in which He, acting directly and not through natural means (as in Providence, q.v.), steps into the stream of history and time, to supersede natural laws by supernatural ones.

Monotheism—Belief in one God. Christians are monotheists (who believe in one God in three Persons) but not unitarians (who believe in one god who is but one person).

Mystery—Not some incomprehensible truth, but that which God has hidden until the appointed time for it to be revealed (Rom. 16: 25-26).

Omnipotence—The power of God, which is unlimited. God is all-powerful and can do anything He wants to do. He cannot (and, of course, does not wish to) do anything contrary to Himself.

Omnipresence—The ability of God to be everywhere at the same time. God alone is omnipresent. Some persons speak (erroneously) as if Satan were too.

Omniscience—God's all-comprehensive knowledge of every past, present, and future event.

Original sin—The doctrine of Scripture that states that humans are born sinners (cf. Ps. 51:5; 58:3; Prov. 22:15; Gen. 8:21; Eph. 2:3). Proof that infants are sinners from the earliest age is found in the fact that they are subject to death, and the wages of SIN is death (Rom. 6:23).

Orthodoxy—Literally, "straight opinion or thought." Orthodoxy is conformity to historical biblical Christianity.

Pantheism—The belief that the universe is god. Examples: Christian Science, Unity.

Passover—One of the three annual festivals of the Jews, which commemorates the deliverance from Egypt, and especially the accompanying plague upon the firstborn (cf. Ex. 12).

Perfectionism—Sinless perfection. Though set forth as the Christian's goal (Matt. 5:4-8), it is an impossibility in this life because of sinful human nature. Those who claim such perfection, John says (I John 1:8-10), deceive themselves (by representing sin not to be sin), do not possess the truth, make God a liar (this false doctrine is a very serious heresy), and do not have the Word of God in them.

Perseverance—(see **Eternal security**).

Polytheism—Belief in many gods. Examples: paganism (Roman and Greek religion), Mormonism.

Prayer—Simply talking with God. There are four kinds of prayer: adoration, confession, thanksgiving, and supplication (ACTS).

Preaching—The communication of biblical truth through human personality to change human beings.

Predestination—The scriptural teaching that from all eternity God has planned everything that happens (cf. Eph. 1:11; Rom. 8:29, etc.).

Priest—One who offers sacrifices, and who stands between man and God as a mediator. Today, there is no need for a special priesthood, since all Christians are priests, offering spiritual sacrifices of thanksgiving and praise (cf. I Pet. 2:5).

Prophet—One who *forth*tells the word of God; a preacher. Most of the inspired prophets also had the power to *fore*tell the future.

Providence—God's superintending and ordering of all events through natural means so as to infallibly work out His purposes in history. Sometimes the word is used to refer only to God's benevolent acts toward Christians.

Redemption—The purchasing (or buying back) of God's people at the cost of Christ's sufferings and death. The price is not paid to Satan, but to God. Salvation brings *more* than redemption since (in Christ) man has been raised to God's throne in the heavenlies.

Reformed—The system of doctrine stemming from the Reformation that includes Calvinism (q.v.), presbyterian government, and covenant theology.

Regeneration—A new birth, brought about through the implantation of spiritual life by the Holy Spirit.

Repentance—To repent means to "change one's mind." True repentance is, therefore, a thorough change of outlook with reference to God, Christ, and one's self. It leads to a change of life. It is not necessarily connected with great emotional experiences.

Resurrection—The raising of a body from the grave in order to reunite it to its non-body part (spirit).

Revelation—An "unveiling." The Bible is God's revelation to us of the facts we need to know about Himself, the universe, and ourselves. God has revealed truth through creation (general revelation) and through the Bible (special revelation). The former is insufficient to lead to salvation, though adequate to lead to condemnation. This necessitates the latter. The former can be interpreted correctly only by means of the latter.

Righteousness—Rightness in God's sight. The only righteousness acceptable to God is that which He Himself reckons to us through faith. All self-righteousness is condemned (cf. Rom. 10:2-4; Tit. 3:5, et al.).

Saints—"Set apart or holy (q.v.) ones." All Christians are saints while yet alive, even though far from perfect (I Cor. 1:2; Rom. 1:7).

Salvation—Rescue from a desperate situation; specifically, from condemnation in hell (q.v.). Our salvation may be fully described in three tenses:

Past—we HAVE BEEN SAVED from the penalty of sin = justification.

Present—we ARE BEING SAVED from the power of sin = sanctification.

Prospective—we SHALL BE SAVED from the presence of sin = glorification.

Satan—(see **Devil**).

Sanctification—"Separation, setting apart" (from the same root as "holy" and "saint," q.v.). The gradual *process* whereby the believer is set apart more and more from sin to God is called sanctification. It covers the entire earthly lifespan from justification to glorification, and is not to be thought of as an *act* (like justification). Counseling is part of the process of sanctification, by which one puts off the old person and puts on the new person.

Separation—The Christian is to be distinct and different from the unsaved. He is to have no close ties of fellowship with them socially or ecclesiastically (cf. II Cor. 6:14-18).

Sin—Disobedience to the law of God, manifested by doing that which is forbidden or failure to do that which is commanded. At bottom sin is disobedience to God. While it has a horizontal dimension, sin must be viewed essentially vertically as (above all else) an affront against God.

Soteriology—The study of the doctrine (biblical teaching) of salvation.

Soul—The same as the spirit but with a different shade of meaning. The soul is a spirit viewed as united with a body, while a spirit is a soul viewed as disembodied.

Spirit—(see **Soul**). A person without a body.

Temptation—Seduction to sin. Men are tempted by the world system, the flesh (their own sinful habits and desires), and the devil. Temptation is not sin; yielding to it is.

Testimony—The witness (good or bad) that the life and words of a Christian bear toward the unsaved, especially concerning the way of salvation and the truth of the Christian faith.

Theism—Belief in a personal God. Christian theism is belief in the true God.

Theology—The study and systematic formulation of scriptural doctrine (q.v.).

Tongue—A language (cf. Acts 2). As a sign to unbelievers, to attest to one's apostleship (II Cor. 12:12) and his call to write Scripture (Heb. 2:4); a means for the conversion of the lost. In the early days of the church God gave some Christians the ability to speak in foreign languages without learning them. Regulations for the use of this gift may be found in I Corinthians 14.

Trinity—The word refers to one God, who is three Persons: Father, Son, Spirit. Christians do not believe in three Gods.

Unitarianism—The belief that God is but one Person; a denial of the Christian doctrine of the Trinity.

Version—A translation of the Scriptures. No versions are inspired; only the original writings were.

Vicarious—Substitutionary. Christ became the Substitute for His people on the cross, bearing the punishment for their sins.

Virgin birth—This is the miracle by which the Holy Spirit effected the incarnation (q.v.) without ordinary natural means. It assured both the sinlessness of Christ and His two natures.

Worship—The respect and honor which one shows to that thing or Person which he considers divine (or uppermost in life).

Wrath—The just judgment and vengeance of God upon those who persist in sin and do not accept His offer of salvation.

These definitions are brief, because of the nature of this work. My hope, however, is that this list will provide a handy ready-reference for the Christian, and that he will spend time studying it in the fashion described at the beginning.

Update on Christian Counseling
Volume 2

To
my new daughter,
Lucy Anne

Introduction

Over the past 12 years I have worked assiduously to produce a body of literature in a field that, prior to that time, virtually did not exist: the field of biblical counseling. In some measure, I believe that I have succeeded. But, because important issues crop up from time to time and constantly studies on vital topics must be done, that do not appropriately fit into any given book that is currently being prepared, I began to publish the reports on these in an open-ended series of books entitled, *Update on Christian Counseling,* of which this is the second volume.

In volume II, I treat mostly current miscellaneous matters, as you would expect from the title. But, for the first time, I have also made available a valuable article, from a past era, that has for long been out of print. Though it might seem inappropriate to reprint anything in a volume entitled *Update,* I have discovered that the old is often the newest and most up-to-date of all. Apart from a few dated references, the article is as fresh and timely as if it had just been written.

I consider the study in I Corinthians 13 significant and hope that it will become a useful resource for counseling. Two very recent trends have been considered: (1) extra-biblical guidance, (2) father-images of God, and one that has troubled us for some years: transactional analysis.

Other matters also have been touched upon. All are calculated to help biblical counselors to do a more effective job *today*.

Blessings!
Jay Adams
The Millhouse
1981

1
Do Fathers Make Atheists of Their Children?

The other day I received a phone call from a sympathetic, well-meaning pastor who raised a question that I have been hearing increasingly, in one place or another, over the last few years. It was, in substance, this:

> If a child has been raised by a father whose life is a miserable example, won't that child grow up with a wrong conception of God and find it difficult to trust and obey Him, since he will base his ideas of what God is like on his own father's behavior?

This is a very serious question, which—if the assumption on which it is based is true—has widespread implications for counseling as well as for Christian education. The teaching behind the question must be considered and all confusion that is connected with it must be dispelled in the pure light of biblical clarity.

To begin with, I told him, "Of course, all sorts of things are possible. It is altogether possible, therefore (although in all my counseling I have never seen it), that some child, somewhere, because of the sinful perverseness of his adamic nature, has done just what the questioner suggests.[1] If a child does so, obviously he will get an entirely wrong view of God. This will be true whether his earthly father succeeds or fails. (All fail somewhere; and even in their successes there are great limitations.) To learn about God from looking at even the best father is to develop erroneous and sinful concepts of God. All sorts of difficulties in one's relationship to God are bound to crop up as a result."

But, let us look at the question again. It *presupposes* that children grow up

---

1. Perhaps more and more we shall see this occurring if children are taught to learn of God by looking at their fathers (to teach them to do so, naturally, is the logical implication of this strange unbiblical doctrine). The notion is beginning to spread: cf. Bruce Narramore, *Parenting with Love and Limits* (Zondervan: Grand Rapids, 1979), pp. 29, 90ff.

1

identifying God with their own fathers.[2] Does this really happen? Does it take place in the life of *every* child or even in the life of most—or many? And if so, what does the Bible have to say about this supposedly powerful and most important way of teaching children about God, the heavenly Father? Surely, if this is where children learn their earliest and most basic ideas of God, the Bible must not be silent about it! But, strange to say, that is just the point—the Bible knows nothing, absolutely nothing, about this notion.

Where, then, does the notion come from? Paul Meier, assistant professor of practical theology at Dallas Theological Seminary, writes:

> In psychiatry, we learn that an adult's attitudes toward God are influenced greatly by his attitudes toward his own father while he was growing up.[3]

He tells of a "patient" (notice the medical model) who was a "devout atheist" (a strange combination of words for an evangelical theology professor) and comments: "And I would have expected him to be, given the kind of father image he grew up with." (Notice again the psychological jargon.) Of persons raised in such situations, in general, he says (note, throughout the psychological rather than biblical orientation Meier takes):

> In their subconscious minds [not a biblical construct], they want to believe there is no God because they resent the fact that they had no father, or one who was nearly always absent and negativistic. . . . Some of these patients hated their fathers so much that they became atheists as an unconscious rebellion against the existence of their fathers.[4]

Meier is clear enough about the source of such views. He gets the notion not from the Bible, but from "psychiatry." Of course, he cannot mean *all* psychiatrists. They disagree so greatly among themselves that it is almost

---

2. Imitation of fathers is one thing (and even that is far from inevitable, as Ezek. 18 indicates), but identification of God with one's father is quite another.

3. To indicate by the phrase "In psychiatry, we learn" that there is anything like agreement on the part of most psychiatrists about this—or anything else—indicates either naivete by Meier or (what is more likely) his assumption of naivete on the part of his readers. What is a psychiatrist doing teaching "practical theology"? And from "psychiatry" rather than the Bible?

4 Paul Meier, *Christian Child Rearing and Personality Development* (Grand Rapids: Baker Book House, 1977), pp. 29, 30.

ludicrous to say "psychiatrists think," "psychiatrists teach," "psychiatrists believe," or (as he does) to speak of "psychiatry" as though this were a monolithic science holding to any particular view. From his description of the belief, however, it would seem that he refers to some psychiatrist(s) of a Freudian or neo-Freudian bent.[5] Just whom, he does not say.

Be that as it may, the important thing to see is that the notion that children identify God with their fathers, Meier says, comes not from the Bible, but from an outside (pagan) source. In that, he is correct.

Consistently, Meier finds that good fathers develop in their children "a healthy concept of God," and that, "If they haven't already put their faith in Jesus Christ, they do so readily when I show them God's simple plan of salvation."[6]

It all sounds so simple, so neat and compact! But is it? Is the predisposition of a child to trust Christ as Savior directly linked to his "father image"?[7]

As I have said already, in a rare case or so, possibly this dynamic could occur, without all the Freudian embellishments, of course; but it certainly could not be considered a common thing—surely not a *rule* of personality development, the basic principle of Christian education and the predisposing factor in grace, as Meier makes it—because the Bible never, not even once, makes a point of it! If it is so important in the raising of children to give them their earliest views of God through their earthly fathers that, with Meier, we must say, "I hope those of us who are fathers, or who someday will be fathers, will grasp the heavy responsibility that God has given us,"[8] then why doesn't he show us where, in the Bible, God tells us this is so? We cannot base theological doctrine on "psychiatry"! Has God allowed His church to exist for 1900 years (and the OT church for a longer period prior to that) without this vital information? Did He allow us to go all that time condemning our children to atheism because we did not yet have Freud's (or Meier's) insights? Was our doctrine of salvation defective until Meier told us what to believe about this crucial matter?

---

5. Note the jargon "father image," "subconscious mind," etc.
6. Ibid., p. 31.
7. There is some strange preparationist theology in this notion and an incipient weakening of the doctrine of total depravity.
8. Meier, op. cit., p. 31.

3

If this idea were really all that important, the God who told us that He had given us "all things that pertain to life and godliness" (II Pet. 1:3) must have said so somewhere. But search the Bible from stem to stern, and you will find neither a hint nor a whisper of this "father image" doctrine that supposedly leads either to atheism or to the ready acceptance of the gospel.

We can only conclude that Meier is wrong in importing into the church (and her doctrine) any such ideas. Sad, that at Dallas seminary, a school that over the years purported to base its teaching on biblical exposition alone, someone now teaches doctrine based on the wild theories of some outmoded psychiatrists! Students who accept such teaching will now go out to place responsibilities (erroneously said to be from God) on the shoulders of the members of their congregations that neither they nor their fathers should have borne! Think of it—admittedly pagan psychiatric dogma taught as Christian doctrine!

Now, of course, I would not want to deny the importance of parental teaching—especially by the father, whom the Bible singles out for such a responsibility (Deut. 8; Eph. 6:1-4; Col. 3:21). Parental influence on a child, by word and by life, is enormous. That is not at issue.

The nub of my argument with Meier's doctrine is this: he lays additional burdens on parents' shoulders that the Bible does not, and he calls these responsibilities God-given. It is one thing to say that one's teaching, by word and life, will be of major significance (but not utterly determinative) to a child's development. It is quite another to say,

1. his salvation or lack of it will depend on whether an earthly father lives like the heavenly Father (who ever did?),
2. that this child's concepts of God will be developed from the father's image,
3. and that the child necessarily will be influenced even into adult life by this image. (Meier tells us about a Ph.D. supposedly affected that way[9] and says those influenced negatively "never really feel forgiven,"[10] etc.)

---

9. Ibid., p. 29.

10. Ibid., p. 30. *Feeling* forgiven is also a nonbiblical construct (cf. my detailed comments on the nature and effects of forgiveness in *More than Redemption: A Theology of Christian Counseling* [Phillipsburg, N.J.: Presbyterian and Reformed, 1979]).

4

It is *such a construct* of parental responsibility—not parental responsibility itself—against which I must protest.

First, no child will ever grow up with a proper concept of God if he must depend on getting it from his father—even a good father. No father, in any way, even comes close to reflecting the heavenly Father accurately. If what Meier says is true, *all* children are doomed; not just some.

Secondly, Meier has put the cart before the horse (a hallmark of psychiatric thinking). Biblically, the father learns how to be a father by emulating the way that God treats him as His child: "bring them up with the nurture and admonition of the Lord" (Eph. 6:4). That is to say, an earthly father is to discipline his children as God does His. God's fatherhood is the standard against which all others are measured; God, the Father, is the model for all earthly fathers. One does not measure good money against counterfeit; he measures the counterfeit against the good. Never are earthly fathers held forth as the model for children to determine what God is like.

Thirdly, no "father image" could properly teach a child about God's love, justice, omniscience, omnipotence, omnipresence, wrath, mercy, etc. All these truths about God must be learned from the Bible and what it teaches by precept and example. God's love, for instance, is not taught through observing the love of one's father (that may, of course, get a hearing for it), but by pointing a child to the cross (I John 4:10).

Fourthly, fathers are to *teach* their children about God *from the Bible* (Deut. 6, etc.). It is their task to teach all that God revealed in the Scriptures about Himself (Deut. 29:29), pointing not to themselves—except perhaps now and then by contrast—but to the God who has made Himself known in special revelation.

Fifthly, and, as for Ph.D.s (and other adults) who are supposedly stuck with their infantile concepts of God, being adversely influenced all their later life (see Meier's fuller account of this: pp. 30ff.), all one can say is that it is time to teach them to give up childish ways now that they have become adults![11]

Sixthly, it is doubtful, however, that there exists such a widespread influence of fathers on their children's concept of God with such bad effects.

---

11. Strange, that the Corinthians (and others like them) could come to Christ with no such difficulty even though their parents were not Christians but pagans.

(What the Ph.D.'s problem *really* was would be interesting to know.) Meier, like the rest of us, doubtless tends to find what he is looking for. We all come to the counseling room with presuppositions, i.e., views, and viewpoints that grow out of them, that we hold as true, and upon which, therefore, we base other views and actions. These presuppositions, indeed, make us all selective of the data upon which we focus attention, and color our interpretations of them. There is no such thing as uninterpreted "objective" data for any counselor.

A typical, obvious example is Tim LaHaye's viewpoint on temperament. Having once adopted this (admittedly) unbiblical, pagan Greek construct for typing individuals, he sees counselees, Bible characters, people who want their future predicted, etc., in the light of the presuppositions inherent in that dogma. Even the Bible is interpreted in terms of the four temperaments (and combinations thereof). The pigeonholes in the framework are built out of nonbiblical materials; then Bible characters (Paul, Peter), as well as Tom and Suzie counselee, are fitted into the holes their characters seem best to approximate. In this system, the Bible is used to support and illustrate the extra-biblical theory rather than the reverse. If temperament were as big a thing as LaHaye says it is, the Bible would be full of it. But, like Meier (and all others who reverse the proper procedure) the framework of the theory is constructed out of pagan materials (i.e., from unbiblical presuppositions, about man, God, and the universe). We do not have to reach *beyond* the Bible for our presuppositions; they should always be biblical. Only then can we evaluate, judge and control our other beliefs based on them in a way that keeps us on track. Since one's presuppositions determine how he will handle data, it is important for him to be sure that those presuppositions are scriptural. That is the only way to be sure that his presuppositions will not lead him astray.

Take Meier's case. He is off the track scripturally because of his presuppositions. Not only does he presuppose a kind of Freudianism to be true, but he seems to presuppose that, at least at times, God Himself speaks as authoritatively through Freud as through the Bible. What "psychiatry" says is taken as "the heavy responsibility that God has given us" (p. 31). That presupposition itself is perhaps the most dangerous of all. Yet, I am fairly certain that Meier would never articulate it himself as true. Nevertheless,

6

unwittingly, he has adopted a method that grows out of and is appropriate to such a presupposition.

If so important a matter as one's concept of God (surely a central biblical concern if there ever was one) depends on the image of God seen in his father, why is the Bible as silent as it is on the temperament issue? Why does Meier find it necessary to go beyond Scriptures to "psychiatry" for the concept? Here is where so much danger lies. To Meier, LaHaye[12] and others who tend to do so, Paul's warning should serve as a needed corrective:

> Now these things I have applied figuratively to myself and to Apollos for your sakes, brothers, in order that you may learn from us not to go beyond what has been written (I Cor. 4:6, *The NT in Everyday English*).

---

12. On this point. Other things LaHaye teaches are biblical. What makes him become so unbiblical at this point?

2

Liberty with a Limit

(Including a Note on Questionable Sexual Practices)

The problem at Corinth that gave rise to the important discussion of the limits of Christian liberty concerned the matter of eating food sacrificed to pagan idols. After an animal had been dedicated and sacrificed to a heathen god or goddess, it was sold in the meat market at a bargain price because, in effect, it was used, secondhand meat. Many of the early Christians, at Corinth at least (cf. 1:26), were of the poorer classes, and some even were slaves. Quite naturally, it would be advantageous for them to purchase this more reasonably priced meat. But they had broken with paganism, and wanted rightly to avoid all that smacked of pagan worship. Consequently, the question arose, "May Christians eat food that has been sacrificed to idols without participating in idolatry?"

In answering this specific question, Paul lays down a general principle that we must study because of its pertinence to many counseling problems. The counselor will find that a clear perspective on this matter will stand him in good stead when he is required to give biblical direction in cases of conscience.

We shall look at Paul's teaching in order to discover the general principle involved, how it applies to Christian living and its place in counseling.

What did Paul tell the Corinthians?

The question first arises in chapter eight of I Corinthians. Then he takes a detour to touch on other matters, only to return to the subject in chapter 10. As concisely as possible, I shall try to restate Paul's answers to the various inquiries that had been made, as he gives them in these two chapters.

First, Paul sketches the situation, pointing up the major issue. He says all have some knowledge about the matter, but it is possible that some are misinformed (8:1-3). He says, furthermore, that a person who may not be

8

correctly informed may have problems with his conscience because of habits formed when still a participant in an idolatrous religion:

> There are some who, out of habit formed in idolatry, still eat food as if it were offered to an idol, and because their conscience is weak, they are defiled (v. 7b).

Then, he says, the one who has no problem with knowledge or with his own conscience nevertheless may have missed entirely another important issue—his influence upon another brother whose conscience is weak.[1]

Strong Christians (i.e., those with a strong conscience on the matter) realize that there is no harm in eating meat that has been sacrificed to idols, since idols are nothing; there is only one true God (4-6). But "everybody doesn't know this" (7a). The brother who thinks that it is idolatry to eat (or that it *might* be idolatry to do so) is the one with the weak conscience. Therefore, since it is sin for such weak brothers to eat, they are "defiled" (7c) by doing so. The *meat* did not defile them, of course. They were defiled by doing what they thought was or might have been sin. For them, to eat was to slip back into idolatry in their hearts. It is important to be clear about this fact: because the *food* was not contaminated (the weak brother himself is said to be contaminated),[2] some (strong brothers) could eat righteously, but others (weak brothers) could not; if they ate, for them it was sin. In other words, it is a Christian principle that the very same act under conditions stated here can for some be perfectly acceptable, but for others be sin.[3]

But that is not all. While strong brothers have liberty to eat whatever is pure in God's sight, there is a limitation to that liberty. If the brother with the stronger (better informed) conscience pursues a course of life in which he freely enjoys his rights and privileges in a selfish and thoughtless way, his freedom becomes license and he sins. His freedom to partake of food offered

---

1. A conscience is said to be weak when improperly informed. The capacity to make self-evaluation and to trigger peaceful or painful bodily responses is called conscience; it functions in accordance with standards that may or may not be biblical. Weak consciences are those that operate according to faulty, unbiblical values.

2. Cf. Titus 1:15 for a similar comment. Again, the defiling comes from within; not from without.

3. Paul put it well in Romans when he wrote: "Whatever isn't of faith is sin" (Rom. 14:23). There, he says that if one eats doubting, he sins. He must know fully that what he is doing is proper before God or he shouldn't do it at all.

to idols may not be pushed to the point where he becomes a stumbling block in the path of his weaker brother. He must forego his right (v. 9) whenever it becomes the occasion for tempting a weaker brother to sin.

If a brother who doesn't have his knowledge (perhaps a recent, uninstructed convert) should see him eating, this may tempt him to do the same. But, since persons who have a different conscience about the act can do the same thing righteously or sinfully, the stronger brother will have led his weaker brother into sin, and possibly back into idolatry (8:10-13). Thus, the conscience of another cannot be ignored when his acts are influenced by one's own example. No man is an island. Such thoughtlessness is sin—against the weaker brother and against Christ (v. 12).

Again, N.B., it is not the eating, in and of itself, that is sin, but rather the careless or indifferent attitude of the one who eats, heedless of its effect upon others. Here, in no uncertain terms, Paul affirms the truth that a Christian is his brother's keeper! It is, therefore, an unqualified principle that the indifferent practices one has the *right* (v. 9 uses the word) to enjoy become moral issues for him when their exercise becomes a hindrance to the life of another Christian.

The privilege must be abandoned, the right relinquished and in love the brother's welfare considered of the foremost importance in the matter. Thus, the eighth chapter of I Corinthians closes (cf. v. 13).

In chapter 9, Paul illustrates how he applied this principle in a different context. In his missionary work (and, indeed, in his work at Corinth) he followed this principle. For the sake of unbelievers, young converts and the witness of the church, he laid aside his rights to marriage, to receiving pay under certain circumstances, etc., lest in any way he might hinder the progress of the gospel or become a stumbling block. (Note the recurring emphasis on rights in this chapter. Those who teach that we have no rights are wrong. God has granted rights of various sorts.)

There is, as I previously indicated, a resumption of the theme set forth in chapter 8. That begins in the middle of chapter 10. Paul reiterates his earlier points, and then discusses the role of conscience more fully. Let us consider what he says.

First, there is a summary: "Everything is lawful, but not all things are advantageous; all sorts of things are lawful, but not all things build up"

(10:23). Moreover, no Christian is to put himself or his interests first, but rather he is to have his brother's interests higher on his list (v. 24).

Then Paul considers various cases and applies his principles to each. These case studies are important because they show us how to use biblical principles in concrete situations:

1. Food sacrificed to idols may be eaten for one's own personal use if there is no danger of leading anyone astray in any manner (v. 25). Those who have no conscience against eating know that all such things belong to the Lord—not to idols or false gods (v. 26). So, when Paul says that he'll "never eat meat" (8:13), he means *in situations where it might cause another to sin*. It is clear that neither he nor others would refrain from personal use where there was no such danger.

2. If an unbeliever invites a Christian to dinner, the Christian is to eat whatever meat that is set before him and ask no questions. He is to raise no issue about whether this meat was offered to idols (v. 27). Why should he? He has no conscience about the matter.

3. However, in the third case, if someone (the Greek is *tis*=anybody—believer or unbeliever) else makes an issue of the matter saying, "This was offered in sacrifice" (or words to that effect), then the Christian should refuse it (v. 28). He does so for the sake of *others*, however, and not for his own sake (he has no conscience about eating *per se*). The other may regard the idol as a god or as contaminating the meat (cf. v. 28).

But this leads Paul to ask, "Why should my freedom be determined by another's conscience?" (v. 29). If I share a meal thankfully, why should I be criticized for eating that for which I gave thanks (vv. 29, 30)? Is Paul now contradicting what he said before? Is he now claiming rights that he said he would abandon under such circumstances? No, in these words he is taking the side of the reader who may object to what he has been teaching in chapter 8 and which he has just reaffirmed.

In verses 31ff. he answers those objections, and, in doing so, pushes the matter at least one step further along. He argues, you must "do everything for God's glory" (31b). When all is said and done, it isn't the brother's conscience, or even his welfare that is uppermost in the exercise of limits on your liberty. You must allow another's conscience to dictate *in order to glorify God*. If you become a stumbling block for *anyone*—Jew, Greek, believer—you thereby hurt His cause and dishonor God. As I (Paul) always adapt to the culture and situation in missionary work, even when it means that to do so puts me at a disadvantage personally, so too should you be willing to do so in whatever you do in order to please God. In this "imitate" me as you have seen me imitate Christ (11:1), who likewise put others first (cf. Phil. 2).

* * *

Let us now summarize what we have learned.

1. Situations arise in which the very same act may be sin for one person and not for another. This is not due to any relativism in biblical ethics, but to a relativism in the sinners who must follow them! The difference lies in knowledge, interpretations and attitudes. The best summary statement of the principle is found in Romans 14:23.

2. A Christian's personal freedom is limited by a consideration of whether or not the exercise of his freedom tempts a brother to stumble (sin) or gives an unbeliever cause to reject or criticize the gospel. In such cases an act thus becomes sin for him to do what under other circumstances would not be sin, not because of the act itself, but because of its adverse effects on others and on God's name.

* * *

These Pauline principles, as I stated earlier, are of great significance to Christian counselors. Often counselees will demand a yes/no answer to questions involving certain indifferent practices. Counselors must be careful not to give an unqualified "go ahead" signal before examining all the surrounding facts in the case, and (in particular) the knowledge and attitudes that form the standard in the counselee's conscience. Always try to determine where his conscience stands with reference to matters of this sort. A too quick response by the counselor could send the counselee out to sin.

On the other hand, counselors must maintain the right of a believer to do whatever the Bible permits *even when another believer doesn't like him to do so.* So long as his participation in a practice leads to no danger of others following his example and thereby falling into sin, he may exercise his rights.[4]

Thus it is fair to say, as a final word, that Christians have liberty, but with a limit.

A Note on Questionable Sexual Practices

Regularly, in counseling, in question and answer periods and in private conversations, I am asked about various sexual practices. The questioner usually asks: "Is such-and-such a practice legitimate? I don't know because the Bible doesn't mention it."

Has God left us without guidance on these matters? In making decisions, is one purely on his own?

No. There are both a broad principle and a narrower one that pertain to the question; we are not without guidance.

A. The broad principle: Here is what I have called the "holding principle" (see also *More than Redemption* [Phillipsburg, N.J.: Presbyterian and Reformed, 1979]). According to Romans 14:23, whatever is not of faith is sin. It is *not* right to participate in any practice if one either

(1) thinks it is sin to do so, or,

(2) thinks it might be sin to do so (doubts).

Either way he sins, not because a given practice necessarily is wrong (it may be legitimate in God's sight) but because the person *thinks* it is or *might be wrong and does it anyway*. That *attitude* toward God is itself sinful.

B. The narrow principle: In I Corinthians 7:4, Paul says, "The wife doesn't have authority over her own body; rather it is her husband who does. Also, the husband doesn't have authority over his own body; rather it is the wife who does." This basic principle of love—that in sexual relations one's task is to please his marriage partner, not himself, has a number of ramifications. First, it eliminates autoeroticism, including masturbation. Secondly, it allows the other person's needs to dictate the frequency of sexual relations,

---

4. So often the passages in I Cor. and Rom. have been misused to justify curtailing another's freedom simply because another—who will tell you he is not tempted to follow the example— merely objects to a practice. The two things—offending/causing to offend—must be distinguished. Objection to and influence over are two quite distinct concepts.

and, thirdly, it means *one may never demand of his/her partner any practice that he/she finds questionable or abhorrent.* So God *has* spoken on the subject. If the *principle of love*—putting others first—is combined with the *holding principle,* there can never be a time when the partners get into arguments or impasses over such practices. It simply won't happen. It will be, rather, like two cars arriving simultaneously at a four-way stop sign and each driver saying "You first." Each partner will respect the wishes and the conscience of the other.

So, the Christian counselor will not speculate about the numerous practices that people ask about. Rather, he will articulate these general principles. How much better to have guiding principles like these that

(1) stress *love toward a partner* in solving problems;

(2) stress one's *attitude toward God* in doing so, rather than merely receiving a list of dos and don'ts.

In such situations, God wants us not only to obey and do the right thing, but to grow closer to Him and to one another in coming to decisions.

3

Counseling the Disabled

"How do you help a disabled person? Isn't it harder for him to make it in life? Isn't it cruel to talk to him about responsibility, the way you nouthetic counselors always seem to do?"

Those questions are good ones. And there may be some disabled persons reading this who need to hear the answers to them. Those who live with disabled persons surely do, and those who minister to them in some way or counsel them also should be interested in a biblical approach to the disabled.

Let's begin by admitting that the disabled person's lot is hard. Counselors must never minimize the tragedies of life and the effects of the curse on human life. And, we may also acknowledge that the more debilitating and the more highly visible the disability, the harder life becomes. These are givens; there is no way around them. All that I say must take these givens into consideration.

But we also must recognize that sympathizing and making allowances alone will not solve the disabled person's problems. Indeed, sometimes these very approaches make things harder still. Sympathy, if not coupled with true help, and making allowances that have nothing to do with the disability itself, can be downright destructive, no matter how well meant.

Precisely because disabilities usually make life harder, the truly empathetic counselor will *stress* biblical responsibility and *not* allow the disabled counselees to "get away with" anything. It is all too easy for them to adopt sinful patterns by which they wring sympathy from others *in order to be allowed to escape responsibilities* that they could and should assume. The counselor will be on the alert for manipulative patterns and, for their own benefit, will confront disabled persons concerning them. How does he do so?

One way is to point out that Paul was a disabled person; yet he never shirked his responsibilities. His "thorn in the flesh," he said, "slapped him around" (II Cor. 12:7). Many disabled persons can identify with that sort of

15

language. But despite this serious affliction, Paul continued to assume every obligation that he physically could; and throughout he maintained a proper attitude toward his disability. How did he do so?

1. He prayed about it; three times he asked God to remove it. But He didn't (v. 8; the word used means "pleaded"). Disabled persons can identify with that too. Then he stopped. Why?

2. Because he began to interpret his disability. It was given to keep him from becoming "conceited" over the great revelations he had received (v. 7). Counselors must help counselees to interpret their disabilities in a positive manner too as God-given and for a significant purpose. Such interpretations may be tentative or partial, but ought to be forthcoming.

3. Through the disability he found special help from Christ, who is willing to manifest (or make "fully evident") His power through our weakness. Here, in itself, is a significant purpose and a tremendous ministry opened wide for every disabled person (cf. v. 9). Paul was so happy for everyone to see Christ's power evident that he could even become happy about his affliction and "boast" about his "weakness" (v. 9b).

4. This led to contentment (v. 10). There was no continued agonizing "Why? Why this? Why me? Why now?," etc. No, the matter was resolved. God sent it to manifest Christ's power in Paul's life, and he was satisfied for it to do so. That was his conclusion of the matter. So too, the biblical counselor must lead the disabled counselee into just such a ministry of manifest power, and into such a state of contentment as goes along with it.[1]

"But," someone objects (I can almost hear it as I write), "Paul wasn't an invalid. Is it proper to say that he was a disabled person?"

We can be disabled in many ways. Paul's difficulty was quite serious. He had some sort of eye difficulty. That we know. (Perhaps he was partially blind.) In Galatians he says, "You know that it was because of physical sickness that I announced the good news to you. . . (4:13). N.B., the illness didn't keep Paul from fulfilling his God-given responsibility. He continues: ". . . my physical condition was a trial to you," but, he notes, ". . . if it had been possible you would have gouged out your eyes and given them to me" (vv. 14, 15). And, at the conclusion of the letter he points out, "Notice the large letters in which I am writing to you with my

---

1. The story of Joni Eareckson is a modern account of just such a ministry.

16

own hand" (6:11). Probably these words refer to the last paragraph or two since Paul tells us elsewhere, "I [Paul] write this greeting with my own hand, and this is the indication in every letter that I have written it" (II Thess. 3:17).

We must conclude that Paul had continuing serious eye trouble that was so debilitating that he could not pen an entire letter (unless Galatians is an exception over which he must have agonized) but had to use an amanuensis. That kind of a problem is a disability. I say it again, Paul was a disabled person from whom other disabled persons can learn much.

The very fact that we know so little about his disability, and must piece it together in the way that we do, is the surest indication that Paul did not use it in a manipulative way.

What else must the counselor help the handicapped, or disabled, person to do? In addition to the basic considerations already mentioned, I want to point out that the essential nature of a disability is that it *limits* the one disabled. Counselors should discuss thoroughly this matter of limitation with counselees since it is of such central import. Handicaps, as in Paul's case, always limit (Paul could not write whole letters himself, often must have been hindered in travel, etc.). But consider this:

1. Everyone has limitations. Some are less visible than others. One person has limited intelligence, another has a lack of coordination that keeps him from excelling in sports. Others cannot walk; some have no ability to carry a tune. A disabled person is disabled more than others *only in degree*. He is by no means to be considered *a special sort of person*. Like anyone else, he is first and above all else, a human being, created in the image of the living God. The designation "disabled" fits him in some special sense—rather than all of us—only because of the extent to which his disability limits him, its high visibility (i.e., in some way it calls attention to itself), etc. What is extraordinary about a disabled person, then, is in degree, not in kind; it is, finally, a matter of the extent or degree of the limitation involved that marks him out. Counselors who think of their own limitations, and how Christ has enabled them to handle them, already know the *basic* approach to use with the handicapped (II Cor. 1:4).[2]

2. N.B., Paul does not say that we can counsel only those who have the same affliction, but those with *any* affliction. The principles and the power are the same.

2. This basic approach to limitation as something common to all is important because the disabled person (labeled as such on signs in parking lots, in rest rooms, etc.) is in danger of growing resentful over his (as he may come to see it) unique problem. (It isn't; see my booklet on I Cor. 10:13, *Christ and Your Problems* [Phillipsburg, N.J.: Presbyterian and Reformed, 1971].) Counselors must strongly affirm his commonalities over his differences. The temptation to become bitter, the temptation to indulge in self-pity, the temptation to manipulate and the temptation to rationalize one's failure to assume his proper responsibilities may all be traced to a common root: a focus by the disabled counselee on his uniqueness and on his disabilities, rather than on his commonalities and his abilities.[3]

3. Counselors, therefore, must help him assess the God-given abilities that he *does* have, the possibilities for productive work and ministry that do exist, etc. Limitations must be viewed not as disabling the person *in toto*. (He is *not* a disabled *person*, but rather, a *person* who is disabled in only *some* respects.) Limitations are necessary for success. The scientist who achieves something significant limits himself to a narrow field of study. He purposely neglects much that he could be doing in order to focus and concentrate his interests, studies and endeavors. This is true of all highly successful persons who contribute something to the world.

But many of us, with greater abilities, achieve very little because we never learn the lessons of *self*-limitation. The person with disabilities has no such problem; God has limited him already, thus *enabling* him more easily to focus and concentrate on those areas in which his abilities lie. If he only will see it and enter into it, the person with a handicap can capitalize on this limitation. For him the problem is simplified: he doesn't need to decide about what he must eliminate; providentially, much has been eliminated for him already.

Persons who recognize these facts and, in imitation of Paul, handle their limitations righteously, do not fall into the many pits that line the pathway of the disabled. There is, for example, the self-centered attitude that says, "Now look out for me; I have a disability, you know. Put me first in line." Of course, as he thinks this way and tells everybody else such things, he is

---

3. Anyone, even those with far less visible disabilities who would never be labeled "disabled" or "handicapped," may focus on his limitations and become resentful. Many do; counselors meet them daily.

also telling himself. Pretty soon he believes it. Then, when people don't go to extraordinary lengths to accommodate him, he gets angry or sulks. Such talk is evidence of a problem, and should be noted (at length—at the appropriate time) by the counselor.

There is always someone with a greater (or, at least, very different) disability than your counselee. Tell him about that person. Tell him, "Here is someone for whom you might *care,* whom you may be able to help, to whom you may be able to minister." Moreover, many of us who are not so visibly disabled as to be labeled (a heinous practice) need his help. The counselor's task will be to enlighten him about his potential for ministry and to help him gear it into practical activity. Every "disabled" person, like every other Christian, should minister to someone else. But, it is especially good when he can minister to those who do not bear the label, but who are thought of as "normal." Self-centeredness is sin, even for a disabled person. For many, it is the most disabling factor of all.

Self-pity often leads to complacency, depression, worry, and sickness. Self-pitying persons let responsibilities slide, then blame the fact on their disabilities (or the failure of others). When a disabled Christian becomes depressed through self-pity, bitterness and the like as a result of following his feelings rather than assuming his responsibilities (no matter how he feels), his problem is no different from that of any other Christian; and he must be brought to see that. His disabilities never excuse him from the responsibilities that truly fit his abilities.

What does a disabled Christian need? He needs to be challenged to live up to his full capacity in the service of Christ, to the glory of God—exactly as every other Christian does. Even if he is totally paralyzed, he has *time,* the greatest natural gift of God. He must use that time profitably, perhaps in prayer. Perhaps he can record messages to missionaries, pastors or others on tape, etc. He must discover (and counselors must help him to do so) profitable uses for his time. (It is wrong to devote most of one's waking moments to watching TV..)[4]

Remember Paul's point: the disabled person is in some sense "weak" (Paul's word for what we call "disabled"). That weakness is the most fertile soil of all in which the fruit of God's power may grow.

---

4. Though it is possible that he could become a TV critic for a Christian publication.

4

Is Transactional Analysis OK?

Frequently I have been asked to comment on the movement known as Transactional Analysis (T.A., for short). This request often is occasioned by concern over the inroads that this pagan counseling system is making among Christian churches. On that point alone let me say a word before I go on.

It is tragic to see how some Christians grasp frantically for every clever new approach that comes down the pike. Among other things, this shows the theological weakness of those who do so. They seem not to be able to discover and evaluate the presuppositions, principles and practices of a system in order to determine whether it is essentially biblical or anti-biblical. (Some, of course, may not have any concern to do so if their own presuppositions are of an eclectic bent.) Usually this inability stems from the deplorable fact that pastors have been trained in seminaries (too often the fountainheads of all sorts of problems in our churches) to think, do exegesis and theology *abstractly*. They do not know how to use the fruits of their studies in the Bible to discuss, dissect and decide upon the everyday problems of life. They have been trained to handle "theological issues," never realizing that theology is for living (cf. Titus 1:1b).[1] They do not know how to translate doctrine and exegesis into counseling, so they eagerly search for some system that will enable them, they think (wrongly) to help counselees. Most of the seminaries that turn out such men have, themselves, adopted the eclectic spirit in counseling.

Whatever else may be behind the eclectic spirit, we see much evidence of its existence today among Bible-believing people in churches and (particularly) in educational institutions. The widespread acceptance of T.A. (or elements of it) is a case in point.

---

1. For much more on how doctrine may be related to life, see my book *More than Redemption* (Phillipsburg, N.J.: Presbyterian and Reformed, 1979), which is a textbook on the theology of counseling.

Since from its inception T.A. has, in its principles and in their formulations, exhibited a hostility toward the Christian faith, and since T.A. constitutes an attack upon all the fundamental principles of authority, one might conclude that T.A. would be rejected out of hand by conservative Christians. Such is not the case. How come? Because, as I noted, Christians fail to see the presuppositional stance of a movement and its effects because they do not know how to discover these through an analysis of the operative principles embedded in the practices of the system.

Here, there is no opportunity to fully expose and evaluate the system. Therefore, I shall focus on two facts and let the reader judge for himself whether or not the system merits the acceptance of the Christian church. It is not necessary to know whether a piece of fruit is rotten (and if so, where) or whether it tastes sour or sweet, etc., if one has discovered that it is poisonous. That fact alone provides more than adequate reason for rejecting it. We shall look at the poison in the T.A. apple.[2]

Now for the two poisonous facts.

1. What the Bible says can be done only by the Spirit of God working by His Word, T.A. asserts it can do without either. It is, therefore, in conflict and in competition with Christianity.

2. What the Bible says man needs as an authority structure for living, T.A. attacks and attempts to destroy. T.A., thereby, is in rebellion against God's sovereign authoritative structures in the world.

If these two positions can be shown to be true of T.A., then it should be plain that Christians must reject and repel goals, principles and methods of T.A. as a pagan substitute for the Christian faith.

But first, let us take a glimpse at the background of T.A.

Eric Berne, the founder of the movement, was a close friend of Erik Erikson, the neo-Freudian who wrote the shockingly inaccurate and prejudicial study of Martin Luther. Berne was strongly influenced by Erikson. Erikson, in contrast to Freud, emphasized the primacy of the *ego* over the *id*. Yet he remained generally within the Freudian camp. Berne, in this, reflects Erikson. But Berne had a clever mind and a way with words that is

---

2. For those wishing to do so, T.A. can be investigated most thoroughly in the writings of Eric Berne, Claude Steiner and Tom (I'm OK, You're OK) Harris.

unparalleled in the field of counseling. He took some of the basic concepts of neo-Freudianism, mixed them with some of his own ideas (and the ideas of others) and repackaged them in new, very attractive wrappers. To this old product he gave a new name, Transactional Analysis.

Berne no longer spoke in crusty, formidable terms about the *id*, the *ego* and the *superego*. Rather, he renamed them Parent (superego), Adult (ego) and Child (id). This transformation of the Freudian product made it much more salable. The new image modernized Freud; Berne began to talk about "games people play," "life scripts," and used catchy titles ("Ain't It Awful") for these games and scripts. The face-lift gave remarkable new life to limping old theories.

Following Berne's lead, Steiner and (especially) Harris have continued to popularize the viewpoint under similar attractive themes: *Scripts People Live* (Steiner); *I'm O.K.—You're O.K.* (Harris). Harris is the greatest popularizer of the three. It was he who spread the movement widely among the general public. Steiner still retains much of the stiffer, more academic approach from which Berne, in spite of his racy vocabulary, never quite separated.

Now, let us turn to the two areas that I have isolated. In our archeological dig we shall send down but a couple of shafts from which we shall gather samples.

First, I said that T.A. is competitive to Christianity because it claims to provide what the Bible says only Christianity can achieve. And it sees no need for the truth of the Word or the power of the Spirit.

Consider Harris' words,

> I believe that Transactional Analysis may provide an answer to the predicament of man.[3]

Something of the messianic claims and spirit of T.A. can be seen in this statement, which (in its context) clearly indicates the fact. *Time* Magazine wrote this about Harris' book:

> The book itself goes so far as to suggest that it may be able to save man and civilization from extinction.[4]

---

3. Harris, *I'm OK—You're OK*, p. 258.
4. *Time*, Aug. 10, 1973, p. 45.

The writer of the *Time* article observes that

> . . . Harris is convinced that only those who believe the "truth" of transactional analysis can win the battle against neurosis,

and quotes him as saying,

> You have to have absolute faith that T.A. is true; otherwise you'll lose.[5]

These calls for truth and absolute faith are, it seems, religious demands no less exacting than that of Him who said "I am the . . . truth . . . no man comes to the Father but by Me."

And, coupled with that is the idea that this salvation of mankind (and individuals) is realized in those who agree "that the not-OK posture is an illusion."[6] Theologically speaking, that means that man's sinful nature is denied. As Steiner continually puts it, you must *"Trust human nature and believe in your children."*[7] Indeed, the thrust of the movement is that success comes when you deny the reality of non-OKness (sin). Like traditional Freudianism, T.A. thinks that guilt feelings can be removed by denying sin. T.A. approaches human problems humanistically, rejecting the need for grace and a Savior. To accept T.A. principles is, therefore, to deny Jesus Christ and His cross any place. As a matter of fact, this conflict goes even deeper. God, whom Berne calls Santa Claus, is called an illusion. The would-be T.A. counselor is warned that "it takes enormous power to shatter these primal illusions," and is told that

> In order for the patient to get better, his illusion, upon which his whole life is based, must be undermined so that he can live in a world which is here today . . . the script analyst . . . [must] tell his patients finally that there is no Santa Claus.[8]

Clearly these samples show how T.A. is at odds with Christianity and is in the business of trying to undermine faith in God while seeking to establish belief in man—and (even more specifically) unquestioned trust in its own dogmas.

---

5. Ibid.
6. Alan Reuter, "Psychology and Theory: A Return to Dialog," *Concordia Theological Monthly* 44, no. 3 (May, 1973).
7. Claude Steiner, *Scripts People Live* (New York: Grove Press, 1974), p. 309.
8. Eric Berne, *What Do You Say After You Say Hello?* (New York: Bantam Press, 1973), pp. 152, 153.

"But why don't you think that God can reveal truth even through men and systems like this one in His common grace? Isn't all truth God's truth?" One grows weary of such questions; but questioners seem never to grow weary of asking them. By the theological gymnastics that are used to justify T.A. (and other counseling systems that, in fact, are in direct competition and conflict with Christianity), the door of common grace is opened widely enough to admit even avowed atheism as in some respects "a good and useful system" that we "ought not reject out of hand," from which we may "learn a good bit" and from which we most certainly may adopt "any number of helpful methods."

Well, of course God works in common grace! Certainly all truth is God's truth. But what has that to do with T.A.? Such arguments are specious; they beg the question. The issue is this:

1. Is T.A., as it claims, truth (we may not simply *assume* so as eclectic persons who misuse the words "common grace" so often do)? We must ask, does T.A. reveal truth from God or is it a godless system set up to rival Christianity?[9] That question cannot be answered by *asserting* it; saying something is true doesn't make it so. There is a way, however, to determine whether T.A. is a medium by which God reveals truth and that is to ask, Does T.A. square with the Bible? God never contradicts in common grace what He teaches in special grace (i.e., in the Scriptures).

2. We can be sure that God did not set up a system in common grace to do what He says (in the Bible) can be done only by the Spirit working through the ministry of the Word. Common grace never *replaces* special grace. God is not a God of confusion, telling us one thing in the Scriptures and something different somewhere else.

All of us find much help in those truths that do come through God's common grace. However, the area with which we are dealing is not one in which we should expect the same sort of help that we receive in other areas of life. Human living is the area to which the *Bible* addresses itself. In the Scriptures, and in the Scriptures alone, can one discover how to love God and one's neighbor (and that is the core of what counseling is all about). And

9. I have shown how pagan counseling systems fail to measure up to the claim of common grace and, indeed, constitute systems that propagate the "counsel of the ungodly" in my book, *More than Redemption*.

24

these very Scriptures teach that such love begins and ends with Jesus Christ. Yet T.A. says,

Dogma is the enemy of truth and the enemy of persons,[10]

and

Truth is not something which has been bound in a black book.[11]

Can we believe that this sort of thing is a blessing of God's common grace, or that it could be the channel for it? Can a system based on such views be integrated with Christianity, as some think?

Certainly not! They are wrong; God told us that all things necessary for life and godliness have been given in special revelation. Surely, generations of Christians prior to Berne and Harris were not wrong in believing so! Any addition to the Scriptures claiming to better tell us how to live (not to speak of substitutions and conflicting views) therefore must be suspect. Did Jesus Christ have all He needed to live a perfect life and to become the perfect Counselor from the O.T. Bible alone? Or, was He lacking in much that T.A. could have taught Him?

We have been seeing how my second charge against T.A. holds up: T.A. attacks the authority structure God gave us by viewing truth as relative. It will have no absolutes. Children must not be restricted, but left free to do as they please.[12] The authority of God in the home is eroded as it is in the church. The authority of God Himself is opposed. Authority demands a submissive relationship, the kind that is undercut by T.A.'s goal of autonomy. The T.A. concept of the naughty parent, whose authority must be rejected by the Adult shows this clearly.

Consider the following:

Truth is a growing body of data of what we observe to be true.[13]

This bald statement taken in conjunction with Harris' rejection of truth in a "black book" leads to a subjectivism in which T.A. is found to be superior

---

10. Harris, op. cit., p. 260. Of course, T.A. dogma is excepted.
11. Ibid., p. 265. It is perfectly clear what book the writer had in mind.
12. Cf. Steiner, op. cit., pp. 303-9. He says that children must "not be prevented from doing things they want to do" (p. 306).
13. Harris, op. cit., p. 265.

to the Bible! On this basis, of course, there is no final standard or authority beyond one's self. Indeed, we do not have to guess at any such conclusion; we are told so frankly and openly:

> . . . when morality is encased in the structure of relit is essentially Parent. It is dated, frequently unexamined, and often contradictory. . . . Parent morality . . . impedes the formulation of a universal ethic. The position I'm OK—You're OK is not possible if it hinges on your accepting what I believe. [14]

In speaking of what he considers to be the true religious experience, Harris wrote,

> I believe that what is emptied is the Parent. [15]

From this brief survey (much more could be said) it should be evident to all concerned Christians that T.A. is incompatible with the Christian faith and that those who become involved in its tenets do so at great peril.

14. Ibid., pp. 260, 261.
15. Ibid., p. 268. Remember, the parent is religion, authority, dogma, etc.

5

How to Win an Unsaved Wife to Christ

A listener to my radio broadcast once wrote:

> Have been enjoying your short messages. Lately you've been talking
> about the way that wives can win their unsaved husbands for Christ.
> Many authors and speakers deal with the above topic. I haven't heard
> any tackle the opposite—how a saved husband can win his wife to
> Christ. Do we just reverse what we hear about wives' roles? It is just
> "love your wives, as Christ loved His Church"?

The question is a good one. The listener is right; we do hear little or
nothing about this matter. One reason for that is that the Scriptures speak so
much more fully about what wives must do.[1] But, as we shall see, the
question is a matter of emphasis, not a question of exclusion.

We all know that in I Peter 3:1-6, a passage that I was discussing on the
radio when this letter was written, Peter clearly outlines how a Christian wife
is to behave in order to please God and (possibly) win her unsaved husband
to the Lord. There he stresses the need for aggressive submission, a beautiful
inner spirit and respectful obedience in doing good.

At first it seems that there is no comparable instruction for Christian
husbands. Perhaps, in Peter's day (as in ours) there were more wives than
husbands in this position. But, as I said, Peter is concerned mainly about the
issue of submission to an unsaved authority under whom one might suffer for
her faith. But what passages tell the Christian husband what to do?

Paul mentions the problem in I Corinthians 7:12ff.: Apart from expressing
his concern for winning an unsaved wife to Christ, and requiring husbands to

---

1. In I Peter 3 the *emphasis* is on the wife of an unsaved husband because, in the context,
Peter is dealing principally with various authority situations in which the believer suffers in
submission.

27

continue living with them in order to win them, he says nothing more about *how* to do so. When he speaks of the unsaved wife as being "sanctified" by her Christian husband, he does not mean that the wife is automatically saved because of her association with him or anything else of the sort. The word *sanctified* has a wide band of uses in the Scriptures. Fundamentally it means to "set apart," and can be used even of the pots and pans that were used in the OT temple. These were *special* (*set apart* from others) and could be used nowhere else and for no other purposes than those for which they had been set apart. So, too, the unsaved wife who lives with a Christian husband is in a *special* or *privileged* position. She lives in constant contact with one in whom the Spirit is at work, with one who is praying for her salvation and with one who not only can instruct her in the gospel, but who (in his daily living) can demonstrate what Jesus Christ has done for him. Truly, she is in a sanctified (or special) situation in that covenant home on which God promises His special blessings. This teaching should be of great encouragement to a Christian husband who is married to an unbelieving wife.

But the question remains, *"How* does he go about demonstrating Christ to his wife?" The listener is on the right track in making the suggestion that he did: "Do we just reverse what we hear about the wife's role? . . . Do we just love our wives as Christ loved the church?" However, two comments must be made:

1. Let's remove those "justs" from his suggestions. Winning a wife by one's life isn't a snap—as those words might indicate. It means proper attitudes, hard work, prayer, obedience to God and patient endurance and persistence. It will demand everything of him. And—of utmost importance— he can never do any of this as a gimmick to win his wife. He must do it *because God says so, to please Him*—whether his wife becomes a Christian or not.

2. There is more "how to" than at first might seem available to the casual reader of the Scriptures. And, perhaps surprisingly, it is in I Peter 3:7, immediately following the directions given to Christian wives.

Looking at I Peter 3:7, we must notice first the word "likewise." Clearly, this word (like its counterpart in v. 1) points back to the behavior of Jesus Christ described at the end of chapter 2. (See my commentary on I Peter, *Trust and Obey* [Phillipsburg, N.J.: Presbyterian and Reformed, 1978], for more details.) But it also serves the function of linking the directions given to

28

wives (vv. 1-6) with those given to husbands (v. 7). Both take their impetus from the same source. Both sets of directions tell Christians how to win lost spouses; both, therefore, point to living out respective roles properly.

What does I Peter 3:7 require? That husbands live with their wives

> in an understanding way, showing respect for the woman as you would for a fragile container, and as joint heirs of the grace of life, so that your prayers may not be interrupted.

Echoes of Paul's better known requirements for loving leadership, as the head of the home, assuming and fulfilling all of the responsibilities of that headship, willingness to die (if need be) for one's wife (as Christ died for the church) and a desire to treat her as one's self,[2] may all be found in Peter's lesser known words, plus some other elements. It is those other elements, which constitute the "how to," to which we now turn.

Paul's call for love—a love like Christ had for His church—is often held out, and rightly so. But little is said about *how* one may begin to love his wife as Christ loved the church. Frequently (but not often enough) the point is made that this love is *unconditional,* i.e., it does not depend on anything in the one who is loved (cf. Rom. 5:6, 8, 10). Its source, its impetus, etc., is wholly within the one who loves, who (like Christ) determines to *set* his love on his wife *regardless* of whether there is anything loving, lovely or lovable about her (the church, before becoming such, was weak, sinful, rebellious). But still, *how* does one love like that? Specifically, *how* does he show unconditional love? Where does he begin?

A step closer to the answer is the observation (made even less frequently) that love isn't (first of all) an emotion; in the first instance love is giving. One loves an unlovely person as Christ did—by *giving* Himself (Eph. 5:25). One loves a hungry or thirsty enemy by *giving* (something to eat; a cup of cold water). That is to say, one *gives* whatever it is that he has that the one on whom he sets his love needs. That is closer to an operational answer; but what of the husband who says, "I don't know *what* my wife wants. I don't know how to please her; I simply don't understand her at all"? How does he begin to love (i.e., begin to give)?

Here is where I Peter 3:7 becomes most practical. Peter insists that

2. Cf. Eph. 5:25-33. For a detailed study of the passage, see my book, *Christian Living in the Home* (Phillipsburg, N.J.: Presbyterian and Reformed, 1972).

husbands must "live with" their wives "in an understanding way." His focus is on the fact that love—intelligent giving of one's time, possessions or self—grows out of understanding.

"But," he may insist, "you'll never understand a woman." That old cliché has done much harm. Like many other false sayings by which people live, this one has helped to destroy many marriages. If God commands Christian husbands to understand their wives, then it is possible as well as necessary for them to do so. But until both the possibility and the necessity of doing it are accepted by a husband, we may be sure that he will fail in any (half-hearted, hope-against-hope) attempts that he may make. God never commands His children to do anything that He fails to provide directions and power (in His Word and by His Spirit) to accomplish. We must believe this and obediently avail ourselves of these provisions. Well, then, how does one understand a wife?

The answer lies in the Greek words that have been translated "in an understanding way." Literally, they read "live with your wives *according to knowledge.*" Many husbands have been living for years in nearly total ignorance of all the true concerns, felt needs, etc., that their wives have.

"OK, but how does one obtain this knowledge?"

How do you get knowledge about something else? You seek it, arrange ways of getting it, etc.; in short, you do research to obtain it.

"Research my wife?"

Why not? Most men have spent more time researching far less important matters.

"Well. . . ."

You could begin by interviewing her.

"Interview her? How do you interview a wife?"

First, you set an appointment.

"Ask my *wife* for an appointment?"

Certainly. You wouldn't think of barging in on a client at any old time to ask questions whether or not he was prepared, or whether or not he had the time, would you?

"Well, . . . I guess not . . . but. . . ."

No buts about it. Your wife deserves every bit as much consideration and more.

"But when I try to talk to her I get nowhere. . . ."

Perhaps one of the major reasons is that, like many couples, you do it at inappropriate times and in inappropriate ways. That's one reason for making a definite appointment that suits both of you for a time and place you set aside for this purpose only. Make sure there will be no interruptions. Then, you might begin to get somewhere.

"But she won't tell me what I want to know. I've tried before and. . . ."

You've never tried doing so on an appointment, have you?

"No, but. . . ."

Well, then you don't know whether she will or won't. Besides, I haven't finished making my full suggestion.

"Go ahead."

Well, making an appointment to interview your wife, rather than trying to find out what you want to know about her when you both are rushed and on the run, will create different conditions. Making the appointment itself ought to show her that you mean business.

"OK, so I make the appointment. What do I do when I interview her? I haven't the slightest idea where to begin or what to say. What next?"

The answer to that is *preparation*. You must spend the better part of every waking free moment for at least a week before you interview her, thinking about what you want to know about her concerns, joys, fears, expectations, likes, dislikes, and whatever else you want to know. And you should write down every question and work hard on how you word each one to make sure you do it well. (I'll be glad to go over the list with you beforehand to make suggestions on wording or content.) When your wife sees what extensive preparations you have made, she will be much more likely to understand that you are serious about this matter and give you good responses. And, incidentally, let me point out a very significant fact—you will have already begun to express love toward her by giving. You will have given of your time and thought to this list. I'd be sure to have *at least* 25 well-thought-through, well-worded, fairly specific questions on that list.

"Well, it just might work. At least, it is worth a try. Do you have any other ideas for understanding a woman?"

Yes. Another thing you can do is *observe* her.

"How do I go about doing that?"

Well, the next time the two of you go to the department store together. . . .

"I don't go to department stores with her!"

Then let me put it differently: The *first* time that you go to the department store with her, as you pass through (let us say) the china section and she stops to admire a plate, *observe*. If she lingers with it, holds it up to the light, looks at it from various angles, etc., make a note of it—she likes it. Then, if she stops, looks at it again on the way out, put a mental check mark next to your note and buy her a piece of it for your anniversary. You can also observe her needs, her concerns, etc.

"What else do you suggest?"

I'll give you one more idea; you can add others if you like: Use feedback. For one week, do one small thing for your wife daily—just to please her.

"Feedback? Sometimes I get too much of that from her!"

Well, what I have in mind will tend to generate useful feedback if you do it well. Be sure that you give plenty of thought each day to what you do for her. Try to determine in your mind, from past experience, what she might like and what she might not. Then do it. But make it something small, just in case you fail to hit the target! And, by the way, do something that doesn't cost any money. (It's too easy just to buy some flowers on the way home from work. It might be better to stop along the road and pick some dried wild flowers instead.) At any rate, whatever you do, *give*. (Remember that's how love begins—with giving; cf. John 3:16; Gal. 2:20); give of your thought, your time, your effort. That is to say, give of your*self!*

"I can see some value in that—it gives me a chance to start thinking about her and expressing love in concrete ways by giving, but where, exactly, does the feedback come in?"

From the response you get to what you did. Be satisfied with "A" for effort (love) even if she "fails" you on the item itself. In other words, you will begin (as you put it) in "concrete ways" to discover what she likes and doesn't like by the feedback. Ask for an honest response, and be as satisfied with a negative one as you would with a positive one. During the first few weeks of this you are *mainly* interested in gathering data from feedback to help you to live with your wife in an understanding way. If you get positive or negative feedback it doesn't matter. Both help you achieve your goal of gathering significant *data* about your wife's likes and dislikes in order to understand her better. But as the understanding comes, you'll hit the target more and more, and the increase in positive feedback will make you aware of the fact. All along, your wife should be drawn closer to you (and you to her), not just because you do score a hit or two, but mainly because she sees you making such an effort. And, the more time, thought and effort you invest in your wife, the more your concern for her will grow: "Where your treasure is, there your heart will be also."

There is a second element in this verse for counselors to emphasize to Christian husbands. They must treat their wives as "weaker vessels" (KJV). When reading this, one husband responded, "Weaker vessel? You should have seen her throw the TV set across the room at me!!" The translation in my *Christian Counselor's NT* clears up the problem:

> showing respect for the woman as you would for a fragile container.

The verse doesn't call the woman a weaker vessel, but tells you to treat her with the same respect that you would give a fragile vase. This is compatible to Paul's "nourish and cherish" her. Husbands truly are to be *gentle*men to their wives.

Some men treat their wives like old tin garbage cans; Christian husbands verbally, physically, and in every other way, must treat their wives like a fragile vase—Ming dynasty!

Finally, notice that a husband also must treat his wife as a joint heir to the grace of life. She too has participated in bringing birth to his children and has a crucial influence upon them. If he doesn't want his prayers for her salvation and the salvation of his children hindered (lit., "cut off"), the Christian will honor his wife as God has commanded. He will respect her for who she is, bearing an equal relationship to their children, and for the sort of influence (for good or for ill) that she brings to bear on those children.

So, in conclusion, let us encourage Christian husbands about this matter, so that they will enthusiastically assume the responsibilities of loving headship in their homes, that their wives and children alike may see the evidence of Christ living in them and may come to faith in response to their prayers.

6

The Use of I Corinthians 13 in Counseling

In any number of places in my books I have referred to I Corinthians 13 as an important passage for Christian counselors to know and use. And I have commented on various verses in that chapter on occasion.[1] Yet nowhere have I discussed the chapter as a whole. That I propose to do here. I do not (however) intend to become involved in detailed exegesis. There are too many good commentaries on I Corinthians for me to do that. Rather, my emphasis will be on meaning (without giving arguments for why I have reached certain conclusions about the text I shall simply go ahead with my interpretations) and on the application of those meanings to counseling. Throughout I shall use *The New Testament in Everyday English* (the text of *The Christian Counselor's New Testament*[2]).

First, it is important to notice that I Corinthians 13 does not stand alone. It links chapters 12 and 14, and is an essential part of Paul's argument that there is something better (12:31) than the exercise of the special gifts of the Holy Spirit: love. Moreover, the discussion is a part of a larger context. The Corinthian church had been involved in unloving acts of disunity, lawsuits, etc. Surely, Paul's words in this chapter, though immediately dealing with their unloving use of gifts, also were calculated to meet the total situation. As such, the passage is pivotal and takes on an unparalleled importance in the letter. No wonder it has become a favorite among Christians. Yet, so often (like other favorites—the Lord's prayer, Ps. 23, etc.), it is known more for the familiar cadence of words, the melody of their structure, and the

---

1. Cf. *Shepherding God's Flock* (Phillipsburg, N.J.: Presbyterian and Reformed, 1980), pp. 18, 99, 178; *Lectures on Counseling* (Grand Rapids: Baker Book House, 1978), pp. 36, 243, 119f.; *The Manual* (Phillipsburg, N.J.: Presbyterian and Reformed, 1973), pp. 39, 153, 414, 369.

2. Also printed and published separately in a revised form without the counseling notes by Baker Book House, Grand Rapids, 1979.

general impression it makes than for its exact meanings and their applications to specific life situations. I propose to break out of the former and into the latter in this essay; unless the counselor does so, he will (1) contribute to faulty use of the Scriptures, and (2) fail to help counselees through the passage. So, then, it is *absolutely* necessary for the Christian counselor to do more than assign the reading of the chapter to counselees.[3]

The form of Paul's poem (or hymn) of love is striking. Rather than give any sort of formal definition (the Bible is not big on giving definitions, so why should I be?), Paul *describes* love in both positive and negative terms. In doing so, he makes but little direct application of his words to the problems that occasioned the poem; there are, of course, transitional, introductory sentences (12:31) and the simple hortatory statement in 14:1: "pursue love." So, while I Corinthians 13 plainly is an essential part of the discussion of the misuse of spiritual gifts, the passage stands squarely on its own two feet as the richest repository of biblical data on love, no matter what the problem lacking love may be.

Indeed, it may well be that Paul wrote the bulk of the words in this chapter for another occasion, or even as a hymn on love that, because of its appropriateness, he inserted at this point. Be that as it may, there is good warrant for considering the timeless truths taught here by themselves, and for making use of them in entirely different contexts, since there is nothing about the love passage that requires us to link it inextricably and solely to the loving use of gifts. Its form, as I have noted, gives no such impression but, rather, argues for seeing a more universal character in the poem.

I shall so treat it in this essay.

I shall not spend time here comparing and contrasting *agape* love (the word used throughout this chapter) with other biblical and extra-biblical terms for love as others have done.[4] That procedure, though it has its place, seems largely to miss the point. The principal way to learn about love, as Paul used the word in the New Testament, is to study I Corinthians 13, though, of course, in doing so the use of other portions of the Bible will be

---

3. Perhaps he could assign the reading of chapter 13 along with a part of my essay on love in this book.

4. For the best of such discussions, see B. B. Warfield, "The Terminology of Love in the N.T., II," *The Princeton Theological Review* 16, no. 2 (April, 1918):153ff. Avoid the several neoorthodox discussions that tend to lead astray.

appropriate (and at times necessary) in clarifying and deepening our understanding of I Corinthians 13. Consequently, I shall focus our attention on what Paul has said to us in the remarkable words that follow:

1 If I speak the languages of men and angels, but don't have love, I am a noisy gong or clanging cymbal.
2 And if I have a gift of prophecy and know all sorts of secrets and have all kinds of knowledge, and if I have all the faith that is necessary to move mountains but I don't have love, I am nothing.
3 And if I give food to the needy and even give away all my possessions, and if I allow my body to be burned, but I don't have love, I have gained absolutely nothing.

4 Love is patient, love is kind; it is not jealous. Love doesn't boast, isn't proud,
5 doesn't act in an ugly way, isn't self-seeking, isn't easily irritated, doesn't keep records of wrongs,
6 isn't happy about injustice but happily stands on the side of truth.
7 It covers all things, believes all things, hopes all things, endures all things.

8 Love never fails. If there are prophecies, they will be set aside; if there are languages, they will cease; if there is knowledge, it will be set aside.
9 We know in part and we prophesy in part,
10 but when that which is complete comes, that which is partial will be set aside.
11 When I was a child I spoke like a child, I reasoned like a child; but now that I have become a man I have set aside childish ways.
12 Now we see dimly as if looking in a bronze mirror, then face to face; now I know partially, but then I shall know fully just as I am fully known.
13 And now these three things continue: faith, hope, love; and the greatest of these is love.

The passage as a whole may be divided into three sections:
   I. Empty Substitutes for Love (1-3)
  II. Essential Factors in Love (4-8)
 III. Everlasting Aspects of Love (8-13)

I shall spend little time with sections 1 (vv. 1-3) or 3 (vv. 8-13) since they are not so directly descriptive of love itself. Rather, I shall concentrate on verses 4-8, in which many (not all) of the essential characteristics of love appear.

36

I. *Empty Substitutes for Love* (vv. 1-3)

None of the acts that are listed in verses 1 to 3 are wrong in themselves (indeed, each one of them can be *good when done in love*. As a matter of fact, that is the very point: N.B., the threefold qualifying phrase, "but don't have love," is what negates the act—not the nature of the act *per se*). These acts are valueless to one's self, to others or to God's kingdom *when separated from love*. Not only the ability to speak in an unknown language (tongue) without studying it, but the instant ability to speak *all* the languages on earth and in the heavens is useless (to Paul it's just so much meaningless noise) unless the use of that ability is motivated by love and used in a loving way for loving purposes (v. 1). In addition, even the use of the more profitable gift of prophecy (here defined as the knowledge, or understanding, of all sorts of hidden truths and the possession of deep truths revealed by God coupled with a powerful and active faith) is empty without love (v. 2). Indeed, more than that, the *possessor* of these coveted things is *himself* said to be "nothing" (*outhen*). He is an empty person, outwardly displaying knowledge and power, but a hollow person inwardly. And, he may engage in the giving of food or property (abstractly, out of guilt, under pressure, etc.) or even follow ascetic, self-centered courses of action (out of stubbornness, for fame or in unbiblical causes), leading ultimately to martyrdom (for such causes). But it is all (every bit of it) *profitless;* as far as Paul is concerned, it is mere waste. All these acts without love are worthless to the one doing them (though, in His providence, God may use them for His purposes). How much of what we have done must be junked when we evaluate it by such a standard!

Christians, therefore, must be concerned to act out of love—for God and for their neighbors. Love alone lifts such acts to a plane of eternal significance. Otherwise, they have but temporary and questionable value and meaning.

II. *Essential Factors in Love* (vv. 4-7).

I have already noted that the factors discussed in verses 4 to 7 do not constitute the whole of love. But they clearly are illustrative of it; i.e., they show us the sorts of things love does and doesn't do. They describe love *adequately* if not exhaustively. It is to this description, then, that the

37

counselor will turn again and again in counseling, to find direction from God. That is why he must be utterly familiar with it. Let us consider each element in the passage separately. One way to think (or speak to a counselee) concretely about these factors in love is to see how each portrays some quality that we see in the Lord Jesus Christ. What we have here is, of course, a clear portrait of Him. I mention this, though I shall not elaborate on it.

The first factor is this:

(1) *"Love is patient."*

The word translated *patient* here is *makrothumia*. It means "long-tempered" and is the exact opposite of our expression "short-fused." It has to do with the restraint of anger, wrath and temper. A person with *makrothumia* has learned how to put up with others. He has learned to restrain himself in all sorts of life-situations. Apply it to the list of items in verses 1 to 3: What good does it do to speak in foreign languages if one says what he says in bad temper? What kind of a martyr is a short-fused martyr, etc.? It is clear, therefore, how important love is in giving value to these acts.

Very many counselees need this quality of *makrothumia*. There is no sense discussing all of the circumstances in which *patience* is essential in human lives. It is, perhaps, *the* factor in stressful situations that makes it possible for one to take whatever other biblical courses that are required of him. For details on how to obtain it, see my discussion of this in *More than Redemption* (Phillipsburg, N.J.: Presbyterian and Reformed, 1979) under my treatment of the fruit of the Spirit.[5]

A mother (or Christian school teacher) who shows no evidence of such patience with her children, for instance, may claim that she loves them—and indeed, that because of this love she is upset with them—but, according to Paul, to the extent that she loses her temper in disciplining them, she does not love them. Lack of patience is evidence of lack of love; patience—the willingness to restrain one's self for the sake of another—is one of the factors in love. A lack of patience indicates defective love.

Love thinks of the other person first; lack of patience puts one's self first

---

5. *More than Redemption* (Phillipsburg, N.J.: Presbyterian and Reformed, 1979), pp. 225ff.

and says, "Look what you did [to me]." Throughout this section, love will be shown to be a giving of one's self (time, interests, etc.) to another while giving up one's own rights, privileges, concerns, etc.

Love, in none of the statements that follow, is set forth as something that one *possesses* in the abstract (in and of itself, for himself). Rather, it is *always* seen as an attitude of self-giving for the sake of another. Love is always related to God or neighbor; it never stands alone.

(2) *"Love is kind."*

Again, I have considered this word (*chrestotes*) more fully in *More than Redemption*.[6] Consequently, I shall not develop it here. Let me say this about kindness, however: The word describes a condition in the lover that is opposed to all that is cruel or severe. Certainly, that which is deliberately cruel is outlawed. But also those severities that flow from thoughtlessness toward others (usually because of selfish concerns and pursuits) are eliminated as well. The *kind* person has a sort of gentleness that is active, not merely passive; it encompasses a desire to be outgoing and shows a vital interest in others and in their affairs. A *kind* person is one who cares about others enough so seek their welfare actively in some concrete way. Many counselees typically manifest self-centered traits, many of which involve severity and border on cruelty. Any call to love—the *one* call that all Christian counselors issue to every counselee in one way or another—therefore, *must* consider this matter. It may never be bypassed. No one claiming to love another can be either calculatingly (or thoughtlessly) harsh or cruel toward him.[7]

(3) *"Love is not jealous."*

This phrase is the beginning of a list of eight negative factors that Paul contrasts with love; each implies its opposite. When one loves another, he has no feelings of jealousy. He isn't sorry but, rather, joyous to see the other

---

6. Ibid.
7. Firmness is not necessarily cruelty or thoughtless severity. A loving firmness moved Paul to write I Corinthians, in which he shows firmness again and again. But that firmness grew out of deep concern for God and the Corinthian church.

possessing whatever good he has (again, the focus is on the welfare of the other rather than of one's self). There is no desire to lessen (in any way) the virtues, achievements or happiness of another. A lover *prefers* to put another before himself. Few counselees who learn to adopt this attitude toward others will have any serious difficulties left to counsel about. They may need direction, etc., but once given that, they will move ahead quickly to the solution of most of their interpersonal problems.

A jealous person is zealous (the two words are related) to hold onto and maintain his own rights and possessions at all costs. That is a sign or clear indicator of the presence of this unloving factor that chokes out the tender sprouts of love that from time to time spring forth. Let every counselor look for it and point it out in the lives of counselees whenever he encounters it.

On the other hand, a loving person wants to share what he possesses or has attained and enjoys helping others to attain whatever skills, status, etc., he himself has. Such a positive attitude *itself* would go far toward splitting apart many of the logjams that occur in counseling sessions. Whenever these standstills are experienced in counseling, check on this negative factor. As in all eight items, the way out begins with confession and repentance.[8] Following the softening of the heart through these, a counselor may assign the counselee specific ways in which (in his particular situation) he may begin to practice the positive actions implied as the opposites of this negative factor. Prayerful practice in time will lead to the enjoyment of seeing others possess and enjoy even that which he himself has never been able to attain.

(4) *"Love doesn't boast."*

The word has to do with *bragging, parading one's self before others*. Love doesn't seek such approval from others. The Adlerian emphasis on one's personal "need" for *significance* in the eyes of others has been imported into Christian circles by Larry Crabb and others. But Paul was not in agreement with Adler. Indeed, his views loudly clash with Adler's emphasis. A Christian doesn't need to feel significant in the eyes of others; he doesn't need fame (no matter how narrow its impact), admiration or applause. Rather, he will give proper praise to others; to be capable of doing that is his real "need."

---

8. Cf. the index in *More than Redemption* for discussions of confession and repentance.

Love doesn't show off. It makes no odious comparisons; it doesn't down others in order to lift self. Rather, it keeps quiet about even genuine achievements, preferring others to praise (if they will), but not *needing* their praise at all. Even when well-deserved praise comes, glory and honor is deflected from one's self in an *honest,* non-hypocritical effort to praise God, who made success possible.[9] This factor leads easily to the next.

(5) *"Love isn't proud."*

In love there is a humility (not a false humility, which is really a kind of pride) that always acknowledges behind achievement, beauty, brains, etc., the providential work of God. The humble man may acknowledge his successes, but he doesn't grow conceited because he knows that all that is worthwhile in his life has come from God through Jesus Christ. Such persons, again, don't demand much (rights, acknowledgment, praise, significance). Instead, their stock in trade is thankfulness. The counselor who wants to help a counselee to overcome the problem of boastfulness will focus on teaching him to acknowledge God's hand in all things and to thank Him for them.

(6) *"Love doesn't act in an ugly way."*

Coming to verse 6 we encounter a word that is related to *shame*. The unloving person will do things, say things, assume attitudes of which he (or others) will later be ashamed. Love never acts in an ugly, shameful way—with violence, foul language or anything else disgraceful. Love is concerned, therefore, about *manner* as well as matter. Love never offends by indelicate or crude acts and words. Certainly the use of four-letter "shock" words that some counselors seem to stock and use in good supply is to be condemned (as well as in the way counselees must learn to deal with one another) as unloving. How counselors who indulge in such practices expect to help counselees become more loving by their poor example is beyond me. Love, in contrast, works hard at doing always what is fitting, appropriate and mannerly (many parts of our land have lost all sense of that which is

---

9. That is not to say that one may not accept such appreciation with thanks. But (at the very least, in his heart) one may not focus on himself primarily or to the exclusion of God.

appropriate and mannerly), so long as these ways do not conflict with God's standards. Love tries always to do that which the Bible calls *fine*.[10]

(7) *"Love isn't self-seeking"* (cf. 10:24, 33).

Whatever love does, it accomplishes in a disinterested way. That is to say, it seeks the other person's welfare and does not calculate what benefits (or lack of benefits) may accrue to one's self in return. There is no boomerang thinking. Counselors continually must make it clear that counselees may not do what they do for others as a gimmick to gain certain personal ends. Perhaps no other sinful tendency intrudes itself more frequently into faulty Christian living. One sees it all the time in counseling sessions. Counselees, in one way or another, will say, "If I do this, what's in it for me?" Again and again they must be challenged to do what God says in order to please Him, whether any benefits return to them or not. One may not choose to do God's will in a *calculated* way.[11]

(8) *"Love is not easily irritated."*

The word here refers to *rousing to anger;* the basic idea behind it is "to sharpen." Sharp, pointed, spiked responses growing out of irritability do not readily flow from one who considers another's words and actions thoughtfully (i.e., lovingly). It is those who do not take the time to think through the situation and the words that they use in responding to it who sin in this respect. Again, they think about themselves. As we have seen throughout, so we see here again, the law of love means giving up our plans, our schedules, our ways, etc., in the interest of others'.

And it may extend to so seemingly a mundane matter as being sure to get enough sleep. Inadequate sleep leads to the temptation to respond in an irritable manner. Some persons who are constantly irritable, when put on a regular, eight-hour schedule find that the problem soon disappears. Sometimes, for the benefit of others, counselees must be willing to discipline themselves in their sleeping habits. But clearly, since sleep loss so fre-

---

10. Cf. my discussion of this term in *How to Overcome Evil* (Phillipsburg, N.J.: Presbyterian and Reformed, 1977), pp. 70ff.

11. Cf. my *What Do You Do When . . . ?* pamphlets in each of which this crucial point is made about the issue at hand.

quently leads to irritability, anyone working on the problem of irritability (or any other, for that matter), no matter what the occasion, should get regular sleep (and plenty of it) to create an atmosphere that is conducive to achieving good results. A sleep-starved person is exposing himself needlessly to temptation.

(9) *"Love doesn't keep records of wrongs."*

How often counselees do precisely what this law of love forbids: they count up, recall and throw up to another all the offenses that he has committed. Sometimes they actually keep writtens records!

Reading the phrase to a counselee from the *New Testament in Everyday English* (or *The Christian Counselor's New Testament*), with its literal translation, is one way to make the point. The fault is as clear an indication of the lack of love as any other. Forgiveness (in which one promises to remember the other's offenses against him no more, and then keeps his promise[12]) is the answer to this failure.

(10) *"Love isn't happy about injustice but happily stands on the side of truth."*

Love doesn't sit idly by when God's Word is attacked. It isn't mute about unfair actions against others. How often counselees need to take a stand for God, for righteousness, for truth (and for the ways of truth)! Often coward-ice — paralyzing concern over what others will do or say — is a clear sign of lack of love. Again, self-concern, rather than concern for one's neighbor, rears its unloving head. The solution to the problem is to get counselees to begin to take a stand for all that is right and against all that is wrong, wherever the lines may be drawn—regardless of the consequences to one's self. If there is no immediate issue to resolve, that beginning should take place at the counselee's next point of choice.

(11) *"Love covers all things."*

Here, in verse 7, we turn at last to four essential *positive* factors. The counselor will find himself pointing to them rather frequently. All four are

---

12. See my detailed and definitive discussion of forgiveness in *More than Redemption*, chapter 13.

rather broad in application (to each is appended the words "all things," or, possibly, "all sorts of things").

Rather than make a point of every offense against himself, as the unloving person does, the lover bears wrongdoing patiently. Indeed, out of love he even *covers* what has been done. He covers a *multitude* of sins. Now, this is not like the Watergate coverup, in which what ought to have been exposed was not (but instead, was covered with lies). Instead, it is the one who was wronged who covered the wrong with *love* (not with *lies*). It was not ignored, distorted, etc., but acknowledged—then covered in love (cf. I Pet. 4:8[13]). Not every wrong must be made an issue. Love doesn't allow these little rubs to come between believers. Instead, it covers these from his own eyes as well as from the eyes of all others.

(12) *"Love believes all things."*

True love, perhaps, is seen most clearly in the trust that it manifests in another. When others would doubt, the one who loves firmly believes. Only hard evidence[14] (never suspicion, general distrust or prejudice) would make him doubt another's word.

Surely this makes the lover vulnerable to others. When one lays his heart on the table, he invites others to run over it with track shoes. But love thinks first not of itself, but of others. That is why the lover is willing to run such risks. He would rather be injured himself than to injure another. The *disposition* of love always is to believe another if it is at all possible to do so. This quality is needed in counseling.

(13) *"Love hopes all things."*

Love always gives the other fellow the benefit of the doubt; it hopes for the best in another. It doesn't go around looking for what is wrong. This biblically realistic optimism doesn't grow out of faith in men, but in the God who can change them. So that, contrary to what so many counselees say ("He'll never do it; he never has before"), love says, "Perhaps this time

---

13. For more on this point, see my commentary on I Peter, *Trust and Obey* (Phillipsburg, N.J.: Presbyterian and Reformed, 1978).

14. Often this involves 2 or 3 witnesses. But even in the face of evidence, the lover always hears what the person has to say by way of explanation before condemning him (Prov. 18:17).

God will make him different." These two opposite attitudes tend to generate (or at least encourage) what they anticipate. And God (blessing His Word when it is obediently followed) may use the hopeful attitude in one person to stimulate change in another. Conversely, a spirit of hopelessness or resignation, when sensed by another, often provides further occasion for him to despair of change—even when he has been contemplating it.

(14) *"Love endures all things."*

Notice, again, in all four positive elements the words "all things" appear. There are no situations so bad that they allow an exception to what is said. All sorts of things can be covered, believed and hoped for in others when there is love. Similarly, we find in this phrase that every sort of offense, pressure, affliction and persecution can be endured in love. Because counselees so often deny the fact, claiming that their situation is unique—worse than anyone else's—the point in this verse must be stressed. All that is contained in I Corinthians 10:13 (see my exposition of that verse in my pamphlet, *Christ and Your Problems* [Phillipsburg, N.J.: Presbyterian and Reformed, 1971]) must be emphasized when helping a counselee. Basically there are three facts stressed in I Corinthians 10:13:

1. There are (at bottom) no unique problems;
2. But every problem is uniquely suited to the believer by God so that he can endure it (if he handles the problem God's way);
3. Every problem has a solution and will come to an end. Looking for the end helps one to endure it.

Counselees need both the hope and the responsibility that are spelled out by these two verses.

We have come to the close of section 2—the major emphasis of this discussion. One thing stands out (especially in contrast to vv. 1-3). The essentials of love outlined in verses 4 to 7 all boil down to this: love means putting others first. Every positive quality examined can only be destroyed by self-seeking; each can be enhanced by giving one's self more and more to others.

The route to love, therefore, is essentially the route to discipleship: to deny (crucify or put to death) the desires of self for Christ's sake, and then to follow Him by losing one's life for His sake and the gospel's (i.e., for God and others who will believe)—and (as a consequence; *not* as an end), thereby *finding* it. To love God and to love one's neighbor, indeed, does summarize the whole teaching of the Bible.

III. *Everlasting Aspects of Love* (vv. 8-13)

Prophecies, languages and knowledge (i.e., extraordinary revelatory prophecy—not mere preaching; extraordinary language capabilities—not normal human speech; and extraordinary discernment of God's ways and will—not the ordinary knowledge that comes from studying the Scriptures) will all come to an end.[15] But love will never fail (lit., "fall"—as a house falls into ruins).

Conclusion

Now, what can we learn about counseling from all of this? Much, much more than I can begin to describe. Let me therefore indicate just some general principles that (suggestively) may lead to other uses as well:

1. Clearly, Paul had more than the local *situation* in mind. He determined to meet their need for love in one area by teaching them (and us) all about love in general.[16]

2. Since counseling has to do with the relationship of counselees to God and to other persons, I Corinthians 13 is altogether pertinent to counselee problems. Of great significance in this regard is the fact that Jesus, when referring to the basic requirement in this twofold relationship, says that it is *love*.

---

15. Note: in v. 9, "languages" is omitted. When the completion of the N.T. takes place, special revelation and direction by prophecy and gifts of knowledge will be terminated. Languages, given to preach to unbelievers, will simply run out as the last missionary dies. In contrast, faith, hope and love will continue after these special gifts have disappeared.

The words used to describe how the other gifts "fall" are of significance: prophecies and knowledge will be "set aside" (*katargeo*="to cancel, destroy, do away with"), whereas languages (specially given) will "cease" (*pauo*="stop, come to an end"). The first two will be brought to an end, whereas tongues will cease.

16. Cf. Paul's general view of Scripture and its application that had it in mind when he wrote I Cor. (cf. 10:6, 11; 9:10). This expression precludes the idea of a *merely* local reference.

3. All that is said about love—in contrast to love*less* acts and states described in verses 1 to 3—has to do with others. The loveless life is the one that is focused and centered on one's self rather than on others. Even when one outwardly does something for another—to the extreme of giving his life—in a loveless way (to acquire fame and glory for himself, etc.), he is still self-centered.

Love moves out toward others, embracing them in attitude as well as act. Heart and hands, heart and lip agree.[17] Lovelessness moves inwardly toward one's self, ever seeking new ways to enhance and aggrandize the self—usually at the expense of others.

Thus, the same act—giving one's body to be burned, for instance—can be done in a loveless way (v. 3) or in a loving way (by standing for truth to help another; v. 6). That is one of the great lessons of the passage. That is the point that the Corinthians needed to learn as they used their gifts. Those gifts could be used lovingly or lovelessly. And that made all the difference.

4. Paul's description of love is a most useful source to which Christian counselors may turn—

a. to find descriptions of unloving attitudes and acts. The negative factors (4b-6a) are particularly helpful for this purpose. Often counselors must identify sinful behavior for their counselees for what it is (e.g., "That is an unmistakable instance of lovelessness that Paul here calls 'keeping records of wrongs,' John").

b. to find descriptions of loving acts and attitudes. Sometimes one counselee refuses to acknowlege that another is making progress. Here is one way to deal with that problem: "Mary, notice how he lovingly covered those rubs and didn't bring them up to you?"

c. to discover concrete counseling goals for which to shoot. Apart from such descriptions of love, it might seem to be an amorphous quality that is singularly elusive.

d. to give impetus to love by using these words to motivate counselees to please God.

---

17. Heart=the inner life we live before God and ourselves.

Much, much more could be said. Actual cases could be given in which each of these elements that we have discussed could be shown to bear on some counseling problem in one of the four ways just mentioned. But rather than do this for you, I suggest that you do the following as a practical exercise that will help prepare you for more effective counseling by learning how to use I Corinthians 13 in actual cases.

1. Purchase a copy of *The Christian Counselor's Casebook* (this volume contains 140 slices of actual cases).

2. Go through each case, using I Corinthians 13 for the four purposes just listed (a-d) wherever possible,[18] in one way or another bringing the principles and practices of the chapter to bear upon it.

3. Work out answers to the questions opposite each case selected, identifying the problems and solutions in terms of the biblical language and terminology that Paul uses in I Corinthians 13.

4. Wherever possible, develop concrete homework assignments (specifically adapted to each case) that grow out of and are appropriate to the principles of love described in I Corinthians 13.

Such an effort might be continued regularly, on a daily basis,[19] over a period of time until the principles of the chapter and their practical applications have been etched into your counseling practice. Few other efforts could be more rewarding.

---

18. Verses from I Cor. 13 will apply in almost every case since love (toward God and one's neighbor) is the sum of our whole duty before God.

19. Perhaps at the beginning of each daily study period.

7

Checks and Promptings

There is abroad today, in several forms, a teaching that has the potential to do much harm. It is motivated by a worthy desire to counter the intellectualizing of God's truth in ways that make that truth of little effect for Christian living. While no one can deny the desirability of achieving that goal, I find myself strongly opposing the proposals that this teaching offers as decidedly unscriptural and bound to cause much confusion among Christians.

The bare bones skeleton of the view amounts to this:

1. It is time that Christians stopped depending exclusively on truths handled by the intellect (and which stop there and go no further in influencing one's life style).

2. There is another way of obtaining direction from God—*through one's spirit*. This "spiritual truth," usually given in the form of "checks in one's spirit" (that forbid him to do something), or "promptings in his spirit" (impelling him to pursue various courses of action), is said to come *directly* from God as the Spirit contacts the believer's spirit.

3. One significant corollary of this teaching is that the Bible is not the sole source of divine revelation regarding life and godliness; another is that the Bible is not sufficient for guidance and decision making. Neither of these points is stated quite so flatly as I have expressed them; they are either denied (inconsistently) or reluctantly admitted only when one is driven against the wall by appropriate questioning.

Now, any number of observations may be made about those propositions. Let me make just one: There is no way in which one could ever discern either a "prompting" or a "check" in his spirit.

The spirit of a human being, on this view, is distinguished from his soul and from his body. The soul is said to be the receptor for rational propositional truth, which is perceived intellectually by it; the body is said to handle sense data from the material world. These sense data are discerned in some tangible form (felt, seen, smelled, heard, tasted). But "spiritual" promptings and checks are said to come some other way.

The question is, are such spiritual influences discerned? This is a serious question since neither the senses nor the mind is the perceiving agency. Spirit is invisible, intangible. If promptings and checks take neither a propositional nor a tangible form, what form do they take? How are they perceived? So far as I can see, there is no answer to this question; and none is given. What we can't know intellectually or organically we can't really know.[1]

But, of greater concern than the inherent anomalies is the warped view of guidance that it fosters. By it one is directed away from the sure Word of God (II Pet. 1:19). Instead, he is offered unidentifiable "checks" and "promptings" that are impossible to distinguish from feelings and notions generated by the person from within himself. That trade-off is no bargain.

But some persons, under the false notion that God must guide us when making decisions in a specific, detailed *ad hoc* manner rather than by specific and general principles of the Scriptures, actually do welcome the checks-and-promptings method as an advance over the historic Christian position. To them, there is probably little that I can say or do to dislodge them from such views; they are absolutely bent upon having God do all their detailed thinking for them—one wonders why He gave them either a brain or a Bible! It is amazing to think that the Holy Spirit spent thousands of years producing the Bible, then indwelt Christians for the purpose (among other things) of illuminating their understanding of the Scriptures, only to bypass the Bible and ignore the understanding by giving us unintelligible and intangible checks and promptings![2] They will persist in their ways until they

---

1. It is in this dilemma that the poverty of the triplex view of man which is basic to this teaching becomes so apparent. For a biblical consideration of the matter, see my *More than Redemption* (Phillipsburg, N.J.: Presbyterian and Reformed, 1979), pp. 108ff. In my opinion, one actually ends up interpreting his *feelings* as checks and promptings. But feelings are physiological phenomena.

2. The notion is impossible to conceive: checks and promptings would *have* to be intelligible to be *received and acted upon*.

50

begin to see that the checks and promptings with which they have been so enamored have led them up too many blind alleys or into circumstances that clearly show that the source of these negative and positive influences is not the Holy Spirit.

But to others, who are open to reading more deeply into the historic Christian position, let me refer you to the section of my book, *More than Redemption,* entitled "Personal Guidance" (pp. 22-34). In it, I have shown that a judicious and prayerful use of biblical principles, precepts and examples will yield everything that is needed to decide every question pertaining to life and godliness (II Pet. 1:3).

And, in addition, I wish to make a few observations about the biblical use of the word *spirit* that plainly prove one's spirit is not a separate, non-intellectual side of his human nature.

For starters, notice Acts 19:21, where we are told that "Paul decided in his spirit. . . ." The verb is *tithemi.* It is used with *kardia* ("heart") in Luke 21:14 as well as *pneuma* ("spirit") to mean that one has decided to do this *within himself.* The two expressions mean that something is thought through and determined in one's mind. And notice, especially—this is the point of significance to us—what happens *in the spirit* is decidedly *intellectual:* a determination, a decision, is made. Surely the spirit is conceived of as operating rationally, intellectually.

In Ephesians 4:23, Paul writes of being "renewed in the spirit of your mind." If the word "spirit" here refers to the human spirit, the verse somehow combines this spirit with the mind (*nous*): the spirit is said either (1) to be within, or a part of the mind, or (2) to be composed of mind. However, it is also possible to take the word *spirit* to refer to the Holy Spirit and to interpret the passage as meaning "renewed by the Spirit who works on (or in) your mind." Taking the passage this way, we see that the Spirit works not in some non-intellectual area called the spirit, but in the mind— i.e., He renews us intellectually so that we begin to think God's thoughts after Him (cf. Col. 3:10; Isa. 55:7-9). Probably "spirit" here means attitude: "rejuvenated in your mental attitude," and has nothing to do with the question.

It is not surprising, then, that one is given a "spirit of wisdom of revelation and of full knowledge" (Eph. 1:17) in answer to prayer. Since the

51

spirit is being renewed in knowledge and holiness, it will grow in its ability to make wise choices based upon its accumulation of knowledge. But, once more, don't fail to note the intellectual commodities in which the human spirit traffics.

In its quest for answers, the spirit searches (Ps. 77:6). This search, incidentally, is described in Hebrew synonymous poetic parallelism (i.e., where adjoining lines say the same thing in different words) as identical to *speaking in one's own heart*. It clearly portrays inner intellectual dialog within one's self (cf. Job 20:2, and, especially, Job 32:8; note too Job 32:18). This inner source of thought and decision can be sinful so that the spirit must be cleansed from defilement (II Cor. 7:1), and false prophets may prophesy "out of their own heart" and "after their own spirit" (Ezek. 13:2, 3). Incidentally, here again, as in many places in the Bible, heart and spirit are used synonymously to refer to the inner life. And when Paul says that the Spirit "testifies" (an intellectual term) with (*sun*="together with"; not "to" our spirit) "our spirit that we are God's children," don't fail to note that there is specific, rational, propositional content to that testimony. And, even when some in Corinth attempted to become involved in some sort of ecstatic enthusiasm by which they sought to divorce spiritual influences from the intellect, they were forbidden to do so (cf. I Cor. 14:15, 16). And we are expressly informed that one's spirit is under our intelligent control (I Cor. 14:32).

So, it seems perfectly clear that the check-and-prompting view fails to take into account the biblical evidence. Indeed, it has no biblical warrant at all. The teaching is based on experience (wrongly interpreted) and not on exegesis.

But of what importance is all this to biblical counselors? It has a number of implications for counseling. Here are three:

1. Counselors must be careful about how they speak to counselees; they dare not use language that might be misinterpreted to approve of the checks and promptings view.

2. Counselors must be clear in their own minds about the proper biblical view of guidance.

3. Counselors must begin to look for the effects of this erroneous doctrine in

the lives of counselees. It can lie beneath confusion, behind discouragement or at the base of doubt. Since the view is spreading rapidly, the incidences of counselee difficulty stemming from it doubtlless will be on the increase in the near future. It is important to look ahead and to anticipate problems so that we may be alert to them and prepared to meet them as often as we can.

8

Does the Behaviorist Have a Mind?

In the Volume XXV, Number 1 (January, 1927) issue of *The Princeton Theological Review*, there appeared an article by Prof. Wm. Hallock Johnson entitled "Does the Behaviorist Have a Mind?"

This article, buried among musty periodicals on library shelves, has long since been forgotten. In those early days of behaviorism, though Johnson saw its dangers, few others believed that such a view as Watson's had a chance. We who live some 50 years later see that it has in many ways achieved its purpose.

Of course, the work of B. F. Skinner (who inherited Watson's mantle) was not on the scene as a threat at the time when Johnson wrote. But Johnson took on John B. Watson, the leading exponent in his day. It is interesting to note that if you strip Skinner of his more precise instrumentation, you find Watson beneath the modern clothing. Peeled down to the basics, Johnson, therefore, meets not only Watson but Skinner as well.

The old article is worth exhuming and preserving. In contrast to much evangelical capitulation to behaviorism, it still constitutes an "update on Christian counseling." We have reprinted it in full.

DOES THE BEHAVIORIST HAVE A MIND?

There is a good deal to be said on both sides of this question. The behaviorist himself assures us that he, or at least the subject of his investigations (for he disclaims introspection), has no mind, no instincts, no will or purpose, in fact no consciousness at all as distinct from bodily reaction to physical stimuli. Stimulus and response tell the whole story, and the response is always of the type of congenital or conditioned reflex action. If the behaviorist should be conscious of his reflex actions, he would be acting out of character and would be false to his professed principles. His own answer to the question of our title is in the negative. He does not claim to have a mind, he will not admit that he has a mind as distinguished from the body, and if the stimulus of the question, "Do you have a mind?" should be presented to him, the response to be expected would be an indignant and emphatic, "No."

There is, however, another side to the question. The behaviorist in spite of his protestations certainly acts as if he had a mind. His pursuits are wholly in the intellectual realm. His main business is nothing else than writing books and articles for learned magazines, conducting experiments which demand some mental equipment to estimate their bearing and value, teaching the young idea that there are no such things as ideas, and instructing classes of other minds that there are no minds at all. The behaviorist uses all the weapons in the arsenal of debate, ridicule, assumption of superior intelligence and learning, and calling of names such as "medievalist" and "mystic." His aim, it is true (although he admits no such thing as purpose), is to convert people to his way of thinking and to affect the thinking processes of the scholastic world in such a way as to bring them all to the opinion that there is no mind; but his manner of doing this is that of the "high brow" and the intellectual. He is incurably intellectual even when he vilifies the faculty of reason which is the candle of the Lord within us.

Both sides in the discussion should be aware of the fact that the case is so foolish and so absurd on the face of it that it is in danger of being thrown out of court. The behaviorist who maintains that he has no mind cannot help refuting himself every time he utters a word, or frames an argument, or puts pen to paper. The defender of the affirmative on the other hand—who maintains that the behaviorist has a mind—is placed in the uncomfortable position of one who can simply vociferate the obvious. He cannot use effectively the method of *reductio ad absurdum* because nothing in his view can be more absurd than the position with which the behaviorist begins. He can apparently do little more than ring the changes upon the characterizations, "glaringly inconsistent" and "palpably absurd."

A university president in the Midwest recently said that in taking up administrative duties he was compelled to commit intellectual suicide, and another president in the East admitted that he had become a "talking machine." If the personalities of these two presidents should be merged into one—if the intellectual suicide should be turned into a talking machine—it is to be feared that the resulting utterances would not be very significant. The behaviorist is a kind of dual personality. On the one hand he claims (or admits) that he has no mind or will or purpose, but on the other hand he says that "the interest of the behaviorist in man's doings is more than the interest of the spectator—he wants to control man's reactions as physical scientists want to control and manipulate other natural phenomena."[1] As a behaviorist he has no mind of his own and no purpose of his own and as a strict determinist he cannot control his own conduct, but in his efforts to reduce psychology to a natural science he wishes to control and predict the conduct of everybody else. There must be a contradiction here somewhere. The behaviorist cannot play both roles at once. But if there is an inescapable contradiction or mental twist in the behaviorist's mind in his fundamental assumption that " 'consciousness' is neither a definable nor a usable concept,"[2] we fear that there may be a moral twist in the kind of conduct he wishes to produce and control. If the behaviorist should be allowed full sway in regulating conduct, we fear that the result would be thoughtless activity, and meaningless behavior, and conscienceless conduct.

Psychology is no longer merely an academic discipline fitted to provide pleasant mental exercise for the classroom. It has entered our homes and our business as well as out schools, and has invaded the realms of ethics, jurisprudence and religion. The salesman in approaching his prospect or seeking to become a super-salesman, the corporation executive in selecting his personnel and in promoting efficiency, the advertiser in attracting the public, the struggling clerk aspiring to the presidency of his concern, the statesman who would prevent war and the reformer who would repress crime, the young man in search of a wife and the mother anxious for the upbringing of her children—all are invited to sit at the feet of the psychologist. The educator with his methods and projects and programs of study is

---

1. John B. Watson, *Behaviorism*, p. 11.
2. P. 3.

peculiarly at the mercy of the psychologist, and the church is beginning to realize that her whole program of religious education may, for good or evil, be profoundly modified under the influence of popular psychological theory. As a thoughtful student of the subject has said: "In the new educational enterprises of the church a matter of utmost concern is the selection of a psychological basis on which the new program is to stand. A choice between the schools has to do with something more important than methods and materials. It has to do with the maintenance or the abandonment of certain elements of the Christian religion which have heretofore been considered essential."[3]

When the behaviorist seeks by logical argument to abolish logic, and from his platform of mechanistic determinism announces his ambition to control the thought and conduct of the world, we are tempted to attribute his inconsistencies to mental obtuseness or perversity, and following the advice of the wise man to "answer a fool according to his folly." This, however, is not to deny that the behaviorist in his experiments has made contributions of value to psychological science, or that in spite of his disclaimer of introspection he has sometimes shown a shrewd and penetrating insight into human nature.

It will prove instructive to glance at the newest book in the field of psychology, *Psychologies of 1925*, containing lectures given at Clark University in 1925 and in the early months of 1926 by leading psychologists. Their names in alphabetical order are Madison Bentley, Knight Dunlap, Walter S. Hunter, Kurt Koffka, Wolfgang Köhler, Morton Prince, William McDougall, John B. Watson, and Robert S. Woodworth. McDougall of Harvard tells us that the mechanists in psychology would have us believe that men are "robots," this name being applied in a recent play to ingeniously constructed machines in the shape of human beings. McDougall adds that "the view that men are merely such robots is now being dogmatically taught to thousands of young students in the psychological departments of the universities of this country."[4] He finds that this view is now enjoying an alarming popularity, and that the spread of this way of thinking among

---

3. W. A. Squires, *Psychological Foundations of Religious Education*, pp. 30, 31.
4. P. 275.

psychologists has gone so far that those who do not accept it are regarded as "cranky persons wedded to medieval metaphysics" and as "queer survivors from the dark ages," incapable of joining in the triumphant march of modern science. The behaviorists may be robots in whom reflex action takes the place formerly assigned to reflection, but they are sure that their reflexes are right and that the reflexes of others, the upholders of rival theories, are wrong. They differ also from the real robots in the fact that, as we have seen, they have far-reaching and revolutionary plans for the application of their doctrine not only in the sphere of psychology but in the fields of education, philosophy, ethics and jurisprudence. Look first at the application in the realm of philosophy. Holding that all the objects in our environment are ultimately electric charges, W. S. Hunter adds that "so likewise is the human animal and the aggregations of human animals which make up society. If the phenomenon of a storage battery is a matter of electrons and protons, so is the phenomenon of family life."[5] Hunter is naturally indignant with the older psychological method "which is inseparably bound up with the ancient philosophical concepts of mind and consciousness as aspects of the universe which differ from the physical."[6]

John B. Watson, the recognized leader of the behaviorist group, finds a "mystical" element even in Hunter's exposition. He is uncompromising in his purpose to rule mind and consciousness out of the picture, and in the interest of behaviorism would revise ethics and jurisprudence, and would apparently do away with the church and religion altogether. It would be interesting to see what kind of a code of ethics the new "experimental ethics" of behaviorism (which Watson admits does not yet exist) would formulate. It would be still more interesting to discover the kind of behavior in the moral sphere in which the principles of behaviorism when freely carried out actually eventuate. Watson would like to make some profound changes in the field of jurisprudence. He would do away with punishment in the rearing of children and the treatment of criminals. He tells us that "punishment is a word which never ought to have crept into our language"[7]

---

5. P. 90.
6. P. 107.
7. P. 71.

—which raises the question whether the man who first introduced it ought not to have been punished. Watson is at pains to emphasize the fact that "the behaviorist is a strict determinist."[8] It follows then, as he declares in italics, that "the child or adult has to do what he does. The only way he can be made to act differently is first to untrain him and then retrain him." Naturally the untraining and retraining must be done by the behaviorist; the other people or psychologists of other schools have no power to retrain the behaviorist. There are of course no criminals in the usual sense of persons who have committed acts that deserve punishment. There are only "deviants," and these are of two kinds, the insane and the "socially untrained." The insane should be sent to the asylum and the socially untrained should be sent to school. We may remark here that even Watson has not been able wholly to emancipate himself from the ideas of free-will, responsibility and desert, so deeply imbedded in our thought and our vocabulary. He will allow a gentle rap on the knuckles of the child if promptly adminstered; and if the socially untrained deviants through obtuseness or obstinacy refuse to take on the training that will fit them to re-enter society, he would even for "ten to fifteen years or even longer" make them "earn their daily bread, in vast manufacturing and agricultural institutions, escape from which is impossible."[9] "Strenuous work sixteen hours per day," Watson naively adds, "will hurt no one." Of course, it is insisted that the care of such deviants should be in the hands of behaviorists. Such a reform in criminal jurisprudence, Watson admits, is only a pious dream "until all the lawyers and jurists decide to become behaviorists." Now since every lawyer and jurist together with every other adult "has to do what he does," what probability is there that any lawyer or judge will "decide" to change his mind and act differently? The only way to reform the lawyers and jurists is to put them where they deserve to be, in a "school" (not a prison of course for this would savor too much of the "religious theory" of retaliation) where they could be restrained and made to work for sixteen hours a day, until under the gentle tutelage of behaviorist wardens they come to see the error of their ways and give evidence of true repentance for doing what they couldn't help doing. Like other mechanical determinists who would do away with the guilt

8. P. 71.
9. Pp. 71-74.

59

or fault or responsibility of the offender against society, Watson can only transfer these notions of guilt and responsibility from the criminal to his social environment. It is our own "fault," he says, that is, the fault of parents, teachers and others of the group, if individuals "go wrong" or deviate from set standards of behavior.

If the insane should be placed in asylums and the socially untrained in schools, how can we tell which is which? If it be found that an alleged criminal does not know what he is doing, how does he differ from anyone else? If he does know what he is doing, then there is something—knowledge or awareness or consciousness—that is of a non-material character and is distinct from, and over and above, his bodily action. Again, how can the behaviorist distinguish between the socially trained and the socially untrained? Let us suppose that a gun is discharged and a person is killed. How is the behaviorist, who denies that purpose influences behavior, to distinguish between accidental homicide and deliberate murder? The whole question, as Prince points out, is whether there is "criminal intent," and the question is unanswerable on behaviorist principles. Carl Murchison, the editor of the volume, makes a point as old as the reply of Zeno to his thieving slave when he insists elsewhere that a philosophy of rigid determinism "is sheer nonsense when applied only to the individual offender and not also to the community which contains him. If it has been determined by circumstances that an individual commits a crime, let it also be determined by circumstances that a social community will strike back with sure and swift punishment."

Before going further it may be worthwhile to glance at the historical antecedents of behaviorism and at the criticism which it directs against other psychological schools, and then we may look a little more in detail at the objections which may be made against behaviorism itself.

In taking up the book of Clark University lectures we are bewildered by the present variety of conflicting theories in the psychological field. We find here represented Schools of Behaviorism, Dynamic Psychology, Gestalt, Purposive Groups, Reaction Psychology, and Psychologies called Structural. One lecturer, Knight Dunlap, says: "The announcement of a new book on *The new psychology and the preacher* might, so far as anyone could predict in advance, be a treatise based on the Freudian or some other

60

psychoanalytic system; it might be an exposition of 'new thought' or some other vagary of the Quimby brood; it might be an application of the theories and methods of 'intelligence testing'; it might be propaganda for the theories and practices of M. Coué; it might be one of the numerous embodiments of phrenology under its more recent name of 'character analysis'; it might be a book on psychic research concerning spooks and other magical notions; or it might be one of the less easily nameable nostrums which strut before the public in borrowed plumage, calling themselves 'the new psychology.' "[10] Dunlap himself, in contrast to the host of pseudopsychologists and to the older "Malebranchian psychology," is an exponent of "scientific psychology" which does away with the superstition that "mind" is "distinct from, but miraculously related to the body."[11]

In tracing the pedigree of behaviorism we find that in the past generation at least four different schools of psychology, each of them associated with some movement in science or philosophy, have successively held the field. There was first the psychology of the soul, and this soul had "faculties" such as memory, imagination, will and so forth. It was then objected that the assumption of a soul was unnecessary for purposes of science and that the separate faculties were abstractions, and it was maintained that the proper study of the psychologist was consciousness, or conscious states or processes in more or less close association with brain concomitants. The soul according to James had "worn out both itself and its welcome," and according to Wundt it was "a metaphysical surplusage for which psychology has no use." Later there arose the functional psychology, studying the mind or consciousness as a servant of the organism and as a means of adjustment of the organism to its environment. Finally the behaviorist, denying the utility of introspection, banished consciousness entirely from the psychological field or reduced it to a name for the relation between the nervous system and its stimulating environment. We may remind ourselves that the psychology of consciousness and its processes (or of ideas and their associations) was stimulated by the growing knowledge of brain physiology, and its philosophical background was the traditional English empiricism coming down from Locke and Hume. The functional psychology was an

10. P. 309.
11. P. 312.

61

application of popular biological categories to the study of mind, and it was associated with the pragmatic movement in philosophy. Behaviorism was an outgrowth of the study of animal behavior, and its philosophical affinities are with eighteenth century materialism and with the New Realism which in its revolt from subjective idealism would define consciousness as a name for the relation between the object and the nervous system.

Behaviorism is a sort of "psychological materialism," to borrow a phrase from Dr. Patton's recent volume. It first dismisses the consciousness of animals and then of human beings as inaccessible to knowledge, and holds that when we attempt to peer into the secrets of our own "minds" all we discover is a feeling of flexed muscles, of visceral movements, and of laryngeal movements associated with spoken language or "silent" language. Consciousness as something distinct from bodily movement does not exist. It is either a myth or is only another name for the relation between the bodily organism and the physical stimulus. Plainly behaviorism is directly opposed to the fundamental convictions of religion, that there is a spirit in man and that the inspiration of the Almighty giveth them understanding, and that there will be a conscious existence of the individual after the death of the body.

A characteristic of behaviorism is the boldness of its negations and the thoroughness with which it disposes of the spiritual or non-material element in man. The soul with its faculties, the mind with its categories, the will with its purposes and freedom, consciousness with its processes and concomitant brain process, ideas with their associations, and even the instincts with their evolution are all thrown upon the scrap-heap. Behaviorism has not only cleaned house but has moved out of its house. One behaviorist, Hunter, would give over the term psychology to the exponents of antiquated methods, while coining the term "anthroponomy" to describe behaviorism or the "science of human behavior."[12] We recall the witty criticism directed against Hume, that he went outside his house and looked in at the window and could find no one at home. The behaviorist has not only gone outside his house, but has closed the shutters and moved away.

The defender of spiritual realities and values will find something instruc-

12. P. 83.

tive in the behaviorist's critique of his predecessors and rivals in the psychological field. The same methods by which the psychology of ideas or of consciousness disposed of the soul as a spiritual entity are adopted by the behaviorist in disposing of ideas and consciousness altogether. If the soul was inaccessible to knowledge, so also is the mind or consciousness as a separate entity. If the old-fashioned faculties and functions were abstractions or myths, so also are the more modern ideas and their associations. The weapons used by the psychology-without-a-soul are now turned against itself by the psychology-without-a-mind. Watson insists that consciousness is "merely another word for the 'soul' of more ancient times," and that the metaphysical implications of the two terms are identical.[13] Behaviorism is in fact psychology without a soul reduced to absurdity.

It is interesting and somewhat comforting to notice further that some popular and ultra-modern theories which have been regarded as hostile to a religious view of things are by behaviorism buried as deep as the old soul-psychology. Empiricism with its exploiting of impersonal ideas, physiological psychology with its concomitance of conscious process and brain process, epiphenomenism which treated mind as a fly-wheel of matter, psychophysical parallelism which chained mind to matter without allowing it any influence upon the movements of matter, Freudian psychoanalysis which substituted the unconscious wish for the "will that can," and even evolutionary ideas of mind which assimilated the mind of man to that of the brute, are all junked without ceremony to make way for the up to date machinery of behaviorism.

The behavioristic materialist takes a short method with the spiritualist. He rightly fears that consciousness even if cast in the modest role of epiphenomenon may by some ingenious turn assume the leading role. The only safe way is to exclude it from the cast altogether. Consciousness may start the voyage as a stowaway in the cargo of mechanism, but there is always danger that it may mutiny and take command of the ship. Consciousness may be tied securely to brain process, but Bergson may be right when he says that conscious activity overflows brain activity on all sides. Consciousness may be merely an instrument of adaptation in the struggle for existence, but in the end the servant may become the master and the development of mind

---

13. *Behaviorism*, pp. 3, 5.

and freedom may be seen as the end of the whole process. The only safe way for the mechanical behaviorist is to exclude altogether this uncomfortable and dangerous intruder, consciousness. "Nowhere is it necessary to introduce the concept of consciousness, or experience, conceived as another mode of existence, or as another aspect of the physical world."[14] Of course the intelligence tests will have to go, for there is no such thing as intelligence; and it is to be hoped that the reactions to the College Entrance Board examinations now demanded of young students will be greatly simplified.

The behaviorist has to do his fighting on two fronts. On one front are the introspectionists, the purposivists, and the metaphysical and theological opponents of materialism; but on the other front he finds arrayed against him the popular evolutionary and psycho-analytical schools. Watson is contemptuous of all that has been written about the evolution of instinct and the classification of instincts. Instinct is defined as "a combination of congenital responses unfolding serially under appropriate stimulation." What we call instincts are for the most part "learned" or "conditioned" reflexes. Going as he admits beyond the evidence, Watson holds that there is no inheritance of mental traits or aptitudes, and he makes training and environment all-powerful. Human beings of all geological ages, of all races and conditions have the same set of unlearned responses—"be it in Africa or in Boston, be it in the year six million B.C. or in 1925 A.D."[15]—and these responses are due to the material out of which men are made and the way this is put together. Most of the treatises on instinct have been written by the "armchair" psychologists who have not studied the behavior of young animals or babies from birth. The Darwinian geneticists "are working under the banner of the old 'faculty' psychology."[16] In fact the whole concept of instinct has become "academic and meaningless," and "actual observation thus makes it impossible for us any longer to entertain the concept of instinct."[17]

The behaviorists and the Freudians were quite friendly ten years ago, but now no love is lost between the two schools. Psychoanalysis is in fact

---

14. Hunter, p. 104.
15. P. 3.
16. P. 6.
17. P. 32.

introspectionism and introspectionism raised to the *n*th degree. The Freudian delves into the mysteries not only of consciousness but of the subconscious and the unconscious. He deals with dreams, with suppressed wishes, and with unconscious complexes. He is naturally *persona non grata* with the behaviorist, and the Freudian emotions go the way of the evolutionary instincts. The elaborate writings of the Freudians, enough in the past twenty years we are told to fill a good-sized room,[18] are consigned by Watson to the waste basket.

"The history of modern philosophy," says Will Durant in his *Story of Philosophy,* "might be written in terms of the warfare of physics and psychology." But in recent times these two antagonists seem to have changed sides. The physicists have been spiritualizing matter, interpreting it in terms of energy and even of will, while the psychologists have been busy in banishing the soul and spirit and even consciousness and purpose from the universe. President Butler of Columbia University has said that "psychology has demonstrated its capacity to become both frivolous and inconsequent"; and in his latest annual report he maintains that "The new and numerous Philistines are the proud discoverers and professors of a new doctrine of behavior which finds nothing to behave and no purpose in behaving. Where they have touched education they are reducing it to a costly pantomime." But perhaps we ought to distinguish between varieties or schools of behaviorism. McDougall distingishes three schools, the Strict Behaviorists, the Purposive Behaviorists, and the Near Behaviorists. We are not concerned with the purposive behaviorists, although it must be recognized that some psychologists can use the term "purpose" as if it were something inherent in the object rather than the subject. E. C. Tolman, a purposive behaviorist, is careful to state that his own doctrine is "not a mere Muscle Twitchism of the Watsonian variety."[19] If the strict behaviorists may be called muscle twitchers the near behaviorists should be termed "steam whistlers." Thus Morton Prince (in the volume of lectures before us) reminds us that Huxley as long as fifty years ago spoke of consciousness in brutes and then in men as only a collateral product of the working of the bodily mechanism, and "as completely without the power of modifying that

18. P. 37.
19. P. 279n.

65

working as the steam whistle, which accompanies the work of a locomotive engine, is without influence upon its machinery."[20]

The near behaviorists do not deny that consciousness exists, but adopting the Huxleyan automatism they have as little to do with consciousness as possible and do not allow it to do anything. The strict behaviorists, of whom Watson is the principal spokesman, do away with mind or consciousness altogether. Watson will not admit that mental states exist and he says that behaviorism ignores them just as chemistry ignores alchemy. "The behaviorist does not concern himself with them because as the stream of his science broadens and deepens such older concepts are sucked under, never to reappear."

By his assumption that there is no such thing as mind or consciousness the behaviorist has thrown out a protective mechanism that is impervious to the weapons alike of argument and of ridicule. When he reduces instincts to the congenital responses of fear, love, anger, etc. (he apologizes for the continued use of these "literary" terms), or to love behavior, rage behavior and fear behavior, it is useless to point out to him that there is a conscious content in these primary responses and a great gulf fixed between them and purely mechanical action. When Watson says again: "By 'memory,' then, we mean nothing except the fact that when we meet a stimulus again after an absence, we do the old habitual thing—that we learned to do when we were in the presence of that stimulus in the first place,"[21] we would waste our breath if we insisted that we could never recognize the stimulus as the same nor the response as the same without the aid of the discarded memory. And when, further, responses and reflexes are substituted for purpose it is idle to declare, using the words of John Dewey, that "complete adaptation to environment means death. The essential point in all response is the desire to control the environment." The trenchant arguments of J. B. Pratt in his *Matter and Spirit,* of Lovejoy in his "Paradox of the Thinking Behaviorist,"[22] and of McDougall and Prince in the volume we have been considering seem to make no dent in the behaviorist's armor. Perhaps our

---

20. P. 200.
21. *Behaviorism,* p. 190.
22. *Philosophical Review,* March, 1922.

only refuge is in the hope that you can't fool all the people—even all the psychologists—all the time.

Possibly we may find a vulnerable point in one of Watson's favorite illustrations, used in his lectures in *Psychologies of 1925* and his *Behaviorism* (1925), for the purpose of proving that "psychology is a natural science—a definite part of biology."[23] "I have in my hand a hardwood stick. If I throw it forward and upward it goes a certain distance and drops to the ground. I retrieve the stick, put it in hot water, bend it at a certain angle, throw it out again—it goes outward, revolving as it goes for a short distance, turns to the right then drops down. Again I retrieve the stick, reshape it slightly and make its edges convex. I call it a boomerang. Again I throw it upward and outward. Again it goes forward revolving as it goes. Suddenly it turns, comes back and gracefully and kindly falls at my feet. It is still a stick, still made of the same material, but it has been shaped differently. *Has the boomerang an instinct to return to the hand of the thrower?* No? Well, why does it return? Because it is made in such a manner that when it is thrown upward and outward with a given force it must return (parallelogram of forces)."[24] The application is obvious. "Man is made up of certain kinds of material—put together in certain ways. If he is hurled into action (as a result of stimulation) may he not exhibit movement (in advance of training) just as peculiar as (but no more mysterious than) that of the boomerang?"[25]

Sometimes the boomerang returns to smite the thrower. The two objects compared, boomerang and man, differ in several essential respects. The man knows what he is doing when he makes the boomerang, and he makes it for a special purpose, so that something beside the boomerang illustration is needed to banish consciousness and purpose from the universe. Perhaps the mechanical action of the boomerang will illustrate action of the simple reflex type, but even this is doubtful. Kurt Koffka says that "Marina dissected the inner and outer muscles of monkeys and connected them crossways. An impulse sent to contract the external muscle of the right eye ought now to result in a movement toward the left and vice versa. The monkey should look to the left when a bright spot appears at the right. In reality, nothing of the kind took place. As soon as the wounds healed the animal moved his eyes as

---

23. See p. 34 of the former volume, from which we quote.
24. Pp. 12, 13.
25. P. 13.

normally as before the operation. Thus the conception of a merely contingent connection between situation and response breaks down even at the reflex level."[26]

It is fortunate that the boomerang cannot "deviate" or be guilty of "socially untrained" conduct, but this emphasizes the fact that it cannot be trained to make "learned" or "conditioned" responses. What a world of mental activity in both learner and teacher may be concealed under the term "learned responses"! Why cannot the boomerang learn? Another difference, and one that opens the gap between man and boomerang still wider, is that a man, if he is a behaviorist, can alter or condition the actions of people, if he can catch them young enough, to an indefinite extent. If the behaviorist had his way with children the babies would stop crying (except when in actual pain) and would no longer be frightened by black cats or other animals, the preachers would stop preaching, the introspectionists would stop introspecting, the judges would leave the bench, psychology would become "a natural science," and everybody would be happy. It is a paradox that people who insist upon putting on others the strait jacket of "strict determinism" reserve for themselves the liberty of influencing the thoughts and conduct of their fellows in a way that almost approaches omnipotence. When it comes to pass that boomerangs begin to instruct and reform their fellow boomerangs and teach them to deviate from the path of "congenital response," then the analogy between boomerang and man, between boomerang and behaviorist, will be more convincing.

Another striking fact, not to overdo the matter, is that a boomerang cannot talk. We strongly suspect that man is a talking animal because he is a thinking animal, and we recall the statement of Max Müller to the effect that "the formation of language attests from the very first the presence of a rational mind." To be on safe ground the behaviorist should stop talking and, as one of his critics advises, "content himself with relaxing and contracting his muscles." As soon as the behaviorist (even if it be in Carnegie Hall at two or three dollars per ticket) begins to debate the question, "Is Man a Machine?" he *ipso facto* ceases to be a machine. He should not only stop talking, but should stop being conscious that he is

---

26. P. 131.

stopping. The only consistent behaviorist is the behaviorist when he is asleep and not dreaming.

We suspect that what the behaviorist has in mind when he denies the existence of mind or consciousness is an objection not so much to the existence as to the efficiency of consciousness. With proper scorn and in italics Watson remarks that "no psychologist today would like to be classed as believing in *interaction.—If 'mind' acts on body, then all physical laws are invalid.*"[27] The editor of the Clark University volume, Carl Murchison, shrewdly remarks that he is convinced "that experimental methods are largely instances of the more or less systematic theories of the experimenter." The shortcomings of the behavioristic psychologists are due to the philosophy of materialism and mechanism which underlies their psychology. It is this that leads them sedulously to avoid "anthropomorphism" even when dealing with human nature, and to side-track at all costs the problems of knowledge, of purpose and of the psychophysical relation.

Consciousness—that is, efficient consciousness—is the Great Intruder in a mechanical or naturalistic scheme of the universe. At all costs it must be kept from doing anything, and the only safe way to keep it from doing anything is to exclude it from real existence altogether. Huxley's "steam whistle" theory was only partially satisfactory, and the theory of parallelism, which was popular twenty years ago but is now rather *démodé*, while it effectually side-tracked consciousness and kept it from any influence upon events in the physical world, at least allowed to it a quasi-activity in its own sphere. The method of the modern psychologist is more drastic. He ignores the very existence of consciousness. In haughty disdain he passes it by without recognition. If compelled to notice it at all he at once merges it into the organism on the one hand or the environment on the other. If a behaviorist of the Watson school, he identifies it with bodily movement, especially laryngeal vibration. If an evolutionist of the Dewey school, he characterizes it as a quality of the "real object." The same motives that induce the naturalistic theologian to deny miracle and the supernatural, so as to shut out the activity of a personal God from nature, history and experience, operate with the naturalistic philosopher or psychologist and lead him to exclude an efficient consciousness from his scheme of things altogether.

27. *Behaviorism*, pp. 242, 243.

The result is what may be called an intellectual apostasy in our intellectual centers and our great universities. The intellect in circles in which it should magnify its office, that is in the departments of philosophy and psychology in our universities, sees fit to abdicate its throne, and to immolate itself upon the altar of materialism and mechanism. The young people in our schools are forbidden to believe in that essential quality of human nature which distinguishes man from the brute. They are forbidden to look backward in memory, or inward in introspection and self-examination, or forward in purpose, or upward in worship. They are asked to accept a philosophy which makes the philosopher (to borrow a phrase from Durant's *Story of Philosophy*) "an automaton automatically reflecting upon his own automatism."

After all the strongest indictment against behaviorism is not that it is hopelessly inconsistent and palpably absurd but that it obliterates all moral distinctions. What sort of behavior will behaviorism legitimately promote? This is the most important question when multitudes of the youth in our colleges and universities are being taught its principles. The plain fact is that morality as a binding restraint upon human conduct and with it reverence for life and the sacredness of human personality are by the progress of behaviorism "sucked under, never to reappear." If the conduct of man is first assimilated to that of the animal, and then the behavior of both animal and man is further reduced by a rigid determinism to the type of mechanical action, if unsocial conduct is simply that which the majority dislikes, although a more enlightened minority may think it desirable for its purpose, then the safeguards thrown by morality and religion around human life and the family relation and the obligations of law and the rights of property are broken down. Then the legitimate fruit of behaviorism in the sphere of moral behavior is indicated by the statement of one of the principles in a famous murder case, that it is as justifiable to kill a human being for the purposes of science as to stick a pin through a beetle.

What is needed today is, to use an expression of the late Professor Ormond, the "re-ification of the Ego." When consciousness goes conscience goes with it, and when free-will and responsibility are denied their place is taken by lawless individualism and an ethic of self-assertion.

Lincoln University, Pa.   Wm. Hallock Johnson.

70

9

Eclecticism in Counseling

For some time, in various places, I have been trying to expose and counter the prevailing spirit of eclecticism in counseling that exists among Bible-believing persons. I have been (and am) concerned about this because, in my opinion, the battle with eclecticism is the most important struggle in which we may engage today. And that struggle *must* be won. Perhaps it is time, therefore, to extend the discussion just a bit.

But first, you may wish to inquire, "How is the battle going?" I would say in some sectors quite well; in others, not so well.

Among ministers and key Christian laymen, in general, there has been a significant awakening to the problem together with a clearly discernible trend to solve that problem. Literally thousands upon thousands of Christians have become articulately aware of the inroads of eclecticism and are combining their forces to sweep it out of their churches and church institutions. This is encouraging, but even more gratifying than this necessary negative effort is the evidence that most of these persons are engaged in strong positive endeavors to learn to do biblical counseling instead.

The battle has gone poorly (with some notable exceptions) in the teaching institutions. Here among vested interests in centers and strongholds of eclectic thought, professionalism, as well as other factors, has hindered advance. Then, too, it should be remembered, nouthetic leaders have had their hands so full helping out the sergeants and the troops on the front lines that they have not yet spent much time trying to influence the generals back at home. But the time has now come when that defect must be remedied. There are capable men within the movement who are concerned to work at this and who (indeed) have begun to do so already. Many more are now preparing for it by means of graduate studies recently introduced at the Christian Counseling and Educational Center in Philadelphia.[1]

But, now, let us consider the origin of this strange word, eclecticism. The term comes from a Greek word *eklego* (which itself is a combination of *legein*, "to gather" and *ek*, "out" = "to gather out"), which means "to pick out," or (as we ourselves say in English) "to pick and choose." The Greek "eclectics" were philosophers who belonged to no particular school. Instead, they took bits and pieces from various sources and glued them together. As we know him today, an eclectic is one who makes a patchwork quilt of counseling theory and practice, taking from various schools what seems best to him. We could say that the principle of eclecticism is:

Each counselor himself is the measure of what is best (or right).

But, in this sense, the word *eclectic* does not appear in the New Testament.

Nevertheless, the *idea* of eclecticism (as we currently use the word) does occur in Acts 17:18a in a very picturesque (though derogatory) term that was used by some Athenian Epicurean and Stoic philosophers to speak deprecatingly of the apostle Paul.[2] I have translated the portion of the verse in *The Christian Counselor's New Testament:*

Then some of the Epicurean and stoic philosophers took him on. Some said, "What does this eclectic babbler want to say?"

The Greek term that I have rendered "eclectic babbler" is *spermologos*. This word pictures birds picking up seed here and there. A bird does not stand in one place while feeding; it scurries about from place to place, often missing ground in between, pecking away first at this spot, then at that one. There seems to be no rhyme or reason, no method, no system to what it does. This hopping about from one idea to another, picking up scraps of information here and there to be pasted together in a senseless collage, of which the word *spermologos* speaks, aptly describes the opinion that those Athenians had of Paul. Because of the senseless patchwork quality of the results of such eclecticism, the Greek term in time also acquired the notion of babbling. To

---

1. For information, write: The Director, C.C.E.C., 1790 E. Willow Grove Ave., Laverock, PA 19118.
2. Ramsay says the word was a piece of Athenian slang.

preserve both nuances I translated it by the two words, "eclectic babbler." Of course, the philosophers were wrong; Paul was not a hopping eclectic. Unlike the many speckled birds perched in the towers of Christian institutions today, he had definite views that (as he himself put it) he didn't receive "from a human being" nor was he "taught" by human beings but rather "received as a revelation from Jesus Christ" (Gal. 1:12). In his yet unanswered book, *The Origin of Paul's Religion,* J. Gresham Machen has fully demonstrated the fact that Paul's contention stands. No one with an open mind can read Machen's unparalleled work and still think that Paul was an eclectic.

But it is interesting to note that it was the adherents to two well-defined schools of thought—though diametrically opposed to one another—that united in their disdain of eclecticism as mere seed-picking that leads to babbling. Yet, as Luke describes their own activities in verse 21 (". . . the Athenians . . . spent their time doing nothing else but discussing and listening to new ideas"), it sounds very much as though they were not altogether immune to eclecticism themselves."[3]

I spend time with this Athenian reaction to Paul's market-place preaching because in it there so clearly lies the biblical refutation of the notion that eclecticism is an acceptable stance. By mentioning this incident, Luke intends to point out how erroneous the early opinions of these Greek philosophers were about Paul. The statement of those who called him a babbling seed-picker was as inaccurate as those who thought at first that "he seems to be promulgating some foreign gods" (v. 18b). Luke parenthetically points out that they said this because Paul had been preaching "Jesus and the resurrection (*anastasis*)." Evidently the word *anastasis* (resurrection) at first had been taken by them to be the proper name for a god (note the plural: "some foreign gods"). Because of these differing opinions (v. 18), they asked Paul to address them before the council of the Areopagus to learn just exactly what it was that he had to say (vv. 19, 20). But when he delivered his message, they not only were cleared up on the meaning of *anastasis*

---

3. Of course, like the council that condemned Socrates, they may have had more of a heresy-hunting spirit; but, N.B., even heresy-hunters (in spite of all that they say) at times may be lured into their interest in heresy by what I can only describe as a sort of eclectic curiosity. This seems to be what Luke had in mind when he wrote v. 21.

(vv. 31, 32) but, by his tactful yet ringing call for repentance (vv. 30, 31), understood that he was no tolerant eclectic either.[4]

There is, then, no evidence that eclecticism is condoned in the Scriptures. Indeed, to the contrary, the thrust of the entire Bible is against it. There is one emphasis from fore to aft in the Bible that is pointed up in the question that ought to be put to every eclectic: "How long will you lean to both sides?" (I Kings 18:21, Berkeley).

Down the long corridors of history, both in biblical times and since, Satan has levelled two basic forms of attack against the church. James R. Graham, in his book, *The Divine Unfolding of God's Plan of Redemption,* has called them *murder* and *mixture*. While murder has been successful at times (cf. the Islamic devastation of the church in North Africa), in general it has been a failure. Instead, as Tertullian observed, the blood of the martyrs has been "the seed of the church." But the use of *mixture*—from the beginning in the garden when Satan's counsel was mingled with God's—has proven to be highly effective. And what is eclecticism (in counseling as well as in other areas) within the church if it is not the modern form of that strategy?

How subtly, how easily, has Satan introduced his ideas into Christ's church in this way! And, in doing so, he has even found it possible to induce believing teachers to assist him. By convincing them that the pursuit of eclecticism is valid—and especially by the use of the eureka method (by means of which biblical truth is mistakenly equated with eclectic borrowings[5])—he has enlisted them to cover his tracks. The warnings of II John (especially vv. 8-11) are appropriate:

> 8 Watch yourselves, that you don't lose that which you have worked for, but rather that you may receive a full reward.
> 9 Everybody who goes beyond, and doesn't remain in the teaching of Christ, doesn't have God. The one who remains in the teaching has both the Father and the Son.
> 10 If someone comes to you and doesn't bring this teaching, don't receive him into your home and don't say "greetings" to him.
> 11 I say this because the one who says "greetings" to him shares in his evil deeds.

---

4. Cf. my remarks on this address in *Audience Adaptation in the Sermons and Speeches of Paul,* chapter 6, pp. 25-34; for implications relevant to Christian counseling see *More than Redemption* (Phillipsburg, N.J.: Presbyterian and Reformed, 1979), pp. xii, xiii.

5. For details on the Eureka method, see my *Lectures on Counseling,* pp. 34ff.

Among the grave dangers of eclecticism, I should like to mention four:

1. Satan's teachings are palmed off to unsuspecting persons as God's truth. (I do not say that those who engage in eclectic counseling are aware that this is what they are doing; no, the prevailing situation is that it is unsuspecting persons who thus influence other unsuspecting persons.)

2. The inevitable failures of eclectic approaches, as a result, are attributed to God, thus creating doubt and weakening faith in His Word.

3. Counselors are led further and further away from the study and application of the Scriptures in counseling while they become more and more concerned about the acquisition and implementation of human opinions. Usually this takes place so gradually that those who are involved in the transition are largely unaware of what is happening.

4. The emphasis on eclecticism has tended to encourage the development of a cast of self-styled Christian "professionals" who have been usurping the place of the pastor, who is God's counseling professional (II Tim. 3:15-17); these "professionals" have hung out shingles and on their own have gone into counseling as a business in competition to the church. Professionalism results.

These dangers constitute just cause for the Christian to do all that he can to discourage any further development of this deplorable situation.

I have pointed out before that Freud, Rogers, Skinner and all other such thinking framers of counseling systems, are wise enough to reject eclecticism. They recognize that one cannot adopt methods and procedures that were built on presuppositions about man and his predicaments that are contrary to their own, and that were designed to effect results and achieve goals that they do not share. The incredible fact is that so few Christian leaders see this. Truly, "the sons of this age are more shrewd with people of their own kind than are the sons of light" (Luke 16:8).

I could, of course, cite innumerable instances of eclectic borrowings and demonstrate how each has weakened some aspect of the Christian enterprise, but to do so would extend this chapter too greatly, and would (for those who would appreciate it) be majoring on the obvious. Instead, I wish to conclude with a plea to do all you can in the near future to diminish the influence of eclecticism in counseling and to promote the spread of biblical counseling. I am of the conviction that the spirit and practice of eclecticism is *the* most serious problem that the church faces today. Until that spirit is exposed to all and rooted out, the weaknesses in the church (of which we are all only too well aware) will never be replaced by the strength and might that comes from a strict and loving adherence to God's powerful Word.

10

"CPs," "ACPs" and "SCPs" in Counseling

From time to time I have spoken of complicating or secondary problems (CPs). By these, I refer to difficulties growing out of the presentation, or primary, problem that so complicate the counselee's life that there is no way in which he can solve it without first reaching a solution to them, or that must be dealt with after solving a primary problem before the case can be closed.

The fisherman accidentally gets a knot in his monofilament line. In attempting to untie it he manages instead to put five more knots in the line. Trying to loosen these, he only adds eight more, and so on, until he is ready to cut the line. This is the condition in which a counselee may come to counseling. But when he does,

1. he may not mention any (or some) of the 13 additional knots; he may focus on the first knot as if it were still his only difficulty. It is the counselor's task, through a judicious use of sub-questions stemming largely from the second basic question on the PDI, "What have you done about it?" to uncover every knot;[1]

2. often the complicating problem (or problems) will be like knots further along the line. That is to say, in order to get back to the original knot, the counselee first must be helped to untie all those knots that are encountered on the way up the line to the original knot.

Keeping these two important principles in mind will aid immeasurably in reaching final solutions that can be attained in no other way. Rushing ahead to tackle a presentation problem right off may not be the most efficient way to proceed, and (indeed) may itself lead to new complications. Counselees

---

1. Cf. my discussion of the Personal Data Inventory (PDI) in *Update on Christian Counseling* (Phillipsburg, N.J.: Presbyterian and Reformed, 1979), vol. 1, pp. 41-56.

have enough problems already; they don't need new ones that are manufactured in the counseling room.

The Bible warns against the baneful effects of unresolved complicating problems. In II Corinthians 2, for example, we read of the repentance of the excommunicated member who had been involved in incest. Now that the difficulty had been resolved through repentance, the member needed to be reassimilated into the body. As a result of his sin, the painful punishment of excommunication (a complicating problem) had been inflicted on him (v. 6). This was proper, and led ultimately to his repentance. But until he had been forgiven and comforted and the body had reaffirmed its love to him (vv. 7, 8), he was still in danger. Repentance was not enough. The repentance led to a remorse (a complicating problem) that could be removed only by reassimilation into the body. That is why Paul warns, "so, instead of going on with that [the punishment of excommunication], you should rather forgive and comfort him so that he won't be overwhelmed by too much pain." Note Paul's concern not only about repentance (all *some* would care about today), but also about the resolution of the entire situation, with all its ramifications, including its secondary or complicating features. That is seen clearly in the reason appended: "so that he won't be overwhelmed." There was a real danger of this if the reassimilation in loving forgiveness did not occur.

In this case, mentioned in II Corinthians 2, the primary problem *could* be handled first (as a matter of fact, it *had* to be), so that, unlike the knots that must be undone before it could be reached, *it might easily have been overlooked* had Paul not been aware of it and alerted the congregation to the possibility.

Thus, we see, the complicating (or secondary) problem that grows out of the initial (or primary) one may need to be dealt with either before or after handling the problem from which it has come. The danger in cases where complicating problems must be solved first is the failure to recognize their presence, leading to failure to solve either the primary problem or these secondary ones. In such cases, sessions eventually bog down, often with neither counselor nor counselee ever knowing why. The danger in cases where the complicating problems must be solved after solving the initial problem (again) is the possibility of failure to recognize their existence. But, unlike the former situation, a problem has been solved—indeed, usually the presentation problem itself. The success in doing so makes it very easy for both counselor and counselee to ignore further difficulties. And yet, as Paul noted in his concern for the recent excommunicant, all the good of the former solution could be undone by a failure to follow up the consequences of the original problem.

Thus, we may speak of *antecedent complicating problems* (ACPs) and of *sequential complicating problems* (SCPs, such as the case referred to in II Cor. 2). Of course, both are sequential in the sense that they are both secondary problems that grow out of primary problems. But the word "complicating" serves to indicate that fact. Thus the terms *antecedent* and *sequential* refer not to the origin of the problem but to the point at which the counselor deals with the problem.

A biblical instance of an antecedent complicating problem (ACP) is found in Hebrews 5:11: "We have a lot to say about this [the primary problem: to inform the reader about more advanced matters that they needed to know in order to live properly] but it is hard to explain since you have become dull in hearing [the ACP]."

Sometimes the complicating problem itself can grow as large as or greater than the original problem; *primary* and *secondary,* then, refer not to the significance or intensity of the problem, but to the question of which problem was occasioned by which. The situation in Corinth, in which several sins were being committed by some persons with reference to the Lord's supper, is a case in point. The sins of greed and drunkenness were serious, but the divine judgments that they occasioned (weakness, sickness and death[2])' became an *immediately* greater difficulty. Paul's message, therefore, was: judge yourself before the Lord does. Such circumstances demonstrate the *urgency* of dealing with primary problems immediately. Unless they are resolved quickly, they will lead to serious (or even irreparable) harm. The case here in Corinth clearly was a sequential complicating problem (SCP).

But in some SCP situations it is necessary to deal with the complicating

---

2. Cf. I Cor. 11:30ff.

problem right away. Someone who develops a bleeding ulcer due to worry and bitterness must first treat the ulcer (the SCP) or he may not live to deal with the primary problem (his attitude toward persons and life). The story of Cain in Genesis 4:3-12 involves a warning that God gave of the *possibility* of great complicating problems that would follow any failure to handle another problem immediately.[3] For your own interest, study II John 10, 11 and III John 9 to discover what kinds of complicating problems are mentioned and what must be done about them.

In conclusion, let me note several areas in which complicating problems frequently crop up for Christian counselors.

1. When a counselee has little or no hope, but is depressed, discouraged or in despair, you are faced with an ACP. Until you give him hope (or, perhaps it would be better to say, until hope has been generated within him) often there is no reason to expect that you can help him deal successfully with the difficulties over which he lost hope (cf. the section on hope in the *Manual*).

2. When a communication breakdown between two or more persons occurs as the result of failure to solve other problems (a *very* common phenomenon), what I have called the "communication dilemma" develops. That dilemma is this: to solve the interpersonal problems, including the communication problem, one must be able to communicate. I have shown how to overcome the dilemma in my book, *Christian Living in the Home*,[4] in the chapter on communication. But for now, let me simply observe that the communication breakdown is a striking instance of an ACP.

3. Closely related to the previous point (or as a part of it), the presence of anger, bitterness, mistrust, etc., results in an ACP. The problem here is that the *issue* in question cannot be dealt with until the *relationships* have first been set right. Nasty people, untrusting persons don't deal with issues properly.

Anger, frequently, is secondary to other feelings (such as disappointment, frustration or even fear). A parent may be very worried about the safety of a child who does not come home on time. But when he does show up, fear and worry change to anger. This dynamic must be recognized.

---

3. Cain's downcast attitude was itself a complicating problem growing out of his previous failure to bring a proper sacrifice. But unless *both* knots were unfastened, more would follow.
4. *Christian Living in the Home* (Phillipsburg, N.J.: Presbyterian and Reformed, 1972).

4. The paralyzing or fleeing effects of fear often lead to strong ACPs. The only force greater than fear is love (cf. my pamphlet on fear).

5. Sleep loss, when it leads to a state of easy irritation, inability to persevere in solving other primary problems, or even to perceptual difficulties (as it may in some cases), clearly presents you, as a counselor, with an ACP.

6. Life-dominating problems (LDPs, on which see the *Christian Counselor's Manual*) also give rise to both ACPs and SCPs. Here, in order to overcome the LDP, and a mopping up operation designed to insure against future failure of the same sort, through radical amputation and rehabilitation (see *More than Redemption*, chaps. 10, 16), you must deal with all sorts of other problems around the entire circle of the counselee's life pie that are tied into the LDP. It is not sufficient to focus on the LDP alone. LDPs, like drug addiction, drunkenness, homosexuality, etc., require total restructuring both *as the means* of breaking down the LDP and as a way of guarding against its recurrence.

7. Bad teaching, poor counsel, faulty attempts at solving primary problems also frequently end up producing a number of ACPs.

8. Organic illnesses, divine judgments, etc., may provide occasions for both ACPs and SCPs.

9. In general, it may be said that SCPs grow out of *consequences*. Loss of friends, jobs (and other sorts of losses) are a good example of this phenomenon. *In all cases* when you have reached a solution to a primary problem (and even when along with this some complicating problems have been resolved—particularly if they were ACPs), the question to ask is, "What have been the consequences of this problem?" A check list of these may reveal the necessity for further counseling. N.B., any given case may have one or more primary problems, to each of which may be attached both ACPs and SCPs.

It is my hope that this discussion will be enlightening to counselors who have not thought through the dynamics involved. The problem of CPs is so much a part of everyday counseling that we must all become aware of its presence.

Matters of Concern to Christian Counselors

To my son Todd
with hope that God will give him
a fruitful ministry

INTRODUCTION

From time to time I have sketched out miscellaneous matters of concern to Christian counselors and have jotted down various comments about each, thinking that sooner or later I might write a book about them or use them as a chapter in a volume on a larger subject. Yet, for one reason or another, that time has never come.

Since some important issues are involved, and as the number of such comments began to grow as they accumulated in my files, I decided that it might be of value to put them together in something of a potpourri manner and send them forth for whatever help they might render to Christian counselors. I have made it a practice to make as much help available as quickly as I can because I am anxious to see change *in this generation.*

In many places I haven't reiterated the biblical bases again. I am assuming that the reader is familiar with my other books, in which I have done so with care. Sometimes, but not always, I refer to my other books in which such material may be found. This book is but a piece of the whole. I don't believe in *unnecessary* repetition. Of course, much is a development and elaboration of previous material. But there is a good bit of brand new material too. All is from a fresh perspective.

The questions discussed are both broad and narrow. I tried to group them, but beyond the roughest sort of classification, you will find that I had to give up on that idea. The table of contents and index will help to give a survey of and integration to the subjects discussed.

Some subjects are basic; some have to do with technique. Some of this material may be of real significance to nouthetic counselors.

May He for Whom this book was written be pleased to bless it as He sees fit.

—JAY E. ADAMS, 1977
Editor: *Journal of Pastoral Practice*

1

I DON'T DARE

Pastor, you may wonder from time to time just where the borders of your counseling ministry may lie. Here I would like to give you a guideline that will help you determine.

I have heard pastors say, "I don't dare counsel a depressed person," or "a suicide," or "someone manifesting such bizarre behavior." If you don't dare to counsel persons with such problems, you don't dare to preach about them either. But you'd better preach about all of these when they involve sin. The guideline to which I have referred is this: a pastoral ministry is a ministry of the Word. That ministry of the Word, whether public or private, whether to crowds or to couples, is one and the same. Paul put it this way:

> We proclaim Him [that is the general ministry to which every pastor is called] counseling every person and teaching every person [those are the two specific ways in which that general ministry is carried out].[1]

Paul and the apostles recognized that there were two aspects to the one ministry. These two aspects issued in two activities (nouthetic confrontation and teaching) that were not different in kind; they were merely distinct in function. The same message, the same sources of information and power, and the same goals are in view in both aspects of this one ministry of the Word.

Counseling and preaching came to be considered activities different in kind and in goals only when counseling became something other than a minstry of the *Word*. Biblical counselors, however, have restored the ancient ministry of the Word to its rightful place; as a result, they see no such dichotomy between the two activities. When they leave the pulpit and enter the counseling room, they see no need

---

1. Colossians 1:28: cf. Acts 20:20, 21.

1

to change hats. They do not abandon Christ for Rogers (or Skinner or Freud). Their approach, their manner of ministering and their context all may change (just as these incidentals change under distinct preaching conditions too), but the basic elements of the one fundamental ministry of the Word remain intact.

So then, how broad is the pastor's counseling ministry? It is as broad as his preaching ministry. If depression may be caused by sin, suicide is contrary to God's commandments, and some (non-organic) bizarre behavior stems from neglect of the body, etc. (see the *Christian Counselor's Manual* for details), he can (should) preach about these things and counsel those who become involved in them.

If the Bible has a message of prevention and of redemption from such sin (and it does), it also has a message that may be ministered in both contexts. A holistic view of the ministry of the Word, therefore, calls for counseling that grows out of exegesis and the concrete application of the Scriptures to life situations just as preaching does.

The fact of the matter, then, is that a pastor shouldn't dare preach on an issue until he is also prepared to counsel people who are involved in it. Because counseling demands a personalized concrete application of biblical truth, the subject must be thoroughly understood. There is no way to speak around issues when people cry for help. It, therefore, provides an acid test that can be applied to one's preaching: "If I couldn't use what I am preaching to counsel someone, do I really have a correct and thorough grasp of the subject, or am I only kidding myself?" When a pastor thinks of his preaching this way, it will dramatically affect his preaching. The test will keep him from putting things over on others and himself. Counseling and preaching are of a piece: two aspects of the one ministry of the Word. Since that is true, there is every reason to apply just such a test. The more a pastor sees this and thinks of counseling in preparing his sermons the more practical his preaching will become. Conversely, the more he thinks of preaching when counseling, the more biblical his counseling should be. The test, "Is what I am doing in counseling applicable to preaching?," is also valid. Applied consistently, it will help preaching to be truly preventive in character.

2

ARTIFICIAL INSEMINATION?

Today it is a simple matter for couples who are unable to have children because of the husband's sterility to resort to artificial insemination. More and more Christian counselors will be faced with the problem. Therefore, it is well to think it through beforehand. The donor of the semen, usually a student working his way through medical school, remains unknown, the wife has the opportunity to bear her own child, and the couple have the joys of a family.

"Why not adoption?" you ask. Because, as one writer said: "I inquired about adoption a little over a year ago. Our local state social services office told us that due to unavailability of children for adoption, the usual waiting period (for a child) is 5 years." There once was a time when one family was able to adopt four or even as many as five children. All that, however, has changed since abortion was legalized. Consequently, childless parents now are waiting in line for children to adopt. Usually there are deformed and mixed racial children available. Some still may be obtained from foreign countries like Korea. So the possibilities of adoption have not ceased entirely.

But the question cannot be determined on the basis of whether adoption is still a viable alternative; the issue must be faced biblically.

On two, and possibly three counts, artificial insemination must be rejected by Christians.

1. Christians who understand God's principles for sexual expression will reject artificial insemination because they will see that it requires the obtaining of semen through sinful means. The donor is required to masturbate in order to provide the semen necessary for the act. Masturbation, I have shown elsewhere, is sin.[1]

---

1. *The Christian Counselor's Manual,* pp. 399f.

3

2. Artificial insemination may be adultery. While it does not involve the physical act of sexual intercourse with another, it does require the entrance of another (third) party into the marital relationship in a most intimate manner. Even if fantasies of what the donor (or donee) might be like[2] could be altogether avoided by both parties (a doubtful supposition), still the result of a sexual act (semen obtained by masturbation) has been interposed between the husband and wife. That it thus breaks the intimate oneness that they are called to maintain seems almost certain. But, even if (technically speaking) one could be sure that no physical or heart adultery had been committed,[3]

1. The very great temptation that it puts in the way of those involved in the transaction (donor, donee) would require rejection, and

2. The fact that it is *likely* that artificial insemination does constitute physical adultery by interposing the semen of a third party between the two who have become one flesh, again requires rejection because "Whatsoever is not of faith [i.e., if one is not *sure* that what he is about to do is right in God's sight] is sin" (Rom. 14:23).

On these counts, counselors must give counsel to childless Christian couples to reject artificial insemination.

That is hard counsel. Along with it must be given comfort, direction about how to explore other possible options (some Christian adoption agencies still grant children, etc.), and advice on how to serve Christ fully in the work (perhaps children's work) to which He has called them if no children ever become available.

---

2. Adultery of the heart (Matt. 5:28).
3. How this assurance could be obtained is impossible for me to see.

MORE ON METHODOLOGY

One of the principal areas of discussion among Christians who are counselors has been (and is likely to continue to be) in the area of methodology. I have written already on this subject elsewhere (especially in *What About Nouthetic Counseling?*, pp. 73-76). There I contended that *methods* in distinction from *means*—were, in a thoughtfully constructed system, connected too intimately to the system to be abstracted and used in another: You can't use a metric wrench on an American nut.

There are systems, of course, that are conglomerates. That is to say, their parts are not integrally related to the whole. These "systems," to the extent that they use methods that do not effectively contribute to the intended goals and objectives, are weakened *as systems* (though, of course, the "systems" may be strengthened thereby, particularly if the methods used are borrowed from the biblical source). Many of these lesser systems, attempting to go their own ways without the slightest intention of depending upon the Scriptures, nevertheless (unwittingly) have adopted elements (distorted though these may be) from the waning Christian consensus in which their systematizers grew up and by which they were influenced. In most systems these elements are not substantial enough to greatly influence these systems for good. Rather, their presence synergistically kneaded into the dough of a hostile context may act as a pinch of salt, but hardly as leaven. Usually, the only real effect is in the confusion caused by eclectic persons who delight in discovering parallels (really minute borrowings) to the Christian position.

The great thinkers and systematizers are careful not to become eclectic. Carl Rogers wouldn't think of using Skinnerian manipulation; Skinner would rather be found dead than to adopt Rogerian non-directive techniques. Methods, for them, are designed to achieve the purposes and reach the goals in view. Apart from such methods they have no system—and they know it. Their methods *constitute* the functional part of the system; indeed they sustain it.

Methods have been designed as the functional elements of a theory. "Here is man's problem," say Skinner and Rogers. "He has been wrongly trained (Skinner)/failed to realize his inner potential (Rogers)." So each, then, draws a straight line as the shortest distance between the two points (problem ———→ solution). For Skinner it is conditioning through environmental control and retraining; for Rogers, non-directive reflective counseling. These are the operative elements in the system; that which gives thrust to the theory. How, then, can Christians who see both the problem and solution in biblical terms (sin ———→ Christ), adopt anything less than methods designed to take the shortest and only route from man's problem to God's solution?[1] To adopt methods that have been structured to get along without God and that are designed to achieve humanistic ends is unthinkable. And if it is biblical borrowings that are adopted— why? Wouldn't it be better to go directly to the Bible itself and find these principles and practices in their pure, undiluted form?

Methodology is not neutral. Methods are the functional factors, the operative elements, in a system. Indeed, to the extent to which a system is theoretically inexact, giving a description of the operative elements becomes the only way that one can describe it in anything like a systematic form. Frequently, too, a system may have theoretical elements that—in the final analysis—turn out to be only so many trappings. Their presence may be purely decorative (intentionally or unintentionally so). It is the *methods used* that actually constitute the system proper. Given only the stated problems and goals (or solutions), a system will not function. Given only certain methods it will still function (perhaps not clearly in time). Functions may change as new goals arise, etc., but something still will happen.

So then, rather than be deceived by the response, "We're not Rogerian; we only use some of Roger's *methods*," a Christian ought to respond immediately, "That, at the heart and core of it, is what Rogerianism *is*, because that is what Rogerianism *does*."

---

1. There is something unique about Christianity. All other systems (theoretically) could borrow from one another since all try to solve problems humanistically. But the *only route* to salvation and sanctification is Christ. The Holy Spirit *alone* can achieve the fruit of the Spirit.

4

DON'T TRY TO FORGIVE YOURSELF

"I know God has forgiven me, my husband says he has forgiven me, but I can't seem to forgive myself." This complaint is typical. Christian counselors are hearing it more and more. But even though it is encountered frequently enough to consider here, the problem as stated is unreal.

"Unreal?," the counselee would reply. If you had to face the agonies of gnawing uncertainty and inner misery that I've known over the past three months since it happened, you'd know whether there was a real problem or not!"

That response would be typical too. What would a biblical counselor say at that point?

First, I always make it clear that I am not denying the existence of a true problem[1] (as if I were saying there is no misery, no agony, no struggle; of course there is). That is not my point in saying that the problem *as stated* is unreal (note the italicized words). There is a problem all right, and it is serious, but it is not the one the counselee thinks it is.

Nowhere in the entire Bible is anyone ever exhorted to forgive himself. Nor is there an example—ever so remote—of such a thing. The concept is foreign to the Scriptures. Rather, when Christ declares, "Your sins are forgiven you," people go away lighthearted and rejoicing. The problem—*as stated*—is unknown to biblical writers.

And it was unknown to everyone else until recent psychological and psychiatric speculation became widespread in the church. Many

---

1. Nor am I minimizing it (for more on the dangers of minimizing, cf. my *Lectures on Counseling* (Nutley, N. J.: Presbyterian and Reformed Publishing Co., 1977), p. 108, and *Competent to Counsel* (Nutley: Presbyterian and Reformed Publishing Co., 1970), pp. 112, 113.

Christians have accepted this unbiblical analysis uncritically just because it sounds Christian. After all, it speaks about forgiveness. But the explanation, the analysis and the solution to the problem are all drawn from non-Christian categories based on presuppositions that are contrary to the Bible. Biblical words and concepts can be used in a totally unbiblical way.

God pictures man as quite ready to love himself, make excuses for himself, forgive himself, and sees no need to urge him to do so. All such promptings, instead, are toward loving God and one's neighbor, or forgiving *others*.

"Well then," you ask, "what is happening in such cases and how can we help people to get to the bottom of the misery they are truly experiencing?"

In every case in which I have encountered the problem in counseling (since I have become aware of the true dynamic involved) I have discovered that the issue is not self-forgiveness but rather a problem of self-dissatisfaction.

This dissatisfaction with one's self grows out of real problems either sensed indistinctly or articulated rather sharply in the discussion by the counselee. The problem typically is something like this: the counselee in one or more ways has sinned. She has repented of her sin and has received forgiveness from God and from others (in the case mentioned, from her husband). Yet, gnawing down within is a continuing sense of deep dissatisfaction *because she knows* (or at least partially recognizes) *that there is more to be done*. She has been forgiven; true. *But she has not changed.* Unless something more is done, she will do the same sort of thing again, having to seek and receive forgiveness once more and even more deeply experiencing the same dissatisfaction all over again. *Something more is needed.* It was at this point that the psychologizers got to her and told her, "You must learn to forgive yourself."[2] Tragically, by this they redirect her better understanding and analysis of the problem, and confuse the issue for her.

Usually this problem of *something more* occurs whenever the counselee has had a history of similar offenses (leading to subsequent repentance and forgiveness). That is to say, she has a *pattern* of such activity. She is caught in the vicious circle of a kiss-and-

---

2. Or equally as bad (if not worse), "You must learn to accept yourself."

8

make-up syndrome from which she doesn't know how to emerge. She knows (or half knows) that unless the pattern is broken she will go on (and on) in the same pattern month after month, year after year.

Visualized, here is what is happening:

PATTERN

$$X\ X\ X\ X\ X\ X\ X\ x\ x\ x \longrightarrow \textit{ad infinitum}$$

X = past incidents of the sin $\longrightarrow$ repentance $\longrightarrow$ forgiveness.
X = the most recent incident, leading to present dissatisfaction.
x = similar future incidents unless the pattern is broken and replaced by a biblical one.

The answer to the counselee's problem, then, is clear. She must be pointed to the put off/put on dynamic of Ephesians 4, Colossians 3, etc.[3] The biblical alternative(s) to handling whatever pressure becomes a temptation to sin—learned, practiced and habituated into a new response pattern—provides the needed solution to the dissatisfaction.

Whenever I have helped a counselee to develop a new, biblical response pattern,[4] without fail his sense of dissatisfaction vanishes, his supposed "need to forgive himself" evaporates, and the matter is raised no more.

---

3. For more on this see the *Manual,* chapters 18, 19.
4. This, of course, takes time and effort (cf. ibid.).

5

DON'T FORGET THE FUTURE

In gathering data it is only natural to think of the past or of the present. What data could one find out concerning the future? But, while technically you are correct in thinking that way, you must remember that it is possible for a counselee to be guilty about what he is *planning* to do in the future. Technically, I say, I agree, the planning is past and not future. The sin has already been committed in the heart. But the outworking of the sinful plan is yet future. That means that most of the data will be inner rather than external.

Because of the ability that God has given man to project into the future, he can experience present guilt and misery over his goals, anticipations, plans and hopes just as he can worry today about things that have not yet happened.

At some point in a data gathering session, then, it is wise to ask about the future (technically, one's present plans and preparations for the future). Such questions as the following may prove useful:

1. Are you worrying about something?
2. Have you been making plans to do something that you know is wrong?
3. What sort of preparation(s) are you engaged in that might be causing problems?
4. Have you been seriously considering some sinful course of action?

Questions like these have turned up important answers such as, "Yes, I've been thinking of suicide," "I've wondered about raping a woman down the street," and "I've often thought about molesting my son." These three responses (three of many possible answers) all indicate that (before engaging in such sinful activities for the first time, at least) a lot of thought is given to the contemplated act. Feelings of thrill and of misery intermingle. Before a person can bring himself to committing such acts (many have told me) they had to "talk themselves into it" (through self-pity, rationalization, fantasizing, etc.). How important, then, to stop the process dead in its tracks, before the inner sin of the heart is widened into its outer sinful counterpart.

Ask about . . .
Expectations
Hopes
Goals and objectives
Responsibilities one is planning to shirk
Fears, worries
Plans
Preparations and steps being taken
Then ask . . .
Is it realistic?
Is it sinful?
Is it questionable?
Are you concerned about it?
Do you have enough facts about it?

Romans 13:14 is critical on this point and may be used in counseling with solid effect: "But put on the Lord Jesus Christ and make no provision for [literally, don't plan to satisfy] the flesh with its desires." The preceding verses (12, 13) make it clear that people *do* tend to plan ahead (and the word in verse 14 is *pronoeo,* which means "to make plans for, plan ahead"). This verse indicates that the habituated desires of a wrongly patterned life will strongly tempt one to do so.[1] Particularly is this true of an undisciplined thought life. That is what is involved in all such planning. Philippians 4:8 also indicates that one is responsible for the content of his thought life. By the prayerful use of a Philippians 4 think-list[2] a genuine effort to discipline one's thoughts for godliness can be achieved.

Romans 12:17b says, "Respect [literally, plan ahead for—the same word, *pronoeo,* is used] what is fine in everybody's sight." Here is the "put on" with which the wrong sort of planning must be replaced. The mind cannot be left empty. We all look forward to, anticipate, plan and prepare for *something.* The Christian must replace sinful planning with righteous planning. Wise counselors will help their counselees learn to do so.

---

1. Cf. *Lectures on Counseling,* pp. 231-238.
2. Ibid., pp. 138ff.

WHO ARE YOU COUNSELING?

The counselee very well may be different persons at different times and places to different people. To her husband, she is his wife; to her children, she is their mother; to her brother, she is his sister; to her boss, she is his secretary; to . . . and you can name it from there. Her habit patterns may be different in all these relationships too. A polite, cheerful, well-controlled, capable secretary at home could be an uncontrolled, screaming terror to her children and a weeping, helpless wife to her husband. Unless the counselor obtains data from each area, he may develop very false ideas about the person to whom he is giving counsel.

Knowledge of competence and control in one area may be of considerable importance in demonstrating the possibility of the same in another. She may plead, "That's just how I am." It is not "just how she is"—implying that nothing can be done about her weeping. That's how she is sometimes, but not "just" how she is. She is that way *at home* because she has *learned* to live like that at home. But she is not that way at work. That she can learn to be different at home is obvious because she already has learned to do so at work. She is a whole person.

It is possible that factors that contribute to the problem should also be adjusted in order to help make the change. If, for instance, at this time in life she has taken on too much to try to work at a full-time job while a wife and mother, she may have to quit the former to give the best hours of her life (rather than the dragged out left-overs) to the latter. Later, when the children are grown, she may wish to hold a job again.

But, regardless of the particular elements involved, in data gathering it is well to ask questions calculated to discover all that you can about *all* of the aspects of a person's life.

SLEEP PATTERNS

Every once in a while the Christian counselor encounters people (usually a husband and wife) who are having problems with scheduling. He may say, "Well, I've got to get up early to go to work, so I have to get to bed at a decent hour." She, on the other hand, may say, "I know that, but he's a day person and I'm a night person. That's just the way we are. I don't see how either one of us can change."

For years, perhaps, they have argued and scrapped over this issue. "You're never in bed in time to have sex," he complains bitterly. "Well, you won't even sit up till ten o'clock and watch the news with me on Friday nights," she snaps back. And so it goes.

What can be done? Much, quickly. The solution is in

a. *Convincing them that change is possible:* they are not *"just that way"*; they have developed sleep patterns. *That* is why they are "night persons" or "day persons." And therefore, since love means putting the other person first (Phil. 2:1-11), they are obligated to resolve this difficulty by doing so.

b. *Repentance leading to a willingness to put one another first.* That means they will take the concrete steps for doing so that you help them develop.

"But how do you convince them that such change is possible?" you ask. Here is one way I have found helpful. I say, "The body is capable of undergoing tremendous change quickly. Not only do shift workers demonstrate this—in 2½ days the switch has been effected—but let's take a simple example. If you were to get on an airplane and fly to Europe tonight, your body would have to adjust (hunger habits, sleep habits, etc.) to at least a five- or six-hour change. How long would it take? I have done it a number of times and I can tell you that I—and *everyone else who does so*—can make the change in two or three days, with no difficulty. The discipline of the new structure (when people eat, wake, work, shop, sleep) in the new country is so rigid that the adjustment happens quickly. If you rigidly discipline yourselves, prayerfully seeking to please God by pleasing one another, you too can see rapid change."

A NOTE ON SLEEP LOSS

From time to time in various publications I have mentioned the fact that 2½ days' (or more) loss of the R.E.M. (rapid eye movement) phase sleep can, in some persons, lead to all of the effects of LSD. Any one or more or combination of the perceptions can be adversely affected so that a person may hallucinate, hear voices, etc.

Experience in counseling shows that a large number of the bizarre (usually horrendously labelled "schizophrenic") behaviors manifested by counselees stem from this cause. Yet many psychiatrists and psychologists, because of their theoretical orientation, fail to pick up sleep loss as the true cause of the behavior. They simply never think to ask whether the counselee has been missing sleep. Nouthetic counselors have been made aware of the problem for some time, and I get reports from all over of counselors who were able to save people from hospital experiences, shock treatments, etc., as the result of using this knowledge.

However, I am concerned here to make one thing clear. While occasionally an otherwise growing Christian, leading an exemplary life, reacts this way because he (let us say) sins against the temple of the Holy Spirit, pushing it beyond its limits by studying for exams nonstop for a period of three or four days, this is not the only sort of situation (and perhaps not the most common either) in which such sleep loss occurs. It is possible that a counselor may find that sleep loss leading to bizarre behavior is but the complicating problem that grows out of one or more other problems.

What I am trying to say in this brief note is that when a counselor has explained and arrested the bizarre behavior by telling about the effects of sleep loss and putting the person to bed, he may only have begun his counseling. In some cases, of course, nothing more may need to be done, it is true.

But what of a case in which, because of cyclically escalating worry about financial matters, Fred begins to toss and turn and lose sleep; and this, at length, leads to bizarre bahavior? The sleep loss is secondary and although it seems to be more significant than the worry because of its flamboyant character, it is really a very simple problem by comparison. This is the danger for both counselor and counselee: to think that once the more dramatic problem has been alleviated, the counseling is over (or all but done). The wise counselor will not succumb to this temptation, nor will he allow the counselee to do so if there is truly a primary—though not so plainly headlined—problem that has not yet been solved.

If the problem (worry, guilt, or whatever), over which the counselee lost sleep, was so important and its solution so illusive to the counselee that it led to sleep loss, it would be tragic to miss it in giving all attention to relief from the effects of the sleep loss. It was the danger of doing so that prompted this note.

OTHER FACTORS TO CONSIDER
WHEN GATHERING DATA

The chapters on data gathering in my *Christian Counselor's Manual,* though substantive, are not exhaustive. One area, I have come to see, to which I should give more emphasis has to do with goals, abilities, obligations and resources.

Somewhere, in the early interviews (first or second session, ideally), it might be of great importance to consider the following four factors in relationship to one another. Perhaps a diagram will help.

—Arrows indicate possible interrelationships—

There are a number of ways to go (as this diagram indicates) in analyzing a counselee's present situation and difficulties:
1. His goals may not be clear to him or others, may not be biblical,

may be hidden (even, at times, from himself), may conflict with abilities, resources and obligations, etc. Agenda matters (mentioned elsewhere[1]) should be raised. So often problems lie in this area.[2] If his goals are wrong, everything else will go awry. He will assume improper obligations and waste and prostitute abilities and resources.

2. His goals may be biblically correct, and his statement of them may be fairly precise. But what of his obligations? If he has taken on unbiblical obligations, they will conflict with his goals and work at cross purposes to them. For example, suppose a Christian social worker, whose task is to point people to the resources available to solve their problems, may not use "religious" resources because of the governmental funding of the agency for which she works. She will soon find that her inner goals (to win people to Christ and see dramatic Christian growth and change occur) are frustrated by her commitment to that job. She must consider whether she can go on gagged by obligations like these. She soon begins to ask, "Am I sinning by wasting my abilities and by neglecting God's resources?" Next, she wonders, "Can I continue in this job? After all, how can I justify giving other answers when I know what God's real answers are and am prohibited from giving them?" Finally, she thinks, "Why did this dilemma arise? The job itself must not be biblically legitimate. What business does the government have in social welfare programs, anyway?"

3. If a counselee sets goals or assumes obligations that are beyond (or far less than) his abilities, he sins. Romans 12:3-8 requires a Christian to make a sober evaluation of his gifts, discovering, developing and deploying them to the full.[3] The same may be said of his resources.

I have only indicated some of the principal issues that may arise from such considerations. The little diagram may prove useful to counselors by helping them to remember to probe all the significant relationships among these four factors. In doing so, the analysis of the counselee's problems may be facilitated.

---

1. *Manual*, pp. 230, 238, 265ff., 276.
2. See my *Lectures*, pp. 217, 220, and the pamphlet series, *What Do You Do When. . . .* In each I have tried to help the counselee to examine goals according to biblical standards.
3. Cf. the *Manual*, chapter 30.

10

HALO DATA—YOU MAY BE DECEIVED

When I was doubling as teacher, registrar and dean of students at Westminster Theological Seminary, I learned something of importance about halo data. At Westminster there has always been a goodly number of Oriental students (Koreans, Chinese, Japanese). Frequently, like any others, these students would come to try to make impossible changes in their schedules, try to obtain concessions, etc. I was the ogre who would have to say no. "I'm sorry," I'd say, "it isn't possible to do this." Politely they would smile, say "thank you," and leave. Then, they'd return later on in the same day, or perhaps the next day, asking again and again for the same thing. Each time I'd explain again why it couldn't be done, and each time they would smile more broadly as they left.

Then I discovered in talking with some of them that that is how things are accomplished in the Orient—you get what you want by persistence. "But what of this ever-broadening smile each time a student is turned down?" I asked. "That," I was told, "means he is getting more and more upset."

It is possible, when counseling persons from another culture, to misread the halo data (like smiles) that may remain fairly consistent among persons from a single cultural background. Counselors should be aware of this fact. But the same may also be true of subcultures or even of individuals who may possess certain idiosyncrasies.

Some Americans, for instance, laugh (nervously) when they become concerned. To take the laugh as a sign of happiness and joy would be a mistake. Someone, misreading the smile or laugh (even a husband or wife) could consider it cruel, whereas it might only denote nervousness or concern. Some ethnic groups are much more demonstrative than others (gestures, loudness, etc., for them may not indicate bitterness or anger at all, as they could for another). To others, New York and New England accents may sound "hard" or "harsh." Yet the person from that area may not intend to come across that way at all.

So, beware of stereotyping halo data. Always, instead, read each person for the way *he* or *she* performs. Halo data noted in clear contexts will help you to read it better in those contexts that may not seem quite so clear.

11

SORTING THINGS OUT

Often counselors defeat themselves because they try to handle conglomerate data. But when things remain all mixed up together, counseling tends to be mixed up too. In listening to the reports coming from the church at Corinth Paul too may have been confused at first. So much was wrong. So many interrelated problems were tangled together. How did he handle the situation? He sorted things out. There was no way that he could speak to all the problems at once. One by one, he took up each matter separately until he had dealt with all: pride, division, false wisdom, sophistry, challenge of his apostolic calling, incest, lawsuits, delinquency in fund raising, divorce, abuse of gifts, lack of love, disorder in meetings, denial of the bodily resurrection, etc. By sorting them out, he removed the principal problem that the counselor meets when he first begins to thread his way through a counselee's difficulties: complexity. Paul simplified things for himself and those to whom he was writing.

Sometimes merely sorting things out for the counselee will, itself, be a key to the ultimate solution of his problem. Often counselees allow themselves to become defeated by complexity. When you begin to sort things out for such a counselee, you can tell because as you lay them out in order, he comes to life, responds and on his own, begins to make suggestions about what might be done to resolve the difficulties. Bringing order out of chaos is clearly one way to give hope; it demonstrates that the seemingly out of hand and unmanageable is already beginning to be handled and managed (at least at this preliminary level[1]).

---

1. Of course hope will quickly vanish if further biblical progress is not achieved. But early hope, as I have pointed out in connection with other matters (see *Manual,* pp. 39-48), is itself a significant (essential) factor in helping to bring about attitudes and preparing a climate for further progress.

"I can see that, but where do I begin?," you may ask after listening to the complicated, contradictory, tangled report given by Frank and Fran. "It's all so confused; how can it ever be unravelled?" By the use of the picture-word that you just used you have actually put your finger on the answer to your question—you can unravel the mess *by unravelling it!* Look for the separate threads that hang out (mother-in-law problem, work, sex difficulties, etc.) and grab one. Keep pulling on this thread until it comes to an end. You will have isolated, sorted out, unravelled one strand. Deal with it biblically. Grab another and pull it loose, then another and another until the whole comes apart like a sweater pulled to pieces. Sort out the reds, the greens, the whites, etc., and lay them side by side in an orderly fashion —just like Paul did. The key to doing this is to take one thread at a time and continue to pull on it until it has come loose and lies alone. Then and then alone can its length be determined with any sort of accuracy. While it was still part of the whole, adding to the complexity and itself taking on longer dimensions, it might have seemed endless or (at least) hopelessly intertwined with the rest. Now, there it lies, manageable, less formidable, unravelled.

The analogy to the unravelled sweater does not always hold, because what sometimes appears to be a whole made up of separate parts is, in fact, two or more wholes, each consisting of several parts. This kind of confusion often occurs when the counselee has had his problem for quite awhile and though new, complicating problems have been added to it, he still thinks of his problem in its original form, as if no additions or changes had occurred. Good counselors know that it is necessary to sort out original and complicating problems too. Usually complicating problems, occasioned by new events, faulty attempts to solve the original problem (putting six knots in the fishing line while trying to untie one), and erroneous interpretations of the situation, must be handled first (you can't get to the original knot except by going through the original six).

A common example of a complicating problem that must be solved first is the deterioration of relationships between persons who have been unable to solve the original problem. Bitterness, resentment, aloofness, or whatever form this deterioration may take, has grown so strong that it colors everything. A solution to the issue that occasioned the original problem, even when plainly presented from the Scriptures, will not be adequate. The counselees will have none of it. They will raise objections, find fault, cast doubts on it, etc. A novice counselor may look on this as simple disobedience or unbelief. Disobedience and unbelief it surely is, but *simple* disobedience and unbelief? No. It is complex; complicated by the sinful attitudes of the counselees toward one another. So, until the counselor separates the relational problem from the issue he will get nowhere. The counselees must be brought to repentance, seek and grant forgiveness and begin to develop new Christian attitudes through acts of love *before* any progress in resolving the issue can be made.

So sorting out *problems,* asking "How many are there?," "What sort of problems exist?" and separating original problems from complicating problems, issues from relationships, is one important aspect of sorting things out.

There are other things to be sorted out too. A fundamental sorting out of *responsibilities* is always necessary before the counseling can make any headway. When counselees have been in the habit of blaming others for their sins and failures, it is absolutely necessary to sort out responsibilities. If through erroneous counsel previously given, a young man has come to believe that his current difficulties in getting along with others is his mother's fault, it will take some sorting out of his responsibilities before you can move ahead. He must be shown that even if she did fail to show him love and even if she did reject him, it is his responsibility as a Christian to learn how to handle those admittedly difficult factors in his early life. He is not stuck with the sinful responses that he, as an unsaved child, first developed. Now that he has come to know Christ all that can change by God's grace, and he is responsible to avail himself of that grace by the use of the means of grace. If he doesn't, but goes on blaming his mother for his present failures, he is sinning. If, as he claims, his mother wronged him, that was her sin for which God holds her responsible. How he responds to her sin, however, is what God holds him responsible for. Christ too was wronged, but the constant wrongs done to Him did not *make* Him a failure. Quite to the contrary, He succeeded by responding righteously to those who treated Him so unrighteously. He sorted out His responsibilities in the matter and fulfilled them.

Husbands and wives, employees and employers, as well as a host of people in other relationships, will come for counseling with the conviction (or excuse) that they are what they are because of what

22

someone else did to them. They must be shown that their ulcers are *not* the result of what husbands did to them, but rather have developed as the consequence of the bitterness and resentment that they held within and for which they alone are responsible. Husbands cannot blame the miserable attitudes that they bring home from work on bosses who mistreated them. They are responsible for responding to bosses in a Christian manner. What husbands did to wives and what bosses did to employees are their responsibilities before God. But the wives and the husbands are responsible for their resentments and gloomy attitudes. Sorting things out helps to enable the counselor to see whose responsibilities are whose, thereby enabling him to help each to assume his in a biblical fashion. Blame-shifting began in the garden and has been with us ever since.[2]

In conclusion, the principle of sorting things out is an important one, always to be remembered. At times when counseling is bogging down, one of the ways in which counselors often can remedy the problem is to retrace what they have done, asking, "Have I sorted things out adequately?" Chances are that in doing so, he often will discover where he has left matters confused and complex that could have been greatly simplified by the process.

---

2. Cf. *Competent*, pp. 213ff.

TIMING

In *A Reply to a Response*,[1] I made a promise that I should like to begin to fulfil at this point. There, in replying to Mr. David E. Carlson's objection that I fail to write about timing, I said,

> I do appreciate his suggestion to say more about timing. I have said a good bit about this by implication, but little systematically. I shall try to heed his advice.[2]

While this is no place to do a systematic study of the question, a few observations on the subject made more explicitly, may help some to think more about the issue.

When I said that I had already said a good bit about timing by implication, I was thinking of such things as my discussion of "yanking" in *Competent to Counsel* (pp. 173ff.), "Communication Comes First," in *Christian Living in the Home,* much of the discussion of crisis counseling in *Lectures on Counseling* (pp. 73-142; see esp. pp. 140, 141), and my plea to work on hope (not data gathering) when a person has very little hope.

The Bible recognizes the principles of bad timing and good timing when, e.g., in Proverbs 27:14 we read, "He who blesses his neighbor with a loud voice, rising early in the morning, will have it reckoned to him as a curse (Berkeley). That is to say, bad timing can turn the effect of an intended blessing into cursing. Good intentions, coupled with bad timing (thoughtlessness for another's situation is what is at the bottom of it) can destroy any good effort. A counselor must be acutely aware of this important biblical principle.

From the other side of the coin comes this proverb: "Like apples of

---

1. Reprinted in *What About Nouthetic Counseling?* (Nutley, N. J.: Presbyterian and Reformed Publishing Co., 1976), pp. 82ff.
2. Ibid., p. 85.

gold in settings of silver, so is a word spoken at the right moment" (Prov. 25:11, Berkeley).

The "right moment" *enhances* the words appropriately given (i.e., given at the right time) as a good setting further enhances an artistic object on display. It is not just that good timing avoids the baneful effects of ill-timed action, but rather (according to this verse) *adds something more* to something already valuable. The Bible clearly recognizes the importance of good timing.

In Ecclesiastes 3:1, after we read, "For everything there is an appointed season," the writer has no trouble giving a number of examples. Here, the principle is that some times are better for some things than others, but everything has a right time.

"Buying up the opportunities" (Eph. 5:15) further emphasizes the need for good timing. The point here is that opportunities may be lost in evil days when they are likely to be at a premium.

Well, then, how shall we think biblically about timing? First, let's consider good and bad timing in precounseling (evangelism). The phone rings. The pastor answers, and this is what he hears, "Well, pastor, what are you going to do about this fine Christian wife of mine who has just packed her bags to leave me?" Is that the time to evangelize Joe? Hardly! The pastor's best intentions so timed, would turn a blessing into a cursing for Joe. Instead, as a wise counselor, he says, "Joe, would you put Mary on the phone?" Then he says to Mary, "Mary, I have to leave for a funeral in thirty minutes, so I don't have any time to spare. Listen carefully. I've been over I Corinthians 7 with you before. You know you can't leave Joe, even if he is unsaved, if he wants to keep the marriage intact. What you are doing is contrary to Scripture and, therefore, sin. Now unpack those bags and the two of you get over here as quickly as you can."

Mary reluctantly agrees and fifteen minutes later Joe and Mary arrive at the pastor's study. Both are still ruffled, but Mary has unpacked her bags and Joe is grateful. Is this the time for him to evangelize Joe? Hardly, again! The pastor is pressed for time, an immediate crisis has been averted, but no real commitments have been made. What does he do? He gets two commitments if he can:

"Mary, I want a solid commitment that you won't threaten Joe with this again. To do so is sin, and you know it." Mary makes such a commitment and he continues, "And I want to see both of you at 7 tonight for the first of a series of counseling sessions in which we are going to talk about what has led to this state of affairs and what God says can be done about it."

That is timing. (1) The counselor is careful not to "curse" Joe with the gospel; (2) he knows that there is a proper time for proclaiming the gospel that will enhance it in Joe's eyes, and (3) he sees the opportunity in all of this to evangelize Joe as well as help put a marriage back together again on a new basis. Accordingly, he builds all of his actions on proper timing. Perhaps that night he can begin to present the gospel.

Let's take a different sort of situation. This time the counselor faces a Christian who is rebelling against God's Word, who won't repent: "No! I won't forgive him! Do you know what you are asking me to do? You're asking me to forgive the man who seduced my wife. It was hard enough to forgive Leigh; but forgive him? Never! Pastor, I came here to get help in putting our marriage back together; I didn't come to discuss my relationship to that confounded scoundrel."

Is this the time to discuss the question at hand? Yes and no. It is easy to see that Jim is still reeling under the shock of yesterday's discovery. He has already come a long way in granting forgiveness to his wife and seeking help for his marriage. But there must be growth in his forgiveness; growth that will come more easily in a week or two when he gets a bit of perspective and has begun to see that Leigh's repentance is followed by genuine efforts to make their marriage a success. It might have been proper for the pastor to put the forgiveness of the offender somewhere on the list of possible items that would have to be taken care of in time, supposing the offender also repents and seeks forgiveness. (The pastor may also have shown poor timing in making a big thing of this possibility *before* the offender has even been confronted about his sin.) But it might have been wiser to introduce this matter later on, at a more natural time when it became an unavoidable issue. Introducing it before the need to actually face it might be good, of course, but not so soon. Jim has already come a long way; the counselor must see to it that he doesn't needlessly put a hurdle in his pathway before he has gained enough momentum to leap it. Bad timing; turning a good, biblical action designed to be a blessing into a curse. Good timing; turning a good biblical action into something better because of its timing.

We have seen how bad timing might have been avoided; how might good timing be used to enhance forgiveness?

Let us suppose that through counseling Jim and Leigh are able to demonstrate the many good things that they have received through seeking and granting forgiveness and all that grows out of it. Then the offender repents of his sin. Now, pointing out how many benefits have already come from the forgiveness that they had experienced (even though it was hard to see this at the time) because they obeyed God and He blessed, the pastor can place the forgiveness of the offender in a setting of silver: "Don't miss His further blessings to you for your marriage by disobeying Him in this matter."

Hundreds of situations may be like these two: opportunities come (or are made) that must be seized. But not every time is opportune.

There is a time, however, when the word must be preached not only "in season" but "out of season" (II Tim. 4:2)—when others don't want to hear, but God requires that the rebuke, the exhortation, or the proclamation must be made. In every case, however, the counselor must be sure of this. The rule is to look for the right time; the appropriate season.

13

MOTIVATION...
IN HEBREWS

The Book of Hebrews was written to motivate Jewish Christians to go on with their faith and not drift away. Some of these professed Christians, the writer suspected, might not be Christians at all.[1] Others, he feared, were being influenced by their bad example, and some had even developed the habit of absenting themselves from the regular assembly of God's people (10:25). Persecution (but not to the point of martyrdom—12:4) had begun. Some were wondering whether they had made the right choice in moving from Judaism to Christ. Like Lot's wife, they were tempted to look back. To avoid any such abandonment, this book compares the two covenants, and everywhere concludes (in terms of the key word of the book) that the new covenant is *better*. The entire book is motivational. It should therefore be an excellent basis for the study of scriptural motivation. Such a study could not but yield rich fruit to counselors who continually find themselves faced with the problem of motivating both disaffected, sinning and/or doubting believers and persons who may or may not be genuine believers. As the writer of Hebrews discovered, it is not always easy to tell.

I cannot do a lengthy study of motivation in Hebrews in this place (you can do it for yourself the next time that you study the book[2]), but I should like to point out some of the key elements that any such

---

1. For an excellent discussion of this question see Roger Nicole, "Comments on Hebrews 6:4-6," in Gerald Hawthorne, ed., *Current Issues in Biblical and Patristic Interpretation* (Grand Rapids: Wm. B. Eerdmans, 1975), p. 355.
2. You'll be all the more impressed, I am sure (as I was) when you work through the whole book.

study must uncover. Doubtless, others will appear to you also.

1. Problems that the writer of Hebrews tried to meet:

    a. Drifting
    b. Doubting
    c. Dullness
    d. Defeat
    e. Discouragement

2. Solutions that the writer of Hebrews directed toward his readers in order to solve these problems. These solutions are all motivational:

    a. Hope
    b. Encouragement
    c. Warning
    d. Example
    e. Threat
    f. Reward
    g. Instruction

Using these elements as you see them in the Book of Hebrews, think through ways in which you too can help counselees who may have similar problems.

14

DULL IN HEARING
A COUNSELING PROBLEM DISCUSSED IN HEBREWS 5:11b

The writer of the Book of Hebrews has been comparing and contrasting the old and new covenants, and at every point finding the new superior to the old. This comparison has led him into a discussion of Christ as the great High Priest. There is much more that he would like to say about this important matter, but for the moment despairs of doing so, since, as he puts it, his readers are (literally) "dull *in* hearing."

The word *dull* (*nōthros*) means "sluggish." To be dull *of* hearing is to not hear at all, but to be sluggish (or dull) *in* hearing is to hear and not hear. It is to hear poorly, in an unenthusiastic and largely unreceptive manner. When water drains sluggishly through a pipe, it drains, but not as it should. There are obstructions that must first be removed before the proper action can be realized.

Dullness in hearing often comes to those who hear words but fail to hear their message any longer. This can happen when familiarity with old words, clichés and hackneyed expressions clog communication. New translations, not only of the Scriptures, but also by the counselor as he discusses the old biblical themes in new ways are often essential. The writer of Hebrews often puts things in new and striking ways to achieve this effect (e.g., his reference to Melchizedek is unique in the N.T.).

Sometimes dullness occurs when the listener hears and rejects what he has heard. He hardens his heart (as the writer of Hebrews warns) to what God is saying because he doesn't want to hear. Hardening at length, if persistent, may lead to the dulling of one's conscience (a salesman is easier to reject each time he appears if you have turned him down consistently before).

30

Sometimes persons are dulled by persecution (as were the persons to whom Hebrews was written). And it doesn't even have to be a bloody persecution, either (cf. 12:4). Persecution, if one is not careful, can wear him down. Soon he can reach the point where he no longer responds keenly to persecution but tends to drift into compromise or (at least) discouragement (if not doubt and despair). That is the sort of tactic that is being used in Northern Ireland where, every day (it could be in any part of the country, no matter how small the hamlet or village may be), there is a bombing or a killing or some similar incident. The intention is to wear down the population. Only by continued efforts to maintain normalization has the population kept free from this temptation. Continued efforts at mutual encouragement, provocation to love and good works, etc., are necessary among God's people or they too may become dull in hearing.

So, there is much such dullness among counselees, who infect others with their dullness, who in turn reinfect the counselees, etc.

Counselors can do a number of things to counteract this dullness in hearing (and note: one of them is to not go on using the same old clichés). But in general these boil down to two: warning and hope. There is, for example, in Hebrews 6:1-10 a *warning* for any who have been only "tasters," not eaters, of the good things of God. They are called to examine themselves and believe before it is too late. Believers in the church are compared not to the bad ground (unbelievers), but to the good that received the same rain (blessings) but responded with faith as true Christians do. They are called back to hope (6:11, 12 indicates that lack of hope brings on dullness, sluggishness, lethargy). Through *assurance* of their salvation the writer calls them to hope.

Hope is what enables one to endure. Paul made this point in I Thessalonians 1:3, when he spoke of the "perseverance of hope" (i.e., the perseverance that flows from hope).

So, to counteract dullness, whatever its cause or causes may be, counselors must combine warning and hope. This has always been the basic biblical motivation from the garden, through the wilderness on to the prophets and into the New Testament—threat and promise, reward and penalty, warning and hope.

31

15

MANIPULATION IN COUNSELING

Today, the American public is slowly becoming aware of the massive manipulation that is being practiced in this country. The exposé began with the publication of Vance Packard's *The Hidden Persuaders* in 1958 and has continued to be a reoccurring theme among popular writers in magazines and books ever since. Technical terms, like "managed news," "image" and a specialized and more frequent use of the word "manipulation" itself, testify to the clearer perception that the general public has been gaining about the activities of business, politicians and the various media. Concerned and informed Christian counselors, therefore, must be able and anxious to evaluate every counseling system and method from the standpoint of its possible manipulation of the counselee.

Some schools, like the behavioristic schools (notably the views of B. F. Skinner—the dean of behaviorism), make no bones about the manipulative character of what they do. Everyone manipulates others, they say, either effectively or not so effectively, so why not do it as effectively as possible in a scientific manner? Of course, the manipulated society will be under the control (a good word for Skinner) of an elite, a group of psychologist-experts. It is they who will set up the contingencies in the environment, determine the rewards and punishments (aversive controls) that will motivate people to run through their maze. With the proper random-scheduling of rewards they plan to train the human herd (men are only animals) to do as they wish. (This is for their own good, of course, but that good is not to be thought of as individual good; the only value, these strict Darwinians think, is the preservation of the human race.) Who will determine what is "good" and what is "bad"? "The circumstances themselves," they reply. Science will read reality and whatever reality says, the scientific elite in control will follow. But who will determine the scientific methods and presuppositions by which "reality" will be read? And how do we know that human bias will not strongly enter into any such procedures? It always has in the past. There is silence; no answer.

As Christians, we know of course, that there *will* be bias; sinful bias! The elite will do as they please—not really even for the benefit of the race (a very questionable goal—not the prime Christian goal, for sure) but for the benefit of the elite. The image of God in man, his moral relationship to God and his fellow man, has been totally ignored in Skinner's analysis. Indeed, Skinner has ignored this concept because he thinks man is no more than an animal. That is to say, Skinner ignores morality, love for God and neighbor, etc., because he has rejected them as unscientific, mythological and, thereby, limiting concepts that have kept the human race from becoming scientific in its evaluation and training of men. Freedom and dignity are nonsense terms, as meaningless as such words as spook or poltergeist. They have no referents except in human fantasy: "All that man is, is an animal behaving. When we learn to measure him and completely quantify his every behavior, we can manipulate him completely. Scientific measurement/manipulation is the goal. Already, we have in our hands enough information to go a long way. Give us a chance." This is the basic viewpoint of the Skinnerians, who are gaining ground on many fronts.

Soon, for the sake of the human race(!) by genetic control, cloning, abortion and euthanasia, the elite will be able to breed a superior herd of cattle that will finally realize Hitler's dream of a super race. The extermination of unwanted weaker strains, according to the principle of the survival of the fittest (Skinner is an old-line Darwinian) will at last be a reality—for the sake of the human race(!). The "fittest," presumably, will be those who are fittest according to the "scientific" bias of the elite.

This is all in the wind.[1] Yet, within the church of Jesus Christ, Christians—I don't doubt their Christianity at all (just their judgment)—are propagating the same Darwinian and Skinnerian dogmas that lead to such horrible conclusions. N.B., I didn't say that these Christians adopted or taught these conclusions. What I said was that

---

1. For many quotations and a general picture, read Philip E. Hughes, *The Control of Human Life* (Nutley, N. J.: Presbyterian and Reformed Publishing Co., 1971), an excellent booklet.

they were (unwittingly) propagating the very same behavioristic dogmas that *lead to* these conclusions. It is time that all counselors who name Christ's name awaken to this fact, critically examine biblically the implications of what they say and teach, and change any courses of direction that might fall in line with such manipulative techniques.

"But Skinner is right about one thing—everyone manipulates, even nouthetic counselors," you say.

In one sense you are correct (depending upon one's definition of manipulation, of course. Nouthetic counselors don't want to control every phase of the environment, every movement of every individual, etc., as Skinnerians do, however); everyone wants to influence others. But the fundamental difference in nouthetic counseling lies in this: the use of the Scriptures in the power of the Holy Spirit. Fundamentally, when properly practiced, nouthetic counselors themselves do not manipulate and control others. What they do is prayerfully analyze people's problems according to biblical categories and then point them to God's solutions in the same Book. They will exhort, encourage, warn, persuade or even hold out God's rewards in accordance with the book, but they do not control, nor do they seek to control, the counselee. Rather, they call the counselee to avail himself of the control of the Holy Spirit. ("Be filled with the Spirit," Ephesians 5:18, means "be dominated" or "controlled by" the Spirit in every area of life.)

Thus, in urging the counselee to seek the control of God (which brings about perfect freedom, the welfare of the human race, *and* the benefit of each individual), the nouthetic counselor *points away from himself* and his own acknowledged bias (he admits, indeed warns, that he is a sinner whose unaided judgment is not to be trusted) to God's perfect, impartial Word.

"But even that approach can be used manipulatively," I can hear someone reply. Of course it can; any good thing can be abused. But there is one saving factor in all this: in pointing to the Bible—regardless of his own motives—the counselor *has* pointed to a unique Source of information, value and power that does transcend human bias and error, one that modern scientists do not take into account. And if, as urged (for whatever purpose[2]), the counselee *does* turn to this Book and to the God that he meets in it, he will be in touch

---

2. Cf. Philippians 1:15-18. Paul could distinguish the message, and God's use of it, from the messenger.

with a source of control other than, and free from, even the counselor himself. That is how in the Inquisition—before a highly manipulative, control-oriented church—individuals who had come to know God through the message of that Book which (in God's providence) that very church preserved, could resist controls and punishments as free men who would go to death rather than be manipulated by human reward and punishment to conform to what they believed was unfaithfulness to Jesus Christ.

Those who see nouthetic counseling as simply one more manipulative system, disguising its manipulation under the cloak of Christianity, fail to see that there is something in it that is unique. Even granting the worst, that it is just that—a sham, a scheme designed to gain power and control over other human beings (which I grant *only* for the sake of the argument)—it still has one redeeming factor: it points counselees to the Bible, and to the Bible's God. No other system does so. By using the Bible as the standard, by insisting that people prayerfully read their Bibles every day and seek God's answers to their problems, by urging counselees to engage in personal contact with the God of Scripture through repentance, faith and obedience, nouthetic (biblical) counseling *alone* points men away from human control to the control of the Holy Spirit.

Any factor that militates against this within the nouthetic counseling movement—any person, any principle or any practice—is thereby not biblical and must (by definition) be rooted out of the system as soon as discovered.

16

RECONCILIATION ➤ RELATIONSHIP

Frequently a problem is cleared up by repentance and the seeking and granting of forgiveness. All is warm and well. But in time, weeks or months later, the reconciled parties have grown cold and have drifted apart. Why is this? Shouldn't reconciliation lead to new and better relationships? Yes, it should, but it will not *automatically* do so. After reconciling us to Himself in Christ, God then spends much time changing us and our relationship to Him. New bonds, based on new biblical patterns—not the mere fact of reconciliation— are necessary for a new and growing relationship. Counselors who realize and work for this see results that last and relationships that mature. Others see reconciliation take place and that is all. They often wonder why—beginning, perhaps, to question the sincerity of the parties who sought and effected the reconciliation. They ought, rather, to ask, "Have I taught them how to live together in the future and helped them to get a new and different relationship with one another off the ground?"

Diagrammed, the three relationships look something like this (see next page).

It is easy to see from the diagram that Christian counselors cannot settle for I or II. The reconciled condition is essential because the barrier must be removed. Yet, the put off must be replaced by new biblical bonds (of love) that are put on, or some other sinful barrier will come between them in the future.

It is helpful to analyze where counselees are when they come in for counseling. Some (perhaps most) are in Stage I, with a *barrier* between them. Some have sought and granted forgiveness (Stage II), but recognize that there is still a *break,* and don't know what is wrong. Others have moved to Stage III but are bogged down in the problems of effecting or developing a new relationship. It is useless to

I	II	III
O∥O	O O	O=O
Unreconciled Condition	Reconciled Condition	New Relationship
A BARRIER of bitterness between parties.	A BREAK remains when the barrier is removed by repentance and forgiveness.	A biblical BOND cemented between two parties.
Often left this way.	Sometimes left here.	Rarely left here.

work on a Stage III problem as though it were a Stage I problem, or on a Stage II problem as if it were a Stage III problem.

Counselors, then, must be concerned not merely to effect reconciliation—as important as that is—but must be content only when the *barrier* and the *break* are gone. They will be gone only when Colossians 3:14 is taken seriously. Love alone—the *bond* of new biblical giving relationships that must be developed—can bridge the gap and bring about future fellowship and unity. Work for this!

PUBLIC OR PRIVATE?

There seems to be some confusion among some counselors who, while intending to be biblical, nevertheless end up with an entirely unbiblical approach because they fail to distinguish two things that differ. A public offense—i.e., one against the whole body of Christ—is not the same as a private offense—i.e., one against an individual. The significance of this important distinction is that the process of Matthew 18:15-20 does not apply to offenses that are not personal. Personal offenses leading to an unreconciled condition must be pursued step by step in the manner outlined in these verses. Only as one of the parties refuses to be reconciled is the issue opened progressively (but reluctantly) to other persons (first to a counselor, or counselor team; then to the church; lastly to the world in excommunication). A desire to keep the matter as private as possible pervades the passage.

But let us say that a member of a congregation begins teaching heresy, or sins in some other public manner that harms Christ's name and the work of His church. In such cases it is *not* necessary to keep the matter private. The heresy must be refuted publicly (Titus 1:9-11). It is not a matter of a personal difficulty between two individuals.[1]

However, it is not enough merely to *refute*. There must also be an attempt to *redeem* the one who has gone wrong (cf. Titus 3:10, 11). In the case of the schismatic person, one or two nouthetic confrontations should be held. The attempt is to win the factious person. However, before he divides the flock—if one or two confrontations fail—he must be excommunicated.

Thus, differing processes must be kept in view when dealing with different situations. Counselors must be careful when stressing church discipline to apply those that fit each situation.

---

1. That may be one reason why John uses the plural form in III John 9b-10b, switching from "I" to "we, us."

DISCOURAGED COUNSELEES

Occasionally one finds a counselee in a unique situation. I might describe it as the discouragement of trailing behind. When a child gets hopelessly behind in a course at school, he tends to give up, cause problems, etc. (not that he *should* do any of these things. But he is likely to, because he is a sinner).

The same sort of thing can happen to a Christian who (as a result of his own sin, or because he is only a young Christian) gets behind the rest of the congregation. They have been growing, they have been learning, etc., but he has not; they have passed him by. Pretty soon he gets discouraged. They are talking about "sanctification," "eschatology," etc., and he still lacks assurance of his own salvation. So he withdraws more and more, soon losing interest and perhaps dropping out. He shouldn't; but as a sinner he does.

What can be done to help him? Two things:

(1) Urge him to talk to the pastor (unless you are the pastor) about the church program. In every congregation there should be something for everyone: for new converts, for repentant sinners, for mature, growing Christians. It is wrong to focus on any one of these groups to the exclusion of the others. Yet, the temptation to do so is great. Because of sin we all tend to be unbalanced; and, of course, we "can't do everything."

(2) Urge him to:

    a. Catch up. Help him to lay out a program for doing so.

    b. Take an interest in what the rest are doing and learning. If he doesn't understand, move in all the more (don't withdraw): ask questions, comment, try to do what is expected. In this way, interest will revive, others will become aware of the need to go more slowly, etc.

    c. Find another Christian who will disciple him.

Look for this phenomenon. I have a hunch that it occurs more frequently than we suspect. May your prayer be Paul's in II Thessalonians 2:16, 17 and your actions those described in I Thessalonians 5:14. These verses describe a church for all seasons—of men.

HOW LONG?

"Our marriage is in such bad shape that it will take a long time to put it back together again. After all, it didn't get this way overnight."

It is common for counselors to echo this sentiment. In fact, you even hear them saying things like this: "Now, you can't expect to solve a long-standing problem like this quickly."

The notion that is expressed in statements of this kind is both true and false. It is true if the counselee is looking for instant, miraculous change at the wave of a wand. Clearly, that isn't how change comes about. God doesn't "zap" such changes.

But if by not solving it quickly is meant months or years, that idea is definitely wrong. In response to the comment in the first paragraph a counselor might well find himself saying, "Not necessarily. If you and your wife had made a joint determined effort to destroy your marriage, you could have done so much more rapidly. So too, a joint, determined effort to save it by doing what God says can bring about changes more quickly than you may think."

Ideas like the one expressed in the first two paragraphs sound good, but fall apart when examined. Counselors, of all people, must become highly critical of trite expressions, seeming truisms and the like, which are in no sense biblical.

Let them, then, teach the biblical position: some change can be effected right away. More will come in time. But great changes can take place soon.

WHO NEEDS IT?

"Need!" What a greatly abused term in counseling! Over the last couple of years, again and again the word comes leaping from the page in a jarring way. I am not speaking only of how non-Christian writers misuse it; no, I am especially perturbed at the way believers do. Consider the following:

> The behavior comes not of the Spirit, but of the flesh. It "feels right" because the person is fulfilling the needs of a maladaptive personality.
>
> . . . The narcissist doesn't really believe this himself; this is why he needs many people to assure him repeatedly.
>
> The need to be right and the tendency toward self justification are marks of the exploiter. It is easy for him to confuse good leadership with his need to be right and to win.[1]

Obviously, from these quotations, Bustanoby knows that what he is talking about is sin. He calls the behavior in question "of the flesh," etc. Then why call *sinful* behavior a "need"? Who needs it?

Do you see what I mean? No? Then let me give you another example (and I haven't searched for these quotations; they are taken from books lying on my desk at the moment) or two—this time from non-Christian sources:

> Each person in a marriage must satisfy the basic need called stimulus hunger.[2]

All the rest come from various non-Christians who are discussing

---

1. From André Bustanoby, *You Can Change Your Personality* (Grand Rapids: Zondervan Publishing House, 1976), pp. 40, 41, 42.

2. Hedges and Betty Capers, in Herbert Otto, ed., *Marriage and Family Enrichment* (Nashville: Parthenon Press, 1976), p. 165.

adultery, why they took up swinging (wife, husband swapping), and what they got out of it:

— . . . now I seem to have the need for another lover as well.

— Well, it has to do with our own ego needs.

— This conversation is interesting because we're talking about our needs and trying to identify the tensions and the interplay of our needs.

— So you just sort of construct a world that suits your needs.[3]

Now, do you begin to see what I am talking about? The supposed needs (need to be right, need for someone to assure him, stimulus hunger, sex with someone else's spouse) are not *needs* at all.

According to the Scriptures, one's *needs* are relatively few: "If we have food and clothing, with these we shall be content" (I Tim. 6:8). And even these two needs are not to be a source of concern or worry: "For all these things the Gentiles eagerly seek; your heavenly Father knows that you need all these things."

What, then, are these so-called "needs"? Substitute the word *desire* for *need* wherever it occurs and you will have a biblical picture of what we have been talking about.

Why make so much of the terminology? Because of this important fact: Under the guise of meeting needs, sin is excused (Bustanoby and other Christian writers don't intend to excuse such behavior, of course, but they use terminology that does in a most confusing manner). These are not only desires, you see, but *sinful desires*.

That is why I am not making much ado over nothing when I point out the importance of using correct terminology in counseling. Much harm has been done in this field by those who under the cover of inexact terms have justified or (unwittingly) given counselees excuse to justify just about every error and sin one could imagine.

Biblical counselors must be careful when using the word *need,*[4] to refer to what the Bible calls a need—and nothing else. Especially, with the apostle Peter, must they properly identify sinful desire for what it is (cf. I Pet. 1:14; 2:11; 4:2, 3; II Pet. 2:10, 18; 3:3).

---

3. Wm. H. Masters and Virginia E. Johnson, *The Pleasure Bond* (New York: Bantam Books, 1975), pp. 118, 152, 154, 156.

4. There are, naturally, nontechnical situations in which the word may be used in a more relaxed manner (particularly in its verbal forms). But this semi-technical substitution of *need* for *desire* must always be avoided.

USE OR LOVE

Things are for use; persons are for loving. When people reverse this and love things, they also end up using persons.

That is one thing that Christ had in mind when He spoke about seeking *"first* the kingdom of God and His righteousness" (Matt. 6). "Then," He continued, "all these *things* will be *added* to you." To seek God's kingdom and righteousness is, in effect, to seek to express love toward God. It means to care about Him and His concerns more than about your own. It is the demonstration of a desire to please Him.

The word "first" is a word of priority. Things in themselves are not wrong; but when sought *first* they become idols that take God's rightful place.

It is an important insight into people to know that persons (God and neighbor) or things are set over against one another in the Scriptures in this way. By determining whether a counselee sets a priority on things, the counselor can discover something about his concern for God and other persons. People who love things and use persons must be brought to repentance. Then they can be helped to seek first God's kingdom and righteousness. People who use persons always do so because they are in love with things. The counselor can use this insight to move in either direction. If he discovers a counselee using persons, he can be sure he has a problem in his priorities about things. If he sees that the counselee loves things, he can know that he also uses people.

IS GRACE "CHEAP"?

Bonhoeffer has done us both a service and disservice by popularizing the catch-phrase, "cheap grace." By this he means a forgiveness that does not really forgive because it is granted too easily, demands nothing of the one forgiven and, therefore, fails to erase his sense of guilt. Counselors, who must speak often of guilt and grace, must be aware of the problems raised by this challenge.

True grace is never cheap. By its very nature it cannot be. Bonhoeffer is correct in observing that there can be a kind of forgiveness that is too easy. Jeremiah, for instance, denounces the priests and prophets who "healed" God's people "slightly," saying "Peace, peace, when there is no peace" (Jer. 6:14). Such a "forgiveness" is not Christian forgiveness, however, because it has nothing to do with the grace of God. As a matter of fact, it is not even forgiveness, as the Bible describes forgiveness. Bonhoeffer's straw man really has nothing to do with either *grace* or *forgiveness*. What Bonhoeffer should have said is that there is a cheap *substitute* for Christian grace and forgiveness.

What is grace, and why can it never be "cheap"? Grace is the unmerited favor and love that God shows toward men, who have becomed estranged from Himself and their fellow men. This estrangement is caused by sin. Sin separates. Man is estranged in two dimensions, corresponding to the two aspects of God's law that he has violated. That law, the Ten Commandments, is the standard of man's relationship both to God and to others. This dual reference is inherent in the teaching of the Scriptures of both the Old and the New Testaments. That is why in His summary of the law, Jesus declared that the fulfillment of the law consists of loving God with all the heart and one's neighbor as one's self. This recognition of the vertical as well as the horizontal dimension is necessary to any counseling that would endeavor to reach the whole man. Cheap substitutes for grace heal only slightly; counseling that pays attention to only one dimension heals only slightly more.

But what is grace? It is God's unmerited favor in Christ to persons whose sin has made them His enemies. Through sin they have become thoroughly *self*-centered. Both their sin and God's favor reached definitive expression in Jesus' substitutionary death, when, in stark contrast to man's rejection, He suffered for the sins of His *enemies*. The grace that God gives, then, is not cheap, since it cost Christ His life. Grace is not cheap because of the suffering that it cost Christ to take the sin of another.

Thus, as the grace of God reaches out to reconcile His people to Himself, so their loving favor must reach out to reconcile others to themselves. This movement toward others is not cheap either, because it inevitably involves the bearing of the pain and suffering that the sharing of the burdens caused by their transgressions entails (cf. Gal. 6:1, 2). Moreover, love shown to others makes one vulnerable, as love always does. He who loves runs the risk of rebuff. When he lays bare his heart, others may run over it with track shoes.

But this is one side of the picture. From a different perspective, God's grace is not cheap because it demands the admission on the part of the one to be forgiven that he has been wrong, that he is a sinful rebel, that he is guilty and deserving of hell. He must confess that his sins put Jesus Christ to death. That is what faith confesses: "Christ died for my sins." Otherwise God's grace cannot be appropriated. Yet, while such an admission is hard, it is not meritorious, since no one so confesses his sin apart from the prior gracious work of God's Spirit in his life. This is the meaning of the Christian's confession of faith in Christ; by it he declares that he has sinned against God and man and needs forgiveness. By it he also "loses" his life for Christ's sake (only to truly find it thereby). Yet faith in Christ means total rejection of all else as efficacious—including all that one has done himself.

Whenever such a confession is genuine, it does not end with forgiveness. Repentance is a change of mind leading to a change in one's way of life. It is not enough for him to affirm that he has been wrong in the way that he has lived toward God and others, but he must be sorry enough for it to intend no longer to walk the same road. To do something about it is critical. That means that so far as he is able to, he must demonstrate that change of life by restitution, etc. Counselors must keep this in mind.

But why do some who seek forgiveness fail to receive it? Because they want it on their own terms. Because they want it without any reference to God's way of forgiveness—they want it apart from the death of Christ. That is to say, they want some cheap substitute for true grace. They want to utter a prayer, magically receive a pardon and be done with it all. They want to maintain their integrity, refuse to acknowledge their sins, and want to "save" their lives (thereby "losing" them). But forgiveness is not like that. It costs. It costs God and it costs the sinner. Any forgiveness that costs God nothing is not forgiveness. Some are willing for forgiveness to cost God so long as it costs them nothing! They will accept Christ's work as a *supplement* to their own. (Of course this is impossible since His work is substitutionary, not supplementary.) Others are willing to acknowledge their sin but want to hear nothing of repentance. They avoid words like those of Ezekiel:

> If he turns from his sin, and does what is lawful and fair—he restores the pledge and gives back what he has robbed, follows the statutes of life, and does no wrong—he shall surely live; he shall not die (Ezek. 33:14-15).

Neither of these alternatives is possible. Grace cost Christ His life; faith means sinners giving up theirs too. This emphasis is in no way a repudiation of justification by faith. Saving faith in another *thereby* demands wholehearted abandonment of self. Wholehearted trust in Christ *alone* is what biblical faith is all about. Justification that comes by faith, moreover, always issues in works that are appropriate to repentance. Yes, grace costs. It cost God His Son, and it costs its recipients their lives too.

Carelessly crossing the street, you step into the path of a speeding automobile. A bystander, sizing up the situation, makes the critical decision in a flash and rushes into the street, pushing you to safety, but is himself seriously injured. Here is an instance of grace—unmerited favor. Because of his mercy shown toward you, he became involved, and it cost him dearly. But it also costs you. You too are deeply involved. Surely you don't walk away from the scene leaving him in a pool of blood, musing, "That sure was a close shave for me." His grace toward you has created a new relationship toward him. You

46

render what first aid you can, call an ambulance, accompany him to the hospital, and anxiously await the report of the doctors. During his convalescence you send flowers, express your gratitude in any number of ways, continually asking if there is anything else you can do for him. His grace has made claims on you. His grace, costing him, has captured you, changed you and cost you. Your gratitude has related you to him. So much is this so that, other conditions allowing, it is likely that the two of you will become lifelong friends. Jesus Christ gave His life for His own and has made them His own; they do not walk on heedlessly, saying, "close shave!"

Grace is not cheap; it costs both the giver and the receiver. It costs both their lives. One died for the other; the other must now live for Him. But there are cheap substitutes around. Christian counselors must be clear about these issues. Is the real reason why Christian grace is rejected because it costs *too* much?

23

COUNSELING FOR DISCIPLINE

A TRIPLE PROBLEM—AND OPPORTUNITY

Let me say it right off and be done with it: Every parent who sets out to train his children might as well recognize from the start that he will also be involved in training himself. This is the double challenge and the double opportunity of parenthood. Let it be said too that woe is the counselor who doesn't count on calling parents to this double task in counseling.

From the outset, the counselor must help the parents to come to commitments about their own lives. Until they are willing to regulate their own living patterns and with consistency patiently pursue those things that will lead to new disciplined living in the lives of their children, the prospect of discipline will remain remote. So the counselor must help them to face this fact from the first session.

It is particularly important not to allow the parents of the children needing discipline to start out training in an *undisciplined* way. They will lead to discouragement for both parents and children. Moreover, bad *new* patterns of inconsistency, etc., will develop within the counseling context and this will make it harder for everyone later on. It is stupid to allow or encourage patterns that you will only have to change later. So it is also essential for the counselor to accept the challenge; he too must be willing to be consistent in disciplining the parents in the discipline of their children.

Two vital steps must be followed:

1. The counselor must explain to the parents that discipline comes through patient, persistent and consistent effort. He must help them to analyze their own living patterns (go to bed, get up regularly, on schedule, etc.) and the ways in which they have disciplined their children in the past to discover wrong elements

that must be changed. He must then get a commitment from them that grows out of nothing less than counting the cost of such change as is needed on their part.

2. Thereafter, he must patiently, persistently and consistently check up on how they are applying discipline in the home. Every crucial point in the program must be checked out at *every* session to be sure that the commitment is being kept. The counselor must discipline himself to discipline the discipliners. This, in itself, will help the parents to develop and maintain consistency. It is easy to slip up on weekly checkups, so in order to be sure, it is wise for the counselor to develop a checklist for the parents, keep a copy in his file folder and go over *every* item with the parents at *every* session.

Actually, the triple benefit of such efforts is that not only the children, but parents *and counselor too,* will become more disciplined persons.

24

ON THE TEACHING OF COUNSELING

For close to eleven years I have been teaching Christian counseling with a fair measure of success. Now, by God's grace, I discover that in Bible colleges and theological seminaries, in laymen's seminars and groups, others have been teaching nouthetic counseling too. I think it might be of value, therefore, to share a few of the insights gained during that experience to aid others and to steer them around the many potholes into which they might otherwise fall. What follows is by no means exhaustive, and is offered for whatever value it might have.

Ideally, in the teaching of counseling I have discovered that, as in the teaching of any skill (and counseling *is* a skill, whatever else it also may be), the use of the discipleship method, consisting of the following elements, is essential:

1. *Theory*

—presented didactically and discussed illustratively (together with examples, case histories, role plays, diagrams, etc.). That is why I have used such diagrams as the anger arc[1] (next page).

Visualized, the solution to the anger problem becomes clear, vivid and memorable. Abstract teaching of a complex dynamic such as this one is harder for many to comprehend.

Moreover, vivid language, live illustrations to which trainees vibrate, that (like Christ's parables) "incarnate" a principle or practice in paradigmatic form, are very useful. One can refer, for instance, to the woman with the manuscript of wrongs her husband committed against her at any time to make the point that the counselor must sort

---

1. For more details, see similar diagram: *Manual*, p. 350.

Problem

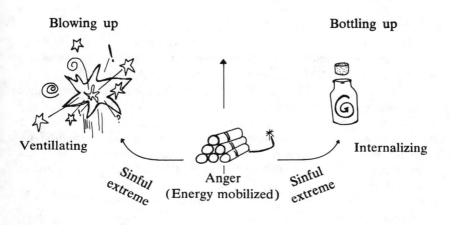

Blowing up   Bottling up

Ventillating   Internalizing

Sinful extreme   Anger   *Sinful extreme*
(Energy mobilized)

Anger released toward others, destroying them	to destroy problem Biblical Center	Anger released toward self, destroying self

Anger released under control

out responsibilities (her husband couldn't put ulcers in her stomach by his sins against her; it was her sinful response to his sins that did so). Bitterness, resentment, etc., can all be tied into this example whenever discussing it.

2. *Observation*

When a painter wants to learn how to paint, he must:
  a. look at paintings (study counseling cases)
  b. watch a painter at work mixing his oils, applying them with the brush (observe counseling).

The same is true of would-be counselors. They need to study cases and sit in on counseling sessions. At the Christian Counseling &

Educational Center and other NANC-approved[2] training centers, such observation is made available to pastors in regular courses.

3. *Discussion*

It is not enough to observe. A trainee needs to be able to discuss what he has observed with the teacher or teachers involved in doing the counseling that he has observed. This was Christ's teaching method. He held seminars with His disciples to discuss the events that they observed. Observation plus discussion ("Why did you do that? What were you trying to accomplish when you said so and so? Did I notice something significant when I saw the counselee brighten up at the mention of homework?" These and hundreds of other such questions need to be asked and answered in detail. NANC centers do this sort of training too).

Discussion also means that the discipling teacher (cf. the last chapter in *The Big Umbrella*) should ask questions of the trainee ("Did you notice how I pressed the issue concerning the mother-in-law?") and make observations that might otherwise be missed ("In the next session I intend to take up this question of priorities again. Notice, when I do, what he *says*").

4. *Practice Under Supervision*

The counselor-trainee can study, observe and discuss counseling until the cows come home, but that will not make him a counselor. He must begin to *do* counseling himself, preferably under supervision (to a limited extent trainees can get such supervised training at NANC training centers. For a few, this sort of supervised training in depth is also provided). Supervision means observation of the trainee as he counsels, help by co-counseling, discussing techniques and practices and help in counseling done outside the center.

5. *Practice*

Practice in counseling on one's own, but with help available when requested, on a consultative and/or general supervision basis, is valuable. By general supervision is meant that the trainee discusses

---

2. The National Association of Nouthetic Counselors (an accrediting association for Christian counselors and training centers founded in October, 1976). For information, write: NANC, 1790 E. Willow Grove Ave., Laverock, Pa. 19118.

his case between sessions with supervisory personnel. (This service is also provided at NANC centers for a limited number of trainees.)

6. *Instruction*

When a person has had opportunity to train others successfully through the use of the same six steps, he will know that he has learned how to counsel. When he can explain theory and practice, show what he is talking about as an example and helpfully discuss what he is doing with others whom he is training, they too will be able to attest to the fact. (For a very limited number, NANC training centers provide such opportunity.)

These six steps constitute the full process of discipleship (or apprenticeship[3]) training. Any system of teaching that omits one or more of these elements is defective. Those whose training consisted of less should recognize the fact and either (by trial and error) get the various elements on their own, or should become involved with others who may be able to help them.[4]

---

3. The two are similar. They stem from the father/son trade relationship. The biblical method is based on the Father/Son relationship that Christ revealed when He said that all that He did or said was what He first had seen or heard the Father do and say (cf. John 3:32; 5:19, 20; 8:28, 31). The discipleship method is more than academic (a pagan Greek model); it involves both show and tell.

4. Cf. my *What About Nouthetic Counseling?*, pp. 90, 91.

25

A NOTE ON HELPING HOMOSEXUALS

One of the most common fears that homosexuals express in counseling is the fear that in marriage they would not be able to "perform" adequately for their wives (i.e., to become sexually aroused for intercourse). The fact is, as we wish to point out scripturally, they do not have to "perform." According to I Corinthians 7:3, 4, God requires that

> . . . the husband fulfill his duty to his wife, and likewise also the wife to her husband.
>
> The wife does not have authority over her own body, but the husband does; and likewise also the husband does not have authority over his own body, but the wife does.

Two facts may be pointed out: (1) Sexual relations are a marriage *duty.* Any duty can be fulfilled if it is done God's way, even when one has problems connected with it. (2) Neither the husband nor the wife is required to "prepare" his/her own body for sexual relations. They have no authority over their own bodies. Thus, the prime fear of the former homosexual is averted. His part of the relationship consists of learning to prepare his wife's body for sexual relations. He must focus upon *giving,* giving pleasure and bringing fulfillment to her. He must not focus upon *getting,* i.e., upon his own body and what pleasure and fulfillment he wants. That is the difference between love and lust. Love *gives* to another; homosexual (or heterosexual) lust focuses upon what one can *get.* His wife's task is to "prepare" him. He has no authority over his own body. Authority and responsibility go together. His wife's authority over his body (and his lack of it) implies *her* responsibility for it.

So, one of the greatest fears of marriage that former homosexuals have is averted, since the Scriptures require him to please and satisfy his wife, not himself. She may need to take special care and make extra efforts (counseling during the first few weeks of marriage would be advisable), but there is no reason why this cannot be achieved, as dozens of former homosexuals and their wives who have consummated Christian marriages successfully have testified. But one of the critical factors to overcome was right at this point. Counselors must understand and be ready to apply the love-giving principle of I Corinthians 7:4.

Incidentally, it is often wise to point out too that, since it is more blessed to give than to receive, pleasing and fulfilling one's wife (or husband) has a boomerang effect—as a by-product it stimulates and excites the other partner too. On two counts, then, the difficulty is erased by application of the biblical principle.

26

JUDGING MOTIVES; BEING SIMPLISTIC

One of the most interesting challenges I have faced in a long time occurred this past year during a 15-minute question-and-answer period following a lecture that I gave at a theological seminary. A charge (not a question) was made by the faculty member of a Christian college who was a guest at the meeting. He accused me of:

1. "flattering" students to gain their acquiescence in my views;

2. trying to get them to read my books by not presenting substantive counseling positions (in the 35 minutes that I had been allotted for my lecture).

The incident came as a surprise (it was the first time I had ever been accused of flattery—usually, I get the opposite objection if I receive any at all). Initially I was somewhat amused—its intended sting failed to materialize and the student body and the professors (so far as I could tell) appeared to be turned off by the tactlessness and bad taste of the visitor. "Well, why not drop the issue then?" That is exactly what I intended to do. But upon reflection I have decided to analyze and discuss it as the background for a vital matter that Christian counselors should consider. It is one that turns out to be not too amusing after all—the tendency of some self-styled "professionals" to attack *persons* rather than the *principles* that they hold; to *call names* rather than to *evaluate viewpoints;* to *judge motives* rather than *words, actions and results.* On every score, this is what happened that day.

But it didn't happen only there. Perhaps you, like I, have become increasingly aware of this tendency in book reviews, magazine articles, etc. Frankly I find it deplorable among Christian writers and speakers, not because it has happened to me, but because it destroys the climate that is necessary for serious discussion and debate.

How can you discuss matters further with a person whose motives you believe are to flatter students and talk them into buying his books? (Incidentally, I didn't so much as mention my books.) The immediate effect of this approach—whether intended or not—is to bypass his views. You certainly don't want to join issues with such an unworthy person, and how can you take his presentation seriously anyway—wasn't it all a cover for his *real* purposes? Immediately debate is silenced, concern is shifted from issues to persons, and principles are undermined in this secondary manner, rather than in a healthy clash of viewpoints.

It is somewhat strange, in light of other remarks (I shall mention) made by the same individual that he should challenge me the way he did; but I have not found that consistency is the general rule among those who attempt to discredit a person's views by discrediting the person himself. Those other remarks were that my lecture was "anti-intellectual." I have examined the lecture and fail to see a shred of evidence upon which to base the charge, since I strongly commended scholarship and urged stringent academic effort and progress. To call another anti-intellectual in a tirade that one of the seminary professors later characterized as "a totally anti-intellectual critique" on his part is the inconsistency to which I refer. But again, you see, if what a man says is dubbed anti-intellectual, why bother to grapple with it? Content can be dismissed as "beneath one." But which is more anti-intellectual, to denounce a person's motives and his lecture or to come to grips with its thrust?

The final charge that he made was that my position was simplistic; yet he didn't specify. Such a generalization needs to be supported by evidence. Otherwise, it becomes merely a name-calling technique that also serves to quash real discussion of issues and allows the one who employs it to slide out of any confrontation of issues. Again, why waste your time discussing a viewpoint that is "simplistic"?

I have taken the time to analyze this incident not out of vindictiveness—I have purposely avoided the names of persons—but as a paradigm for Christian counselors to help make them aware of the kinds of attacks to which they too may be subjected if they persevere in Christian counseling.

One other reason why I have written this is to suggest a response or two that might be made to such charges.

First, let's consider the flattery and wanting-to-sell-your-books charge. The basic problem here was that the accuser was judging motives. At the time I was not quick enough to think through what was happening and I was pressed for time (he had taken all the rest of the 15 minutes allotted for questions) and did not answer adequately—I simply denied the charge. But I now know what to do the next time if I am forced to face this sort of attack again verbally or in print. I suggest that you might consider it too.

I intend, on any future occasion, to do this:

1. I shall explain that the Scriptures do not allow Christians to judge one another's motives. ("Man looks on the outward appearance; God looks on the heart," I Sam. 16:7. See also James 4:11, 12.) God, then, allows us to judge only behavior and words (even then, we must be extremely careful to "make a righteous judgment," John 7:24). Matt 7:1-5 tells how to do so.
2. I shall explain that he has violated that biblical commandment by stating that my motives were flattery and avarice.
3. I shall call on him to repent before God and man and to seek forgiveness of both.

In dealing with charges of a simplistic approach, the basic problem is that confrontation of viewpoints is thereby avoided by denouncing an opposing view as unworthy of serious discussion. Such name-calling coupled with charges of anti-intellectualism attacks the competence of the one who has set forth the views that are so attacked. I have covered the charge of a simplistic approach elsewhere,[1] and will not develop it further here. Instead, let me suggest that words like "simplistic" and "anti-intellectual" may rightly be used to characterize a system, but when they are so used, they ought to be supported by evidence. Any other use is itself hopelessly simplistic and anti-intellectual. I will, therefore, demand a thoroughgoing explanation, complete with supporting evidence and argumentation. Anything less, I fear, would be simplistic.

---

1. *What About Nouthetic Counseling?*, pp. 2-4.

27

A TEST CASE

"So you've had another run-in with sister Carruthers, Martha?"

"Not exactly. We didn't actually fight or argue . . . but . . .well, you know how it is—we disagreed, she was adamant and so was I and . . . Oh, I just don't want to work with her on that committee any longer. She always has to have her way. . . . She doesn't listen to anybody else's opinions, cares less about their feelings and . . . well, after the meeting, I went right up to the pastor and resigned. I guess that's about all there is to it."

"You resigned! I thought you told me that you had been looking forward to being elected to that committee for months! I remember the first day that you came home after hearing about your election— you were enthusiastic and all excited about how you could do so much to serve the Lord in this way. Why you. . . ."

"I know it; and I haven't changed my mind one bit about the importance of the work that we can do in Pioneer Girls. But I must confess, my enthusiasm certainly has cooled since I discovered that Violet Carruthers intends to carry on in her same old ways. After all, she is only one member of the steering committee; others were elected to express their opinions too!"

"Mmm . . . Honey, I don't think you should resign. I think you ought to *deal* with this problem, not give up. Who knows, maybe you could even help Violet."

"Well, I'd like to—but *how?* That's the real question. It's one thing to tell me to do something, but it's another to tell me *how.*"

"I guess you've got a point there. I'm not sure; but I'll tell you what we can do—we'll go to the pastor and ask him. He'll be able to tell you how."

You are the pastor. What would you say? Where would you begin? What biblical guidelines would you follow?

It is better to think through such problems on paper before you have to face them in your study. Why not take the time to jot down five or six thoughts that would serve as guidelines? It is good from time to time to tackle a test case. This one is relatively simple. To help you, let me ask a few suggestive questions.

1. Would you let Martha talk negatively about Violet?
2. If so, how much would you allow her to say (what sorts of things)?
3. If not, then how would you be able to help Martha with her problem?
4. Would you want to ask Violet to sit in at some point? If so, at what point? For what purposes?
5. What would you advise concerning the resignation?
6. What are some of Martha's problems?
7. How could you help her see them and what would God want her to do about each?
8. Would you want to involve Martha's husband some way, knowing what sort of man he is?

NOTES

NOTES

28

ONE ANOTHER

One of the great things that pastoral counselors can do to help Christian counselees is to introduce them into the fellowship of other members of his congregation. Encouragement is vital to sustain one between counseling sessions and through difficult changes. Yet not all of that encouragement can be given by the counselor himself. That is one reason why it is important to introduce them to others who will show such concern.

The words "one another" appear all over the New Testament. The frequency with which they appear indicates the importance of mutual fellowship in Christian growth. It is clear that we can help one another. But what should they do when they get together as Christians? Hebrews 10:24, 25 reads,

> Let us consider how to stimulate one another to love and good deeds . . . encouraging one another. . . .

Notice there are three things to emphasize to both the counselees and the stronger Christians to whom they are introduced. Tell them:

First, you must *stimulate* one another.

The word "stimulate" is literally "irritate, provoke." It has the idea of shaking loose things in the other person's life that otherwise might stay put. The use of the term in Acts 15:39 shows how powerful the contact indicated by this word can be. Of course, it doesn't really mean to cause trouble. But it certainly is not a mild term. It means contact that shakes up another.

Secondly, you must *consider how* to do this. That means thought and effort. Such things can't be done well off the cuff. It takes work. How? Through hard, exact, prayerful study, discussion and application of the Scriptures.

Lastly, you must stimulate one another *to love and good works*. This is certainly an important qualification to add to the first point.

Contact—shaking up one another—should be calculated to lead to love and good works; and should be encouraging (v. 25). It takes bold contact with impact, but only after prayerful consideration, to do so. All three work together.

Group activities must follow these important biblical rules carefully, or difficulties are bound to arise. Instruction given to couples or individuals whom you *train* in these three critical points will pay off when you have counselees who could benefit from their stimulating encouragement.

PRIORITIES

When Jesus said, "Seek God's kingdom and His righteousness *first*" (Matt. 6:33), He was setting priorities. The Christian counselor learns from this that counselees have problems with priorities. He investigates priorities, and helps counselees to set biblical priorities.

For instance, when helping a missionary family, he may have occasion to challenge them (and their board, if necessary) about the sin of putting work before children. He may have to challenge a wife about putting children before husband, etc. These problems are fairly well known.

But what about the not-quite-so-common problem that arises when the counselor discovers that the counselee has many items on the same level of priority? How does he analyze this, and what does he do about it?

Often, the lack of priorities indicates a lethargic, who-cares attitude. I am not saying which is the chicken and which is the egg (either could be). A wrong attitude readily could lead to a levelling of enthusiasm (neither hot nor cold about anything). On the other hand, an attempt to play no favorites, and thus handle all matters on the same level of priority, first, could lead to frustration and then to a who-cares attitude. Either way—and they spiral in a dog-chasing-his-tail fashion—the result is the same: no real priorities in life.

Too many priorities means that there are no high-priority items. It is the counselor's task, then, to discover just how the counselee is failing to put God's kingdom and righteousness first; how he is putting things first (or on the same level). Then, he must help him (concretely) to figure out what putting the kingdom and righteousness first in his life means.

THE HUMAN / DIVINE IN COUNSELING

There always have been problems in the church in relating the human and divine elements in sanctification. The error of those who have gone astray has been in stressing one element to the exclusion (or at least deemphasis) of the other. At present, there is some danger from a moralistic, do-it-yourself, arm of flesh approach for counseling that ignores the work of the Holy Spirit. I have warned about this elsewhere.[1] But my concern here is to take up an equally persistent and pernicious error—the deemphasis of human responsibility.

There is a very pious-sounding movement abroad that takes many forms. Various leaders might be mentioned. It has been around for some time, but only recently has begun to exert influence into the counseling field. Here, most prominently, it is advocated in one form by Charles Solomon under the name Spirituotherapy, Inc. What I am about to say, however, will approach the problem generally—not in terms of specific authors or viewpoints.

Generally speaking, the movement can be recognized by phrases and expressions such as, "Let Christ live His life through you," "Let go and let God," etc. The intent of this movement is good, but the statement of the problem and the practical outworking of the doctrine in counseling contexts is horrendous.

What is intended, doubtless, is to throw the counselee completely upon God for the solutions to his problems. This is commendable. The desire is to eliminate self-righteous activity in which Christian counselees, like pagans, turn to their own resources rather than depend upon the resources of God. Again, this is commendable. I can find no fault with either of these intentions and teach (and have taught) the same from the beginning. Where, then, does the differ-

1. *Manual*, pp. 3-8.

ence arise? I have said in the statement of the problem. Instead of stating that the Christian is wrong in pursuing a course of activity in his own wisdom and strength, but should prayfully turn instead to God's wisdom in the Bible and seek the Holy Spirit's power to do what the Bible enjoins, they say the Christian is wrong in pursuing the course of activity, and in trying to do what the Bible enjoins— period! What is wrong, say they, is that the Christian, himself, is trying to do anything at all. Rather, he should be getting out of the way and allowing God, the Holy Spirit, to do it instead. If he will stop living his life, Christ will live His life within him. If he will stop doing altogether, the Holy Spirit will start doing instead.

The difference is subtle, but critical. According to the view propounded, just about everything written concerning nouthetic counseling is wrong. Always, our emphasis has been upon *doing* what God commands, *by His strength.* Who is right?

It is useless to try to debate separate texts. The fundamental clash is broader and more structural (although one might with force emphasize a large part of the Book of James, which talks about the doer of the Word). The important main point to grasp is this: doing God's will is not a mystical quiescent experience. It is a matter of Spirit-powered obedience. The Christian is not told to "Let go and let God" in the sense that God does the believing and God does the obeying for him. There is the crux of the matter—*who* does the believing and obeying?

There can be only one *biblical* answer to the question: the Christian himself everywhere (that's why I say it's a structural issue—how you interpret *every* passage) is enjoined to trust and obey. Everywhere (at the same time) he is told that he cannot do so in a way that honors God unless he is given help by the Holy Spirit. Yet it is *he,* not Christ, who believes and does.

If those who hold to the passive view were correct, life would be much simpler. All we would need to do is renounce self, get more and more out of Christ's way every day until soon we would be free from all other responsibilities. In fact, we would have a New Testament that could be written in but a few paragraphs. Instead of those long biblical treatises like I Corinthians on what we must become, how we must shape up, what we must do, it would simply explain, "Let go, and let God."

No, friend, coming down to earth again to the Bible we see a hard road of pruning (John 15), of growth, of change, of struggle like an athlete or soldier. *We* are involved in this, not Christ only. It is "the life *I* live," that I live by Christ who is in me and Who will *strengthen me.* He doesn't weaken me, but strengthens me. When I am weak *in my own strength,* then He strengthens *me* with His glorious might. Why am I strengthened if He is going to do it all? No, He strengthens *me* to enable *me* to live and look like Him. In that way others will come to know that He indwells me.

Occasionally, the Christian counselor will meet counselees who have been marinated in this ideology. The best way I know to combat it is to distinguish clearly between who the Scriptures say must trust and obey; thus we rely wholly on Christ for sanctification. We rely wholly upon Him when we (not He) believe and obey His Word by His strength granted in grace to us.

THREE ENEMIES

Historically Christians, with good biblical reason, have spoken about the believer's three enemies as the world, the flesh and the devil:

The World = problems in the scene (there)
The Flesh = problems in me (here)
The Devil = problems behind the scene (beyond)

The problems that a counselee brings to his counselor, therefore, will have three dimensions—even when the emphasis may be upon only one or two of them. Counseling can be incomplete if it fails to reckon with all three.

It is important for the counselor to make clear to the counselee the multidirectional nature of his struggle. The environment (scene) in which he lives exerts various pressures on him. There are times when he must break old associations (persons, places, activities—cf. I Cor. 15:33[1]) and cement new ones instead. His own habits by which his behavior is patterned (flesh; for more on this, see *Lectures,* pp. 231-238) must be changed. The biblical put off/put on dehabituation/rehabituation dynamic (see chapters on this in the *Manual*) is essential to all change that sticks. And, one must recognize that he is involved in a spiritual struggle behind the scene too (cf. *How to Overcome Evil* on this). Otherwise he may not be aware of the evil one's schemes, and may trip over the many stumblingblocks that Satan puts in his way.

Somewhere, somehow, in every series of counseling sessions then, the counselee must be alerted to the full range of difficulties with which he is grappling. Only then will he avail himself of the full range of resources that God has provided.

---

1. Often the counselor must stress the first half of the verse: "Don't fool yourself. . . ." Counselees proverbially will protest that they don't need to abandon old associates.

CHURCH DISCIPLINE

Many Christians who think that they have done all that they can to solve their problems have not yet begun to do what Jesus Christ requires. So counselors must do all they can to instruct them about this fact.

When you tell them so, it sounds surprising. They may not even believe it. They may protest, "Now wait a minute. My husband and I have been having problems all these years, and I've tried everything . . . *everything*. There isn't *anything* more to do. I even went to a good Christian friend (or to my pastor) and asked if there was anything more, and he said he didn't know of anything. He thought that I was doing everything that I could do."

In response I say, "If you're a Christian, if your husband's a Christian, there is always a way to solve that problem between the two of you."

The answer to the problem does not lie in some kind of mysticism. It isn't a matter of saying, "Well, I'll leave it all in God's hands and hope that it works out for the best. After all, all things work together for good for those who love God, who are the called according to His purpose." Now that verse is a wonderful comfort. And there are times when we can say, "Well, there's nothing more that can be done about this situation." But it's not the time to say that when two Christians are involved in a relationship that has gone sour. The only time to say that is when there is an *unbeliever* and a Christian involved in an impasse (Rom. 12:18).

Many Christians think they have done all God requires when, as I say, they have only begun. "Well," they say, "why don't you get to it and stop all these preliminaries?" All right. Part of your problem may be impatience, but let's go on anyway.

Matthew 18:15, 16 and 17 gives us a very important clue about how to solve problems that don't seem to be getting solved any other way.

It is concerned with how to solve problems between Christians. This is a neglected area, and yet it is an extremely valuable portion of the Word of God to understand. It deals with church discipline. "Church discipline?!" Yes, church discipline. "Aw, c'mon. Church discipline is just the way that you get rid of troublemakers in church." That's the response so many give. If that's what church discipline has meant to you, or if that's what it's meant to your congregation, then that is not church discipline as the Bible looks at it. That's church discipline abused, not properly used.

Church discipline is not intended to get rid of anybody. At every point in the disciplinary process that Christ outlined, the whole concern is to bring about reconciliation, not to get rid of anybody.

Now let's look at that passage a little more clearly. There are three steps in church discipline.

First: Verse 15 says, "If your brother sins, go and reprove him in private. If he listens to you, you have won your brother."

Now that first step I want to discuss briefly. Sometimes Christians go this far, but very rarely. Most of the problems that we have with others, that go on and on and on for weeks or years even, could be solved if we just simply did what this first step says to do. If the counselee has been sinned against, he is to go and tell his brother about it, to go with the facts and the data, and to face him up with the problem, simply, plainly and straightforwardly. Now it doesn't say go in the spirit of nastiness. It doesn't say go, in order to tell the other guy off. It says to tell him about the problem. Counselors must warn about going in the wrong way. Many times problems aren't resolved simply because we don't tell the other person about them. He doesn't even know that we've taken offense. He doesn't know that he's stepped on our toes. And so, he doesn't come to us. No reconciliation takes place. We stand there folding our arms, saying, "Well, let him come," whereas he doesn't even know that there is a problem.

It's the obligation of the offended party to go, as well as the obligation of the offender if he knows that he's offended another. That's the first thing to see in verse 15. "Go and reprove him." but notice . . . "in private." You don't advise him to go to the church, to all of his friends or to his neighbors. You don't let him go talk about another behind his back. You say, "Go and talk to *him*." Keep the facts as private as the offense itself was in the first place.

And the purpose for which he goes is mentioned in the last part of the verse. He wants the other to acknowledge his sin, or to straighten out any misunderstandings. He wants him to hear what he has to say, so that the two may become reconciled once again. It says, "if he listens to you, you have won your brother."

That's what he wants; not to get rid of somebody. But the first step of church discipline, an informal step that any individual in the church may take with any other individual, has one main goal and purpose to it. And that is, to win one's brother.

The counselee may respond, "But you said that I could do this with my husband (or wife), or with my parents, or with my children." The counselor answers: "Yes, I did. If there is any Christian brother or sister with whom you are unable to work out affairs in any other way, you may go and you may talk to that person about what is wrong. If problems continue to separate the two of you, you need to straighten those matters out by first going to that other person."

"But I'm supposed to be subject to my husband." Or, "I'm supposed to be subject to my parents. I can't go and *reprove them*, can I?" Of course you can. Subjection and reproof are two entirely separate and different matters. Reproof, as this passage looks at it, is in no way inconsistent with subjection. Subjection has to do not only with *what* you do, but *how* you do it. If you go in a submissive manner, in the proper recognition of your relationship to that parent or to your husband, who bears the authority of God, you may reprove him. Remember, Nathan reproved David. He was able to reprove the *king,* in spite of all the authority that had been given to him as king. Authority is not limitless. Authority in the Bible is limited by the Bible itself.

And so, what your counselee must do is go in a right and submissive spirit, one that recognizes his proper relationship to the other. He must be certain that he really is seeking to win the brother back. He must be seeking reconciliation. If he goes in that manner, he can speak about anything that's wrong between them. God may straighten out the problem right on that very level itself.

We have been talking about the values, privileges and right of church discipline. Every believer in Jesus Christ has the right to be disciplined. Counselees may say, "That's the kind of right I can do without." No, they can't. Church discipline is extremely important.

Discipline is not some process that God has given to get rid of all kinds of troublemakers in the church, as a lot of people think, though it might do that, at times. But that's not its main purpose. The main purpose of church discipline is to win others back to the Lord, and to bring about reconciled conditions between brothers.

Many people, remember, think they've done all they can do to try to solve a problem, when they haven't even begun to do the things that the Bible tells them to do. And in a super-pious fashion, that isn't pious at all because it isn't biblical, they just leave the whole thing mystically in the hands of God, rather than following His directions in the power of the Spirit of God.

And those directions are found in Matthew 18:15-17. Jesus says that if two brothers are having problems with one another they are to go to one another. That's the first step that we talked about—it does not say wait for him to come. Of course, he's obligated to do so, if he recognizes his sin. But the offended party is always to go to the brother. He is the one who always is aware of the problem because he's the one who hurts. One who is offended is obligated.

He may say, "Well, that doesn't seem right. The offender should come." Of course he should, but suppose he doesn't realize that he has offended you. Then nothing gets done. And that's exactly what happens, week after week, year after year, when people go on with the same old bitternesses and grievances against one another, simply because the one who is offended sinned also. He sinned by not following verse 15. It says, "If your brother sins, you go; you who have been offended, go and reprove him in private. And if he listens to you, you have won your brother."

That, of course, is the purpose of church discipline, to win the brother, to bring about peace—peaceful relations, peaceful communication, peaceful friendship between the two. Brothers ought to be at peace with one another.

But suppose the offender doesn't listen when he goes to him. Suppose that instead of winning him, he gets all the more angry. Suppose he gets upset. Suppose he says, "Look, I've had enough of this. You've come here five or six times. You've been coming here after me, again and again and again, telling me about this thing. And I don't want to do anything about it. I've had it. I don't want to do it, and I don't want to see you." Then what do you tell him to do?

First, make sure he keeps going until he has exhausted that first resource. When the offender says, "Don't come again. Quit. Let's stop this whole business," then turn to verse 16: "If he does not listen to you, take one or two more with you, so that by the mouth of two or three witnesses, every fact may be confirmed."

All right. So he then takes a couple of arbitrators along with him. They stand between the two. They become counselors. They try to get the two to be reconciled to one another. They do everything within their power as neutral observers and concerned, interested parties, who are part of the Body of Christ, to bring about this reconciliation.

In other words, Jesus says, "Don't stop if you yourself fail. Go get an elder, a pastor. Take them along with you. And the three or four of you, sit down and talk this matter through and pray about it." This is the second step.

It is rare that the second step has to be taken if the first is followed. But there are times when the second step has to be taken, and in that case he must take it. He has no option. He can't say, "Oh, well, he won't pay any attention to them." Or, "He'll just get all the more angry." He has no right to talk that way. He has no idea how God is going to work. Everything does not depend on the brother. He may say, "Well, that's why I haven't tried. . . ." He is prejudging the situation, but he has no right to do so.

Jesus works especially in the way in which He Himself has told us that He's going to work. Indeed, at the very end of this section He says, "Where two or three are gathered together in My name, there am I in the midst." That's not some kind of warrant for small prayer meetings. He's not even talking about prayer meetings. He's talking about the question of church discipline. And Jesus promises to be there in a very special way, working through church discipline. The counselor may say, "If you let this go on and on and on between the two of you, bitterness and resentment building up, differences growing, the matter of the two of you and your relationship getting more sour every day (in a marriage, in a home, in personal relationship at church, whatever it may be) don't tell me that you've done everything that you can do!"

"You tell me that the other person isn't going to respond properly, and will make things worse? You don't know that. And even if things get worse, you are to follow what Jesus Christ says anyway. You must do what you have to do; you have to go."

Well, what happens if he doesn't listen to them? Suppose they go back four or five times, and he finally says, "Look. I've had enough of this. Get out of here and don't come back!" Verse 17 makes clear what Christ requires as the third step in church discipline: "And if he refuses to listen to them [that is, the arbitrators, the counselors you bring with you], tell it to the church, and if he refuses to listen even to the church, let him be to you as a Gentile and a tax collector." Now what does that mean?

Well, finally, if he won't listen to you personally, as you go privately, if he won't listen to the arbitrators or counselors you bring with you, then you are to bring the matter officially before the church board, before the elders of the church. And they are to tell him in the Name of Jesus Christ that reconciliation *must* take place. And this power and this authority which Christ has given to them is to be wielded with love, but also with firmness.

Finally, if he refuses to hear even the church, then they are to excommunicate him, not for the particular sin that he committed, but for his arrogance, and his refusal to heed the authority of Jesus Christ, exercised by His Church. And so they excommunicate him. They put him on the outside, where the Gentile, that is, where the heathen, where the tax collector who had been excommunicated were. But even then he is not thrown out to get rid of him. Even then, like that man in Corinth who was excommunicated, his excommunication is to lead him to repentance.

In II Corinthians 2:6-8, after the man did repent, Paul says: "Quickly, lest there be too much sorrow on his part, receive him back, reaffirm your love for him and forgive him." Not only should the church be quick to excommunicate when someone refuses to hear the authority of Christ after all the attempts at reconciliation, but it ought to be even more quick to receive him back, once he has repented of his sin.

And so we have a wonderful process given to us by Jesus Christ. If you've never used it, start today. Start right now. Use the principles in the Word of God that have been given to you. Otherwise you do not counsel properly.

33

DIVORCED OFFICE BEARER

Question: "A man has been nominated as an office bearer in a church. He, his wife and those who nominated him are very upset over the fact that his nomination has been refused. The refusal was due to a church by-law that states that no divorced person may ever hold office in the congregation. They say, "God has forgiven; why doesn't His church forgive?" What is the scriptural position on this matter?"

Because this problem is an urgent one in so many situations, I have responded to this question in a general manner.

Answer: Your question is not unique. In this day of many divorces and remarriages the church is facing such issues more and more. The matters you raise are important. They cannot (and should not) be avoided. On the other hand, they are not easy.

First of all, let's make two things clear:

(1) God does forgive *all* sins in Christ. The couple are absolutely correct about this. There is only *one* unforgivable sin, the sin against the Holy Spirit (attributing the Holy Spirit's work to an *unclean* spirit —the devil). I Corinthians 6:9-11 makes it clear that Christ grants forgiveness for the sin of adultery.

(2) Forgiveness does not clear one from every consequence of his sin. Forgiveness means that God will not hold one's sin against him. The forgiven person will not be judged eternally for that sin; Christ was judged in his place. But social consequences must still be met. If, in a drunken brawl, an unsaved man shoves his arm through a plate glass window with the result that the arm must be amputated, that does not mean that later, when he is saved, he sprouts a new one. No, he will bear the consequences of that sin for life.

Now, there are consequences of sin that are for life, and some that are not. The only issue in question is, how does the Bible speak about this particular question?

The answer, it seems, is that the Bible teaches that some consequences of past sin for eligibility as an officer in Christ's church are lifelong, and others are not. For instance, if before conversion a man married more than one wife, his polygamy does not keep him from membership in Christ's church, but it does prohibit him from bearing office in that church.[1] And this is not because he isn't forgiven by God and the church, but because an office bearer must "be an example in all things" (including monogamous marriage practices).

Now is the question at issue like that? Not quite. A qualification for an office bearer is that he "must be above reproach" (I Tim. 3:2) and also "must have a good reputation with outsiders" (I Tim. 3:7). Titus reiterates this by saying he "must be blameless" (Titus 1:6).

The circumstances of his divorce and/or remarriage may be such that a person for years afterward (perhaps even for the remainder of his life) would fail to qualify because of the bad reputation that he bears as a result. On the other hand, his lifestyle subsequently may be such that God has changed his reputation. Moreover, he may not have sinned at all in obtaining a divorce, if it was granted on biblical grounds.

Since each case differs, and since we have these clear biblical criteria to determine who is eligible for office, it is wrong to add church by-laws, especially when they are less flexible than the Scriptures themselves. The church has no right to forbid what God allows. It is the job of the existing officers in each instance to determine whether or not a given individual fits those qualifications.

On the other hand, if the man in view also is "very upset," and if this means anger, lack of self-control, etc., or if his conversion is quite recent, other qualifications would apply (cf. I Tim. 3:2, 6; Titus 1:7, 8). The attitude with which they deal with this matter itself will say much about qualifications, and (from another perspective) may have a lot to say about the reputation of the nominated office bearer.

---

1. He must be "the husband of one wife" (i.e., only one at a time—I Tim. 3:2; Titus 1:6). The passages do *not* say "married only once" (the normal word for marriage, *gameo*, is not used in these passages).

34

BAD LANGUAGE IN COUNSELING

Of course the Christian counselor himself refrains from the use of all language that could even be classified as questionable. This is a contrast to the language used by many other counselors today who, for various reasons, seem to think that anything goes in counseling and that lewd language and swearing not only are permissible but even desirable. One of the hallmarks of the Christian counselor, in contrast, should be his careful, accurate and judicious use of language. He does not need to engage in shock appeal, prove that he is one of the good ole boys or whatever other purpose one might have in view when filling the counseling room with blue or risqué language.

On the other hand, he will not be prudish about sexual talk. The Bible isn't. In appropriate ways at proper times he will use acceptable sexual vocabulary in a factual (not suggestive) manner. But his terminology will not be scraped out of the gutter. Nor will he find it necessary to emulate the counselee's use of such language, pleading communication as an excuse for doing so. Moreover, he will studiously avoid any language that, in any way whatsover might sexually titillate the counselee. A Christian recognizes the potential constructive and destructive power of language, and he wants to wield it as a weapon for good, not for evil.

Just as he is careful about his own language, he will make every effort to regulate the kind of language that others use in the counseling session. His own example, in a majority of cases, and his avowed Christian stance will set the standard. But there will be times when—for whatever reason: habit, shock value, resentment—counselees will use sinful language in counseling sessions. In such cases, the counselor must take action to bring it to an end.

In cases where a husband and wife are tossing invectives at each other like fiery darts, digging each other, and spitting acidic phrases on each other (even when no lewdness or swearing is involved), as soon as it is apparent that this is going to characterize their conversation,[1] I bring the session to a complete halt. "Whoa!," I am as likely as not to say, "That is no way to talk to one another. No wonder you have had problems, if that is how you try to solve them. Obviously, this is a part of your difficulty, and if I allow you to continue to do this, I will only be contributing to your troubles rather than helping you with them. But even more important is the fact that this is sin—an offense to God. So, every time this happens I'm going to jump in and remind you that this won't do. We intend to solve these problems God's way, and He has told us that we must learn to guard our mouths. Listen to what He says in Ephesians 4: 25-32. . . ."

It is important to let counselees know that you are in charge, that you intend to get things done, that Scripture will set the standard for counseling and that you are concerned about working on every aspect of the counselee's problem, anything—even his language—that contributes to it. At times I have said something like this:

"There may be only one hour in the entire week when you speak to one another as Christians should, but if there is only one—this will be it. Perhaps when you begin to see what good results it brings, you'll be ready to expand such talk to the rest of the week. But ready or not, God requires it, and while you are here I am going to hold you to His requirements. Now, let's get to work again. . . ."

There are times with Christian counselees, when, if the language continues after every attempt has been made, there is nothing left to do but exercise church discipline. With unbelievers, if it continues to get in the way of counseling, and the party fails to consider the gospel seriously, he must be dismissed from counseling with the understanding that he can return any time that he wants to learn about Christ and stop insulting His name.

Incidentally, when I have come to a final session where, for one reason or another, it becomes apparent that I must dismiss the counselee because he rebelliously will not move on from where he is, I usually try to hook a verse into him that he can carry with him when he leaves and that the Holy Spirit may use to bring him to repentance.

---

1. Once or twice may be a different matter that could be commented on later, at a more appropriate time, especially if it seems that they are attempting to control such outbursts, etc.

The verse that I most frequently use is Proverbs 13:15: "The way of the transgressor is hard." I hook it on him by weaving it into my conversation again and again (as often as 15 or 20 times) in that last session, explaining what it means, giving examples of what has happened to others, warning and describing this "way" (or road). I send him off asking God to use the verse to humble him before Christ. I have had such people come back (not all, of course) in six or eight months. When they return, I ask, "What made you return?" Invariably they have said, "I found out that the way of the transgressor is hard." The stories they tell substantiate the fact.

So, counselor, watch your language. Regulate the language others use in your counseling sessions (not because you are shocked by it, but because it is offensive to God and counterproductive to them).

THINGS TO DO

For some time now I have been jotting down ideas for books and articles to be written, as well as other projects that would be profitable for Christ's church. These would especially aid counselors and counselees, I am going to set forth a list of a few of these in the hope that some readers will catch the vision and do the job (we all need to work together).

Games

1. *Confrontation*—a game for teaching trainees the basic principles and practices of Christian counseling (I have already given you the name of the game).
2. *Marriage and Family*—a game for teaching Christian families the responsibilities, role, problems, joys and biblical principles of Christian family life. For use by the entire family.
3. *Courtship*—a game for teaching the biblical principles of interpersonal relationships, dating and courtship, with special emphasis upon God's solutions to typical problems and practical ways of implementing the principles taught.

Books

1. *Prayer and Practice*—a book designed to demonstrate the close biblical links between prayer and practice, the object of which is to show that prayer *alone* is rarely (if ever) enjoined in the Bible. Title: "Practice What You Pray."
2. *Practical Studies in Proverbs*—grouping, explaining and applying proverbs to the many areas of life covered in counseling.
3. *How to Counsel Children*—by someone who has thought through this question biblically.

4. *How to Counsel Teenagers*—ditto.
5. *How to Counsel Singles*—ditto.
6. *How to Counsel the Aged*—ditto.
7. *Case Studies* (full length, all sessions) of biblical counseling.
8. *A Reference Guide to Biblical Counselors and Counseling Resources* (published and updated annually).
9. *A Reference Guide to Biblical Counseling Methods.*
10. *A Biblical Analysis of Theories of Christian Counseling.*
11. *Interpersonal Relationships* (loving neighbors).
12. *Seeking First the Kingdom of God.*
13. *Biblical Principles of Group Work.*
14. *Principles of Suffering in I Peter.*
15. *A Series of Illustrated Children's Books* inculcating preventive principles of living from the Bible.

Pamphlets

1. *On Discouragement.*
2. *Biblical Guidance.*
3. *A Guide for Counselees.*
4. *A Pastor's Invitation*—inviting persons needing help to seek counseling.
5. *How to Do a Homework Assignment.*
6. *Principles of Christian Work.*
7. *How to Find a Mate.*
8. *A Family Workbook*—consisting of things Christian families can do together to strengthen their ties.

Hymns

1. *Having to do with Sanctification and Growth.* Our hymnals sadly lack them.
2. *Having to Do with Christian Fellowship and Mutual Ministry* (how Christians can help one another). The latter are virtually non-existent.

Tests

Tests built on biblical presuppositions according to scriptural norms—
1. *To Determine Gifts.*
2. *To Discover Sinful Habit-Patterns.*
3. *To Uncover Potential Difficulties* among couples engaged in premarital counseling.

4. *Screening in* tests for ministerial and missionary applicants.

Programs

1. *Of Counseling for New Converts* (I have a tape on this suggesting guidelines[1]).
2. *For Teaching Married Couples How to Relate to and Care for Aging Parents.*
3. *On Preparation for Dying.*

---

1. Available from Christian Study Services, 1790 E. Willow Grove Ave., Laverock, Pa. 19118.

36

DON'T COUNSEL

There are times when I refuse to give counsel. For instance, I incessantly receive calls from desperate people about difficulties that they think I can resolve for them in 15 minutes over the telephone. In all such cases I find I must refuse to give counsel, and I refer them to the Christian Counseling & Educational Center, 1790 E. Willow Grove Ave., Laverock, PA, 19118 (Tel. 215-884-7676), where a list of names of pastors who have studied at the center is maintained.

"Why?" you ask. "Why do you refuse to help these people?" For a number of reasons. First, it is impossible to do sactisfactory counseling on the phone. I want to see the responses (halo data) of the person to whom I am talking. Secondly, there isn't time to gather adequate data and I would give wrong responses as a result if I tried to counsel under these conditions. Thirdly, I have a carefully arranged schedule (with flexibility, of course) that will not allow for numbers of unarranged hour-long telephone counseling sessions. Fourthly, in most instances, the person calling is calling about someone else who may or may not have given his/her permission to disclose the information that the party is about to reveal to me. As a Christian I cannot be a party to gossip, to wives talking about their husbands behind their backs, etc., under such circumstances.

This last point leads to another. Over the last few years I have spoken to literally thousands of pastors in meetings in the USA and around the world. During breaks, question-and-answer periods and at the conclusion of meetings inevitably I have a number of pastors who bring a counseling case to me to solve. I try to answer this way:

"I really wish I could help you, but I'm afraid I can't. I hope you don't think I'm copping out (some possibly do, but I'm not), but I would do both you and your counselee a disservice to try to give you advice on the meager amount of data that I could obtain here, and when I have gotten that data from a third party. I don't know what your counselee is like, I haven't been able to ask him the questions that I'd want to ask, look for his reactions, etc. I simply won't try because I'd probably lead you the wrong way."

Some of you—in time, if not already—will find yourselves faced with the same situations. I urge you to refuse. Even though you *want* to help (it isn't easy for me to say "no"; I've had to learn to do so), I am sure that you can see that such "help," more often than not, may turn out not to be help at all, but only a new problem. When someone asks you for directions ("How do I get to 4004 State Street?"), is it kinder to guess and tell him something that you are not sure about, or simply to say, "I don't know"? Similarly, you will recognize those situations in which you *don't know* how to counsel another because the circumstances do not allow for such knowledge. Better than giving wrong directions, you must say, "Not now and here." It is almost always better to postpone counseling to a set time and place (your study, preferably), when *both* of you (or *all* of you—if other persons are involved) have set aside adequate time for it.

Even when people tell you that it is urgent, and *must* be done now you can be sure that most so-called emergencies are not (there are some few, to be sure). In most instances (probably 999 out of 1000) the party would be better to wait until that set time and place. Most "emergencies" have been going on for months or years. A few hours' more delay usually won't make any difference. Be firm. Insist, "It sounds to me like this matter is too important and too complex to handle over the phone. I can see you at 7:30 tonight." Don't allow others to pressure you into poor counseling. Part of their problem may be to learn patience and take the time to do things well.

Most people, if given something to do in the meantime, will be content. So give them a precounseling homework assignment (it will begin to structure things and, incidentally, move counseling ahead): "By the time you get here tonight, please have written out all of the events that led up to the problem, what you have done about it, and what you think I might be able to do to help. Be specific. Also, list any other facts that you think might be of importance."

So, please, don't counsel unless you can counsel. Be sure you have the proper setting, the time to gather all the data you need and that all of the parties who should be there will be present.

37

PREDICTION

There is a danger that is too seldom recognized and countered by Christian counselors. Only recently in counseling have I become aware of the problem and what to do about it.

Take a typical example. Nancy goes alone for counseling. She is a Christian; her husband isn't. One of the first things she says in response to the counselor's question is, "No, pastor, Ray will never come. I've asked him before and I've gotten a negative response. This time I didn't even bother." Nancy is predicting.

Later on in the same counseling session, while discussing some homework assignment, the pastor suggests that it might be helpful to have Ray check her out each day on her assignment. But Nancy replies, "I'm sorry, pastor. There's no use trying that. He won't co-operate; I know him too well. You can forget that suggestion." Again, Nancy is predicting.

But neither Nancy, the pastor, nor any other counselee has the power to make such predictions. Only God can do that. And this fact must be pointed out to the counselee.

It is pagan to suggest by such a prediction that Ray is unchangeable; and yet that is precisely what Nancy is doing. Her mind is made up: because of uniform (and was it really all that uniform?) behavior by Ray in the past, she assumes that his behavior will be the same in the future. I say this is pagan thinking (and Christians often may think like pagans) because it fails to reckon with the most significant factor of all: God. God can change Ray. In His providence the very changes Nancy is making may be used to get to Ray. In fact, even a change in Nancy's viewpoint toward Ray (particularly a change in her "he's hopeless" attitude) could be critical in this. If, instead, she prayerfully asks God to make Ray different while herself becoming different, this itself could make the difference.

Nancy must adopt a biblical attitude toward God ("He is in this, and nothing need be the same tomorrow. God can work in Ray's life just as He has been at work in mine"), and toward Ray (love "hopes all things"; i.e., "If I love Ray, I will not give up on him"). When Nancy adopts these two new attitudes, that, in itself, will give her a new and more pleasant approach toward Ray that he is sure to notice. This has happened frequently in counseling sessions.

All this, and whatever else fits the theme, may need to be said to a counselee who predicts the future behavior of another. It is nothing short of sin to do so, for the reasons already stated. Counselors must point out sinful ways and show instead God's way of approaching such situations.

"No predicting allowed!" is a sign that could well be one wall motto to hang in every counselor's study.

38

WHEN ASSERTING, ASSERT

Quite frequently I have noticed a tendency on the part of counselor-trainees to ask questions of the counselee as a substitute for direct assertation of biblical fact. These questions are not directed to the counselee in order to gather data, to ask for commitment or even to put him on the spot (like most "why"-type questions do). No, rather, the counselor is trying to get a point across to the counselee (usually, he tries to get a number of such points across this way before the session is over), but instead he is

1. dulling the impact of the point by phrasing it in question form rather than in assertive form;

2. aggravating or confusing the counselee, who isn't sure whether he is expected to answer these questions (or if so, how to do so).

If what I am talking about is as clear as mud so far, let me attempt to demonstrate by giving you a couple of examples and then re-phrasing them as indicative statements (assertions). There is some problem in doing this because the peculiar intonation put on the question is often a part of the technique, and that is all but impossible to reproduce on paper (so I haven't tried).

Question (meant as assertion of a truth): "John, do you know that the Bible teaches that this is sin?"

Answer: "I'm not sure, pastor, I . . ."

Question: "Well, don't you know that Paul says, 'Be worried about nothing'?"

Answer: "Uh . . . I guess I've read that."

Question: "Isn't it clear then, that both Jesus and Paul teach that you must stop worrying?"

Answer: "I suppose so," etc.

Well, perhaps the counselee should have known all of these things, but is that the point? This is not a quiz on the counselee's Bible knowledge (if that *were* the point, then the series of questions would be appropriate). The counselor really isn't interested in how much John already knows—he wants to be sure that before he leaves this session he knows this biblical truth. It would be better simply to make the point, relieve the counselee of the obligation to give inane answers and, if there was any question about his understanding or acceptance leave that to the end. Here is how that might look:

"John, the Bible teaches that worry is sin. In Matthew 6, Jesus says . . . [here read and give explanation of the passage] and Paul also writes, 'Be worried about nothing.' So it is plain that God wants you to stop worrying. How does all that strike you?"

You can see that the counselee would feel less crowded and pushed by this approach. He has been given time to think through your whole presentation before asked to give a response. You may elicit negative responses, questions, objection or all sorts of diverting comments by opening the possibility for response by the counselee *before he has had the opportunity to hear you out.* I have seen this happen to the consternation of the counselor.

Let your rule be to assert what you want to assert and to ask questions not as a habit, not as a supposed softening technique (it is actually more pushy than making a statement), but when you really want an answer. There is, of course, a place for a rhetorical question (one to which you don't expect an answer). But the one I am talking about is neither fish nor fowl. The counselee is perplexed, thinking he must answer, but wondering whether the question isn't more rhetorical than not. Let your yea be yea. The counselee doen't need any added confusion created by the counselor!

39

COMMON GRACE AND COUNSELING

Elsewhere in this book I have taken note of the fact that sleep loss can lead to the same sort of effects as LSD. The information comes from science, not from the Bible. The biblical principle is for Christians to avoid whatever harms the body, the temple of the Holy Spirit. Under that absolute principle one seeks as best he can from observation (not infallible) as well as the latest results of science (these are not absolute, but always changing) to discover the sorts of things to which the biblical principle may apply. Whenever there seems to be a substantial risk that one, by pursuing a practice or course of action, may harm his body (and thereby sin), he avoids the practice or action until he has substantial evidence to the contrary.

It is by the common grace of God, a goodness which He extends to those who do not serve and love Him as well as to His children who do, that such facts as this one concerning sleep loss have come to light. We can all be grateful for them and utilize them.

However—and here comes the kicker—there are those who (intentionally and otherwise) slip in all kinds of false teaching about man under the guise of "common grace." Freud's irresponsibility, Rogers' reflections, Skinner's reward schedules, etc., cannot be accepted as common grace. *Nothing in common grace contradicts what God has given in special grace* (in the Scriptures). Hence, the standard, in all cases, of what one accepts from observation, science, etc., always must be the Bible.

There is a second factor too. A godless system designed to do precisely what the Scriptures themselves were designed to do—to change men's lives so as to function in proper ways (i.e., designed to teach people how to live)—can never be syncretistically blended with Scripture. I do not have space here to demonstrate how such systems function competitively over against the Bible, but those acquainted with my other writings already know my position, and others might consult *What About Nouthetic Counseling?*[1] as a starting point.

The major issues, then, that must be kept in mind in regard to the claim that nonscriptural data are true by God's common grace are:

1. Are they in competition with a principle or practice already enjoined in the Scriptures?

2. Are they in harmony with the principles and practices of the Scriptures?

---

1. Especially pp. 16-20, 31, 35, 37-39, 73-75.

40

DON'T TRY TO LOVE YOURSELF

A good friend of mine, Bob Smith, M.D., who is deeply involved in the work of the Christian Counseling Center of Lafayette, Indiana, a center patterned after the Christian Counseling & Educational Center of Laverock, Pennsylvania, where pastors are trained in nouthetic counseling, recently sent me an article that he had written concerning the topic at the head of this page. He told me to do what I wanted with it. So, since this is the first opportunity that I have had to publish it, I take the opportunity to do so here.

I have revised it somewhat, while retaining most of his style, and send it forth as a further statement on a subject that I have been trying to bring to the light of day in my writings. I offer it here because it throws light on the matter from a few new viewpoints as well as the previous ones. We should be grateful to Dr. Smith for making his thoughts known to us.

DON'T TRY TO LOVE YOURSELF

"It was difficult for her to love others because she did not love herself enough. It is impossible for us to accept the other one as he is if we have not accepted ourselves as we are."[1] This statement presents a concept that is finding ready acceptance among modern Christians. Its supporters use the statement of Jesus recorded in Matthew 19:19, "Thou shalt love thy neighbor as thyself." This same phrase is also found in Leviticus 19:18; Matthew 22:39; Mark 12:31; Luke 10:27; Romans 13:9; Galatians 5:14; and James 2:8.

These passages all teach that we are to love our neighbor as ourselves, but something has been added. Today we are being told that

---

1. Walter Trobish, *Love Yourself* (Downers Grove: InterVarsity Press. 1976), pp. 10-11.

it is impossible for a person to love his neighbor if he does not first love himself. This self-love is being taught as a commandment of God. "The command to love your neighbor is never given without the command to love yourself." "Self-love is thus the prerequisite and criterion for our conduct toward our neighbor."[2]

But if you will carefully examine all of these verses you will notice there is only one command given: Love your neighbor. In none of these is there a specific or implied command to love yourself. In each of these passages love of self is considered to be present naturally. Self-love is assumed in the same way the existence of God is assumed. In no place in the Word of God can it be demonstrated that there is a specific or implied command or encouragement to love ourselves. The philosophy of self-love (and it is more than merely an exegetical fault about which we are speaking; the teaching has overarching dimensions) has reached epidemic proportions in contemporary Christianity. Many harmful conclusions have been drawn from it.

We are told that by not loving himself a person fails to love what God loves and therefore disrespects God's creation. God loved us so we must love ourselves. As can be seen from the opening quotation, the concept of self-acceptance arises out of the teachings of self-love. Self-acceptance then becomes the basis for accepting others. Regretfully, some who are biblical in their teachings have used the term *self-acceptance* in a confusing way. They are not guilty of the bad theology of the self-acceptance movement, since what they describe is not the self referred to by the self-love proponents, but one's physical make-up. Accepting what God has done in our physical body—large noses, short stature, defects, handicaps, etc. (with which many people are dissatisfied), is what is called self-acceptance. We would prefer to call this an acceptance of God providence. What is our self? What does the Bible mean when it refers to the self? What did Jesus mean when He taught that we must deny self (Luke 9:23)? "By the self, He meant the old desires, the old ways, the old practices, the old habit patterns that were acquired before conversion."[3] It is thus something that can be readily identified. The Bible doesn't refer to some vague, ill-defined, hard to understand concept, as is

---

2. Ibid., p. 11.
3. Jay E. Adams, *The Christian Counselor's Manual* (Nutley, N. J.: Presbyterian and Reformed Publishing Co., 1973), p. 211.

found in such words as personhood, the holistic person, etc.

As stated earlier, that human beings love themselves is a biblical assumption. Instead of encouraging self-love, the Word of God either uses it as an illustration or restricts it. As an illustration, self-love provides an example of the depth and intensity of concern that one must show in his love for others. We are to love others in the same way that we already have demonstrated love for ourselves. Christ said love your neighbor as yourself. "He didn't issue a command enjoining self-love but referred to that which is already present as an example to guide us in our love of others; self-love is not something we need to learn. It is something we already do. "Christ says, in effect, do good for your neighbor (or wife) with the same devotion and zeal that you exhibit in doing good for yourself."[4]

An existing self-love is clearly referred to by Paul in Ephesians 5:28-33. Here we are told that the husband is to love his wife *as he loves his own body*. His existing love for himself is a guideline for his love for his wife. The existence of self-love is assumed in the statement that "no man hates his own flesh" (v. 29). What Paul teaches is that no man naturally hates himself, but naturally loves himself. He loves himself in spite of his defects, failures and faults. "Christians must learn to have the same intense love for others as they have developed for themselves. They must learn to cover another's faults in love as they do their own. And similarly, they must learn to give others the benefit of the doubt as they give it to themselves."[5]

So, as we see, self-love is not commanded but is used as an illustration. Yet there is more to the question than that. Since self-love already exists, it is not encouraged, but restricted by God. The problem is not that sinners have inadequate self-love but too much self-love. The desire for food does not need to be learned or encouraged but must be restricted. The same is true of self-love. Improper or unlimited self-love is that which seeks for satisfaction of self as the primary goal. It is self-love that is not subject to Christ in His Word. Self-love enthusiasts use this concept in an attempt to correct bad feelings about one's self. The goal of the self-concept movement is satisfying my needs and desires before yours. Such an approach is self-seeking and self-satisfying and puts self first, and as such, with Ayn Rand, encourages selfishness. To put self first is to think of

---

4. Ibid., p. 144.   5. Ibid., p.144.

one's self more highly than one ought to. It is to seek to satisfy personal desires rather than biblically directed and justifiable goals (Phil. 2:21).

Furthermore, Jesus commanded us to deny self (Luke 9:23; Matt. 16:24). To deny self does not mean hating what God loves. It means rather to hate what He hates. God does love us, but He does not love our sinful behavior. He hates our sin and the source of our sin. He commands us to deny self. This means to put to death on a daily basis (take up the cross daily) all the selfish desires of our being. Included in this is crucifying the passions and desires of the flesh (Gal. 5:24) as well as the lust of the eyes and the pride of life (I John 2:16). One may not spend time pursuing his own interests, but those of others (Phil. 2:4). Self-love puts self first and makes one's desires the guideline for action toward others. The Bible puts others first.

The basis for loving others is not self-love. The statement, "If we cannot love ourselves, we cannot love our neighbors,"[6] is not true. The basis for loving others is obedience to God's commands in His Word. In these commands obedience is not contingent on anything, including feelings.

> This is my commandment, that ye love one another (James 15:12).

> Husbands, love your wives (Eph. 5:25).

> Thou shalt love thy neighbor as thyself (Mark 12:31).

> But I say unto you, love your enemies (Matt. 5:44).

In all of these there is not one prerequisite for the Christian to fulfill in order to love. Nor are love-generated feelings listed as prerequisites for loving actions. The Bible does not say to love when you have good feelings toward a person or when you feel warm, friendly, and kindly toward him. It orders love no matter how one feels; obviously, then, love is not fundamentally a feeling. Love begins with action, the action of giving.

> . . . God so loved the world that He *gave* His only begotten Son (John 3:16).

> . . . the Son of God, who loved me, and *gave* Himself for me (Gal. 2:20).

---

6. R. Lofton Hudson, "Love Yourself," in N. J. Allan Peterson, ed., *The Marriage Affair* (Wheaton: Tyndale House Publishers, 1971), p. 48.

. . . Christ also loved the church, and *gave* Himself for it (Eph. 5:25).

Feelings flow from action. Right feelings flow from right actions. In John 13:17 Jesus said that feeling happy comes from the right action of doing what He said—"If ye know these things, happy are ye if ye do them." A good feeling is not the fundamental basis or motivation for any behavior (that is God's command) but the result of it or the by-product of it. Feelings may add incentive or tend to impede action, but are not determinative of it.

How am I to love if I do not feel like it?

First of all, deny self. Get all of your selfish desires out of the picture.

Secondly, follow the biblical guidelines on love. Love as Christ did. His love was self-sacrificing and self-giving. His concern was not for Himself but for *the spiritual welfare of others,* namely, His church (Eph. 5:26-27; Phil. 2). So to love as Christ did means giving to meet the needs of the loved one.

It is possible to love everyone at least as an enemy. That means to pray for him (Matt. 5:44; Luke 6:28), do good to him in order to overcome evil (Luke 6:27; Rom. 12:20, 21), bless him (Luke 6:28), and never try to get even for wrongs he has done to you (Rom. 12:17, 19). I Corinthians 13:4-7 describes all sorts of loving actions Christians may take. Love is action based on the Word of God to please Him. It is not dependent on how you feel toward yourself or toward others.

Thirdly, love others in the same way you love yourself. Even when you have done something unsatisfactory to yourself, you continue to do good things for yourself.

What of suicides? Do they love self? The suicide takes his life out of a love for self that is too great. He refuses to go on putting self through the ordeals that he tries to escape by self-murder. The same thing is true of the ascetic who tortures his physical body in an attempt to atone for his sins and thus protect himself from divine wrath. Each of these still shows self-love, distorted though it may be, and is using that self-love to avoid dealing with life in a proper way. These points very briefly describe the basis of love.

What *is* the problem with those people who are told they have a poor or negative self-image and do not love themselves enough? If you have been told that, your problem may be not too little self-love

95

but too much. You think more highly of yourself than you should (Rom. 12:3). The problem is that you see that others don't have the same exalted thoughts of yourself that you do. They do not treat you or talk to you or respect you as you think they should. Because you consider yourself so important, you think the problem is someone else's fault and not yours. You may use this excuse to avoid changing your own behavior. Such self-evaluation requires you to be very honest with yourself. It means that you are the source of your problem. You have selfish goals and when they are not achieved you blame others and refuse to change. Selfish people, unless convicted by the Spirit using His Word, find it very difficult to make this kind of evaluation.

Someone may tell you that the reason you aren't treated by others as you'd like to be is because you don't love them as you should, and this lack of love shown by them stems from your own lack of love for yourself. If you were to ask how you are to learn to love yourself, listen to a typical answer. "How can we learn to accept ourselves, to love ourselves? Essentially, there is only one answer to this question: We must learn to let ourselves be loved."[7] ". . . the experience of being loved . . . is so necessary if we want to love others."[8] "The healthy self-love grows out of being loved."[9] Thus, you are told that the way to learn to love self is by being loved by others. In order to love others (which requires self-love) you must be loved by them. You don't have to love others (can't, as a matter of fact) until they start the process by loving you first. If they don't love you first, presumably this excuses you of any God-given command to love them. Your lack of love toward them is their fault!

That is the kind of conclusion you reach when you adopt the self-love logic. As is readily seen, it is contrary to God's Word. You are not allowed any such contingency on which to hang obedience to God. Your treatment of others is not based on their treatment of you. What you must do is confess and receive forgiveness for your sin of pride and love others in a biblical way, no matter how they treat you. Your happiness is found in obeying Jesus Christ (John 13:17) and in pleasing Him (I Thess. 4:1), not in having people treat you the way you think they should.

---

7. Trobish, op. cit., p. 19.
8. Ibid., p. 20.
9. Hudson, op. cit., p. 48.

All of which brings us to the matter of a poor or negative self-image. This is the same problem as lack of love for self, carried a little further. Your problem is not a poor self-image but self-pity. If you are feeling sorry for yourself because of the way people treat you and you are not getting what you want out of the relationship, you reject them. If they fail to accept you or give you all the things you desire out of the relationship, you reject them; they sense the rejection, and return it. Then you condemn them for it.

You may be told that the reason for this is a negative self-image. You may be told that you don't accept others because you don't accept yourself. But according to Romans 2:1 you are condemning them for doing what you are doing. You don't accept others because they don't accept you. Your failure to accept others is not the consequence of a lack of self-acceptance or a negative self-image but is due to selfishness. You don't have a good feeling in the relationship or a sense of security from being accepted by others, so you feel bad.

This bad feeling stems from guilt arising from the sin of selfishness and not from a poor self-image. Dealing with the sin gets rid of the bad feelings and dealing with sin is possible because Christ died for sin. So, the supposed lack of self-love and poor self-image really boil down to bad feelings that result from the sins of selfishness and self-pity. These bad feelings are removed by confession of the sin and changing the selfish behavior to giving. But note—and this is critical—the goal is not to give in love *as a gimmick* in order to feel better, but to give in order to please God, no matter how you feel.

Where did this self-love concept come from? Over the years as psychiatrists and psychologists studied what they call abnormal behavior they tried to figure out the cause of the behavior. For example, they study certain groups of people, say depressed people or alcoholics and hear them say over and over again, "I'm no good. I'm a loser," etc. Such people appear to deal with all of life from that perspective and end up with many problems. So they have concluded that such persons have a bad concept or image of themselves. So the psychologist reasons, "He has a negative self-image. His problem is not that he is really no good or a loser. He just thinks he is. As long as he thinks that way, he will act that way. The solution is for him to change his thinking. He must not think bad of himself, but think good of himself, accept himself, i.e., love himself. Then he can move out into life as a new man or woman."

Christians hear this and because it sounds logical and appears to come from a reliable source, they accept it as truth without measuring it by the standard of God's Word. As a matter of fact, they do what is worse; instead of measuring such philosophies by God's Word, they measure God's Word by contemporary philosophies and assumptions. But even worse, they then take God's Word and twist it to make it agree with this pseudo-truth proposed by unbelievers. They project the teaching into the Scriptures, then claim to find it there.

The concept of self-love is the result of man's attempt to explain human behavior in a way that man can comfortably accept. But the explanation—as agreeable as it may seem to you—is contrary to the biblical description of the problem. And the biblical one—uncomfortable as it may seem to you—is that our sinful behavior is the cause of our bad feelings and the solution is to work on the sinful behavior.

Thus, to command one to love himself is not biblical. Nor is self-acceptance or self-adequacy. ("Not that we are adequate in ourselves to consider anything as coming from ourselves, but our adequacy is from God"; II Cor. 3:5, NASB). We are not to accept or "please ourselves" (Rom. 15:1), "For even Christ pleased not himself" (Rom. 15:3). Our goal is not self-acceptance but obtaining satisfaction from the fact that we are accepted by God through the atonement of Jesus Christ and that He instructs, empowers and uses us to accomplish His purposes. Our goal for satisfaction is not through accepting self or pleasing self or loving self but, in the words of Jesus, to "do always those things that please Him" (John 8:29). This is to be our source of joy and satisfaction. "These things have I spoken unto you, that my joy might remain in you, and that your joy might be full" (John 15:11). "If ye know these things, happy are ye if ye do them" (John 13:17).

DO YOU HAVE AN OPEN MIND?

Objection: "But you don't have an open mind!"

Ever heard it before? Well, it won't be the first or last time if you are involved in trying to be biblical in your counseling. Let's see how you might answer.

Response: Right. And neither do you. Your very objection indicates that you have a position on the matter. As a matter of fact, those who most vigorously advocate open-mindedness often most viciously attack others who believe in being close-minded. It is logically impossible to hold an open-minded *position* with *conviction*. That is, in itself, a contradiction. Either one has no convictions on the subject (which isn't open-mindedness, but simple lack of conviction), or he holds firmly to a position for or against open-mindedness (and in neither case can he be open-minded toward the opposite position)."

An open mind is like an open window; you have to put in screens to keep the bugs out! That is the way that a professor in one seminary puts it. He means, of course, that a person without convictions is open to everyone else's opinions (no matter how outrageous). Many who boast of having an open mind simply don't have convictions about anything much. As the Peanuts crowd puts it, they are wishy-washy.

Christian counselors must be closed-minded about open-mindedness. They are required *not* to be swept along by every wind of doctrine (especially counseling doctrine, which changes at least as often as the breeze) like those without convictions.[1] At the same time, they must be as open-minded as the Holy Spirit will make them toward scriptural truth. Here is *one* place where open-mindedness is both de-

---

1. Ephesians 4:14.

sirable and possible. The Spirit alone can truly open the mind and heart to the changes demanded in the Bible.[2]

When the Christian speaks of closed-mindedness, then he considers it a virtue and not a vice. But the sort of closed-mindedness that he applauds isn't pig-headed bigotry. Rather, it is the conviction that what God says in the Bible is true. And it is that very Bible that insists that he open his mind to *facts* wherever they are found.[3] But such data may not be accepted uncritically. They must be screened. The Scriptures are the screen by which the Christian keeps the bugs out. As his Standard of faith and life, the Bible keeps him from becoming the flypaper to which every sort of belief sticks.

2. Luke 24:32.
3. I Thessalonians 5:21.